WE SET THE BAR

Fighting for Equality, Empowerment
and Change within the
Legal Profession

Jo Delahunty KC

First published in Great Britain in 2026 by

Bristol University Press
University of Bristol
1-9 Old Park Hill
Bristol
BS2 8BB
UK
t: +44 (0)117 374 6645
e: bup-info@bristol.ac.uk

Details of international sales and distribution partners are available at
bristoluniversitypress.co.uk

© Bristol University Press 2026

DOI: 10.51952/9781529221305

British Library Cataloguing in Publication Data
A catalogue record for this book is available from the British Library

ISBN 978-1-5292-2128-2 paperback
ISBN 978-1-5292-2129-9 ePub
ISBN 978-1-5292-2130-5 ePdf

The right of Jo Delahunty to be identified as author of this work has been asserted
by her in accordance with the Copyright, Designs and Patents Act 1988.

All rights reserved: no part of this publication may be reproduced, stored in a
retrieval system, or transmitted in any form or by any means, electronic, mechanical,
photocopying, recording, or otherwise without the prior permission of Bristol
University Press.

Every reasonable effort has been made to obtain permission to reproduce copyrighted
material. If, however, anyone knows of an oversight, please contact the publisher.

The statements and opinions contained within this publication are solely those of the
author and not of the University of Bristol or Bristol University Press. The University
of Bristol and Bristol University Press disclaim responsibility for any injury to persons or
property resulting from any material published in this publication.

Bristol University Press works to counter discrimination on grounds
of gender, race, disability, age and sexuality.

Cover design: Sarah-Louise Deazley
Front cover image: Emily O'Brien Tattoos
Bristol University Press uses environmentally responsible print partners.
Printed and bound in Great Britain by CPI Group (UK) Ltd,
Croydon, CR0 4YY

Bristol University Press' authorised representative in the
European Union is: Easy Access System Europe,
Mustamäe tee 50, 10621 Tallinn, Estonia,
Email: gpsr.requests@easproject.com

'Traces the journey of a woman who rose from a poor, single mother household to succeed at the Bar, navigating entrenched misogyny along the way. Her resilience and determination shine out from the many accounts of how she achieved justice for victims. She throws down the challenge to today's generation, whose social mobility is more limited, by promising that it's worth it and that the Bar can change.'
Baroness Ruth Deech KC (Hon)

'A brave and honest account, relatable for many who have taken a less conventional journey to the Bar. Jo characteristically challenges the power structures and stereotypes which hobble progress and equality, bringing to life their deep-rooted reality. Her "love letter" is an inspiring call to arms for all changemakers.'
Jenny Beck KC (Hon), Solicitor, Director and Chair of the Nuffield Family Justice Observatory's Board

'An important, personal, angry, informative paean of praise for the Legal Aid system and a passionate argument for equity at the Bar. Deeply personal and equally passionate, it should be required reading in all chambers – especially by leaders.'
Martin Elliott, Honorary Master of the Bench at Inner Temple, Professor Emeritus at University College London and Gresham College

'Jo is a hero of the family law Bar. Her book is a raw, compelling and heartfelt forensic dissection of our justice system and what has gone so wrong for so long. Jo speaks truth to power and her voice is our voice. We must strive to do better, much better and quickly.'
Leslie Samuels KC, Chair of the Family Law Bar Association

'A powerful, unflinching book which demands that the Bar must finally look and sound like the society it serves. Celebrating women's contributions to the law, it names the barriers, calls out the hypocrisy and then leans down the ladder to pull others up, insisting that diversity, visibility and voice are non negotiable for a healthy justice system.'
Dana Denis-Smith OBE, First 100 Years and Deputy Vice President, Law Society

'A fundamentally important book to be read by the leaders of the profession who for too long have tolerated the abuses and the failings it catalogues in such pitiless detail and by the politicians who for too long have starved the family justice system and the legal aid fund of the necessary resources. Read, and act! An often angry and impassioned but sadly all too justifiable denunciation of what is so wrong with the Bar and the family justice system – the continuing failures to stamp out sexual harassment and to improve the position of women and ethnic minorities both at the Bar and on the Bench and the cost and corner cutting tolerated by those, including the judges, who ought to know better. A tremendously powerful read. Much of the time I did not know whether to weep or to rage. But the overall message is resolutely positive, delivered by someone who really understands what the Bar and the family justice system are actually about, and concluding with a detailed and very necessary call to arms. What is so depressing is that it all still needs to be said - and the people who most need to read it probably won't. The autobiographical sections give insights into the Bar over the last 40 years that will be of lasting value.'

Sir James Munby (1948–2026), former President of the Family Division of the High Court and Chair of Nuffield Family Justice Observatory, written on 23 December 2025*

---

* *In Memory of James Munby*

James was my mentor, my friend, my champion, my confidante. Our history went back over 25 years. We communicated often and frankly. I cannot believe his brain and energy is no longer mine to plunder. We were speaking up to 23 December 2025. He had just sent me his review for *We Set the Bar*. Few judges would be prepared to take that public stance in support of such hard hitting challenge to the Bar and Bench. We then spoke and laughed about how our edges had been sharpened, not softened, by age. This was his sign-off email to me after we put the phone down because, as often happened, we had more to say than time to say it:

> Although now 77 – tempus fugit – I refuse to see myself as one of the old men, many of whom, of course, are very much younger!

James died suddenly on New Year's Day. That news is still being processed. James was a titan in the legal world. His integrity, intelligence and approachability offered hope in an increasingly hostile and divided world. I can't believe I won't be able to plunder his boundless energy, curiosity and kindness again. RIP James.

This book contains discussion of issues such as sexual harassment and abuse, including child abuse.

Contents

About the Author   viii
Preface   x

1   Introduction   1
2   Wigs and Gowns   25
3   A Life in the Law   66
4   Power and Patronage   103
5   Power Inside the Courtroom   144
6   Women at Work: Glass Ceilings and Sticky Floors   176
7   Advocating for Change   222
8   Is It Worth It?   263

Postscript   283
Index   285

About the Author

Professor Jo Delahunty KC was called to the Bar in 1986, took silk in 2006, became a Recorder in 2009, a Bencher of Middle Temple in 2011, appointed Gresham Professor of Law 2016–2020, and then Emeritus Gresham Professor of Law. Jo is ranked as a '"Star" Silk Individual' by Chambers & Partners and 'Leading Silk' by The Legal 500.

Jo is proud of her history as a child of a single mother, born into a large East Finchley working-class family. She attended state schools, was the first in her family to stay in education beyond the age of 15 and to go to university, attending St Anne's College, Oxford. Jo took the financially perilous path towards the Bar, seeing the law as a weapon for change and challenge in an unequal society and a defence for the vulnerable against the powerful.

A passionate advocate for the legal aid Bar, Jo has stayed true to her vocation to act for the neediest members of society.

In public law family cases she specialises in the most serious child abuse cases involving the death of/catastrophic injuries to a child, fabricated or induced illness (FII) and sex abuse. In private law Jo deals with complex cases of domestic abuse, controlling and coercive behaviour, alienation, child and partner abuse.

To mark the centenary of the Representation of the People Act 1918, Jo was among 100 women to be awarded the Freedom of the City of London and named as one of Middle Temple's 100 Women of Distinction in the Past 100 Years in 2019. Jo is an Ambassador to Bridging the Bar and Patron of the Association of Women Barristers, a Reader for the Queen Elizabeth II Prize for Education and a Speaker for Schools lecturer. It has been said that 'Jo Delahunty is just the godmother of children law now'.

Jo has won multiple industry awards for both her silk and campaigning work and is outspoken on issues affecting diversity, inclusion and wellbeing in the legal profession. She is openly neurodivergent and fearless in calling out toxic issues that the Bar has for too long buried, such as judicial bullying, sexual harassment and mental health stress. She is outspoken about the Bar's failure to reflect the diversity of the society it serves.

In 2025, she was the winner of The Lawyer You Aspire to Be 2025 from the Legal Style Awards and the prestigious Family Law KC of the Year. She was also one of three shortlisted finalists for DEI: Outstanding Contribution for the Chambers UK Bar Awards.

Jo was invited to write this book following her series of lectures delivered for Gresham College during her tenure there. She has taken up the challenge to continue to speak honestly about the highs and lows of life at the Bar. Jo celebrates others who have come to it from non-orthodox backgrounds and have carved out space and reputations for themselves, in multiple disciples, that show why the Bar is a brighter and better place for having a diverse and inclusive professional population.

Preface

This book is my love letter to the legal aid Bar.

This book sprang from my Gresham professorship and the increasing freedom it gave me to speak openly about my working world as a barrister. As I did so I discovered a hunger for knowledge about it allied with a concerning lack of accessible, frank, information about the reality of its expectations and demands. At Gresham, for the legal community and then on the public stage, I opened up the Bar's Pandora's box, confronting its challenges and addictions, discussing myths and misconceptions, and exposing its flaws. This book takes that narrative further and deeper. Becoming a barrister was a defining choice for me. I wanted to make a difference to the fractured society I saw around me and that has informed my choices about what work I do, for whom and why. I consider myself, still, to be an 'outsider' despite progression within the profession I love and I embrace that disconnect. Each barrister's practice is as unique as their own DNA. I know I am not a typical barrister. I come from an atypical background and have an atypical profile. I am Jo Delahunty KC. I am passionate about the future health of the self-employed independent Bar. That means it has to change to be an inclusive, diverse, egalitarian and healthy profession. If that means talking openly about factors that blight the Bar, such as its lack of diversity, its elitism, its toxicity in terms of mental health stress, and a culture that can protect and foster sexual harassment and bullying, then that is what I will do. This book sets my stamp upon matters that were not, but are now, becoming capable of open debate.

The hidden challenge, yet to be tackled, is to recognise that the Bar is in danger of fracturing between those whose practice serves private wealth and those who work in the legal aid sector. The former is thriving, the latter is at risk. The pay, the working conditions, the lack of meaningful respect and financial and political support by politicians of all persuasions is ringing its death knell. As I write this preface the legal aid sector is in crisis as a result of a cyber-attack in April 2025 that has left many firms and barristers in a state of financial and career crisis. Data that affected hundreds of thousands of legal aid users, whether that be members of the public, solicitor's firms or barristers going back to 2010, was accessed and downloaded. Four months on and much of the legal aid system is still offline and we have no date for full restitution. When it returns the legacy of its impact will be long felt in terms of client trust and who, whether solicitor or barrister, remains solvent and willing to continue doing legal aid work. There have long been concerns about legal aid 'deserts' as lawyers have gradually withdrawn from services due to lack of funding, and there are fears the long-term consequence of the hack will be less access to justice for the most vulnerable in society. The data breach was catastrophic, yet it has attracted less media coverage than the attack at the same time on M&S. I believe legal aid to be the fourth emergency service yet its status as such is not appreciated until it is turned to in moments of personal crisis, whether that be immigration, crime, housing or family. It relies upon the dedication and selflessness of its practitioners to keep going when it, and they, have been broken by decades of underfunding and disrespect.

What you will read is coloured by my own history, coming as I do from a single-mother, working-class London background, but I am not alone in finding and making my place at the Bar; not despite but because of lessons learned early on about injustice and inequality. I have been gifted with narratives from colleagues at the Bar and they talk about aspects that are theirs to own – whether that be racism, classism, abuse, sexuality or the intersectionality of any or all of those issues. They don't embody the traditional image of the Bar but they are to me, their clients and colleagues, the personification of what the Bar should aspire to be – inclusive, diverse, creative, courageous, colourful, passionate and principled. This book is written in celebration of them and what they represent.

I would therefore like to acknowledge the support and encouragement of my companions and colleagues who have given their consent to using their accounts within this book: Mary Aspinall-Miles, Julie Fallon, Shelly Glaister-Young, Emma Hughes, Stephen Lue, Ian McArdle, Mass Ndow-Njie, Eve Robinson, Brie Stevens-Hoare KC, Marina Sergides, Srishti Suresh and Colin Wells. You all gave me your trust when you accepted my invitation to speak in your own voice about your journey to the Bar and what the view looks like now you have climbed its hills and are looking around and beyond. Thank you 'Team Jo'. I have some colleagues who have become 'sisters and brothers' in law. You know who you are. You have helped me survive and thrive, and when I have fallen, you have picked me up and held me until I felt strong enough to take up arms ready for battle again.

My legal heroes are pretty obvious as you read into the chapters, but I single out Mike Mansfield KC as the person who showed me, by his deeds as well as words, that one could and should be a change maker by one's actions as a barrister. Mike was and is a 'Champion of the People'. To have his friendship and support meant and means the world to me.

To Baroness Ruth Deech KC (Hon), Sir James Munby and the Hon Dame Mary Hogg – thank you for lifting me up to reach the Bar. I have set my standards high because of your teachings.

I would like to record my appreciation for the platform to the remarkable education institution that is Gresham College for having the confidence in me and what I wanted to say to appoint me as their Professor of Law in 2016. Gresham College has, since 1597, been committed to delivering free education to all who wish to access it without discrimination of income, age, background, belief or country. They appoint those they consider to be leaders and pioneers. Seeing the contributions of Sir Chris Whitty (Physic), Sir Geoffrey Nice KC (Law) and Professor Ronald Hutton (Divinity) by way of example alone is to see the generosity of intellect that is the hallmark of its chosen professors. It was a privilege to be part of this remarkable organisation for over a decade as Professor, Fellow and Council member. I remain a strong advocate for the College through my Emeritus Professorship. Check it out if its work is unknown to you. It is a brains trust of the highest order.

I would also like to thank my editorial team at Bristol University Press. Without the encouragement, patience and support of Helen Davis, I would never have got beyond the starting pistol. Without Rebecca Tomlinson, Grace Carroll and Victoria Pittman, I would never have got to the finish line. They have done more than act as editors; they have been my advisors and champions. I am indebted to them for their skill and generosity of spirit.

My family were and are remarkable people. My huge East Finchley clan of the Edwardses, Norrises and Burkes, with its multi-generational shared love of life ethos, gave me the confidence and skills to be loud or a listener. To be a showstopper, lime-light hugger or to wait in the wings ready to be called in for the chorus. My great aunts and uncles were the life and soul of any party. We lived in each other's pockets in rented flats within shouting distance of one another. Their energy, along with my Nan and Grandad's (slightly more sober) steady, unwavering love, created, for me, a childhood to be proud of. What I've lost from their passing I retain in my links with Al Norman and Devina Solanki. They *are* family. That means something.

Then to my own family. The one I've created with Jonathan Light, the man I got to know in China in 1981 when I was 17 and doing my A levels. Jonathan was 18 and about to start at Imperial College reading chemical engineering. Jonathan galvanised my political interests. He shook up my preconceptions of what I could do and should do if I wanted to put them into action. He saw my place at the Bar before I could and without him, I would not be here. When I've found the professional and personal challenges I've set for myself too much to handle he has spurred me on. As a man of principle himself, he makes me stronger and fiercer. This book is a case in point. I'd have dropped the project but for him picking up the baton and holding it, and me, together until I got to the finish line. It's been a long slog. When I wanted to give up, he spurred me on. He was and is my 'critical' champion. 'Critical' because he is no believer in false praise or anodyne commentary. I get the unvarnished truth from Jonathan, and I need that as my lodestar. 'Critical' because, quite simply, without him by my side I don't know where I would be in life or at work. Without him, I know I would not be the person that has been given three remarkable, very different, kids and this incredible career. Thank you, Jonathan Light.

Lastly, I want to say 'thank you' to the woman who won't read the words in this book but who was front and centre of my being as my mum. Pauline Alberta Delahunty (née Norris) (1939–2007) was a quiet, clever woman made into a softly spoken, quiet warrior. She created a new life for us by necessity of circumstance as an abandoned mother and wife and her love and singular devotion to me. She died a few months after I'd taken silk and was already very ill when I hit that career milestone. I wish she could have seen what I've done with that status and responsibility. I think mum would have been scared for me at times, but she would have been proud of what I have tried to do for women like her and for families like ours who aspired for little but deserved so much more in terms of opportunity. She was and remains my ultimate hero.

JDKC
11 August 2025

Note to the readers ...

While I've been critical of the pace of change at the Bar on issues that matter to me, if my hopes are realised change will happen. The future of the Bar isn't fixed, but the printing date for this book is. A case in point is the Harman Report on bullying, harassment and sexual harassment at the Bar, due to be published later this year. It is an excoriating reaffirmation of the toxic elements of the Bar's culture that I identify and tackle in this book. The book is as up to date as it can be at the time of writing. I've tried to pick up on consistent themes from many Bar and other professional publications and people, so even if statistics change, the trend is clear, as is what needs to be done to change direction and momentum. It will need updating, but that's got to be a good thing if we are heading in the right direction. If it's not, then the fight to set the Bar continues. We have work to do and it must be done.

1

Introduction

This book is about the reality of being a legal aid barrister: the vocation for it, the joys of doing it, and the struggles and integrity of the people that epitomise the best of it. But it's also about the stress of it, the stamina needed to endure it, and what needs to be done to make the Bar a healthier, more inclusive profession. Because, to be frank, it is a damaged one as matters stand.

In many ways the role of a barrister is to be the storyteller on behalf of our clients and to engage the court in their version of history. We excel at that. What we are not good at historically is being prepared to *become* the story by talking openly and honestly about who we are and what we see and think of our profession. If we are to Set the Bar, we have to be prepared to confront the reality of our professional lives, identify where we fall below standard and understand how we can Set the Bar higher.

I have been at the Bar for 40 years. In this book, I identify the people that Set the Bar for me and those who I can hold up to inspire others to join our world – but with their eyes open to its challenges. Readers will not know many of the people I celebrate in this book, because their paths to the Bar have been largely invisible, yet they are its unsung heroes. They are the people I hold close because they show me that the Bar can be a better place, and its independence is worth fighting for. This book is not a 'how to' guide to becoming a barrister,[1] it is about *why* we have become barristers and whether we

---

[1] For anyone who wants to see my take on that steep curve then perhaps as a starting point dive into a lecture (and its notes) I delivered

think, in the main, we made the right choice in so doing. To answer that question, I explore issues that we too rarely speak openly about among ourselves, let alone with the public. On some controversial issues I have been a solo voice until joined by a chorus, on others my colleagues have been the stars and I've been a back up singer.

You might ask why, in a profession which spits out as many able candidates as it embraces, and psychologically damages as many as it intellectually nourishes, I am an advocate for the independent Bar. Although it has been battered by cuts in legal aid and decisions made by our leaders about how to slice the court service to the bone to work the numbers rather than buttress justice, I remain passionate about the integral role the Bar plays in trying to inject fairness, humanity and integrity into a legal aid system. This is despite the system being barely and rarely fit for purpose, after decades of underfunding and governmental disrespect.

One of the obstacles the Bar faces in becoming a truly diverse, inclusive profession is its image of exclusivity, wealth and patronage. That image is founded in historical fact and persistent hurdles to equality of access and achievement. The stark reality is that the Bar does not, in my view, have equity of access for equally able candidates. On top of that, we don't have equal access to all specialisms at the Bar. Of the small proportion of applicants from non-traditional backgrounds ('traditional' applicants historically being white, middle-class, straight men) that get to the Bar and gain a professional foothold in it, we have a higher proportion of Global Ethnic Majority (GEM) peoples[2] and women in the underfunded,

---

for Gresham called 'The Insider's Guide to Becoming a Barrister', available at https://www.gresham.ac.uk/watch-now/barrister-insiders-guide

[2] We need to get away from the cover term BAME (Black, Asian and Minority Ethnic), it brings up the correlation of everyone who isn't white and turns a majority of ethnicities into a minority. There's a lively debate on alternatives; Global Ethnic Majority (which covers 80–85 per cent of the global population and refers to people who are Black, Asian, brown, dual-heritage, indigenous to the global South and/or who have been radicalised as 'ethnic minorities'), people of colour (often used in the United States), ethnically diverse, Black and global majority, and this is an example of where I don't want to

lower-paid and governmentally disrespected legal aid areas of work (for example, crime, immigration, family and housing) than are welcomed into the better-paid commercial, high-status sectors of the Bar (commercial, trusts, and so on). We know we need to target academies to get to the talented young before their career options close off, but we still tend to focus on groups rather than class and income per se, and some groups more than others. White working-class young men, for example, will struggle to find vocal champions or organisations that can speak for them and of their potential. We cannot pretend to have done any more, in the last few decades of so-called 'progress', than scratch the surface to change the Bar's overall make-up. There is potential everywhere but opportunity is a privileged and scarce resource.

We are not neurodiverse-friendly, even though it's likely that there is a considerable number of diagnosed and undiagnosed neurodivergent practitioners. I was one of the first, and am still one of a very few, senior barristers who has gone public about their diagnosis of ADHD, for example. We shed women barristers like floss, in particular at the point of parenthood, because the Bar can be an inflexible place where home and work life battle for supremacy. Losing women at this stage means the loss of professionals with often over five years of working experience.[3] My GEM colleagues still experience racism

---

presume or over speak, so I've asked my colleagues and it seems the current preferred option from those who it directly impacts is Global Ethnic Majority (GEM), with some happy with 'people of colour'. I'm going to be led by the majority of my friends and colleagues who are impacted upon by the term and will use GEM as it makes us think about why a global majority is seen as a minority in my professional space.

[3] Bar Council, 'Key Trends Shaping Recruitment and Retention at the Bar', 31 October 2022, https://www.barcouncil.org.uk/resource/key-trends-shaping-recruitment-and-retention-at-the-bar.html. Since 2000, a roughly equal number of men and women obtain tenancies after pupillage; female barristers aged below 30 are generally more likely than male barristers in the same age range to have stopped practising during year 5 and more likely to have left practice indefinity before year 5; and men by far outnumber women in terms of taking silk, with the proportion of women KCs standing at just 17.9 per cent in December 2021. The Bar Council's 'Race at

and not all of my LGBTQIA+ colleagues are comfortable with being 'out', because they fear their practices will suffer.

My colleagues on the front line of legal aid work have entrusted me with their life stories and career highs and lows for this book, and each of them speaks with integrity and courage. Whether our pronouns are he, she or them, whether we identify as straight or LGBTQIA+, white or GEM, got straight As at school or struggled, come from single families, blended families or screwed up families, we all represent the Bar. It's important to me to deconstruct my success and that of my colleagues, because we are not now as we were when we were making life choices about whether to stay on in education or go to work, what to study let alone what we wanted from life as an adult. My colleagues' stories, and mine, deconstruct many myths about who and what makes a barrister. It is, for example, bollocks to think only 'the best' make it to the Bar. For myself, and many others, chance encounters, luck and the kindness of strangers played as significant a role in our careers as our intelligence and aptitude. This book aims to open up a world that is closed to many, who may only judge it through the selective, and sometimes distorted, lens of the press, social media or the tales of bruised client participants. This book acknowledges the fetid boils of secrecy, power and patronage that fester in our profession. It amplifies the call for constructive, positive change.

Who is this book for? It's for my colleagues, it's for my power masters, it's for the interested public, it's for the young who we need to come into our profession to take it forward and be its champions for the future. It's for anyone involved in the law who is prepared to listen to uncomfortable truths and vocally agitate for change. As barristers we are expected to be eloquent in the cause of our clients, but too often we are poor advocates for ourselves. That needs to change. The public have little understanding of our role. We are too often seen as emblems of the state, fighting to protect it, not defend the public against its excesses. Or we are portrayed by right-wing politicians and the uneducated press as 'fat cat lawyers', making a

---

the Bar Report 2021' revealed only five Black female QCs (as was) at the time of publication and all were London-based (https://www.barcouncil.org.uk/resource/race-at-the-bar-report-2021.html).

killing out of trials for the indefensible, the unworthy and the guilty as though we, the barristers, are entitled to take a view on morality and guilt as individuals and professionals. Such attacks are based on sheer ignorance. As of September 2023, we had a high-ranking government minister who publicly criticised our ethics, carelessly exposing us to racist and misogynistic threats from an enraged public mob.[4] In August 2024 we had riots and public disorder in our cities after inflammatory internet wind-ups by apostles of the far right laying the blame on 'immigrants' for everything wrong in our society. Those men and women alleged to have been involved in racist, fascist marches in our cities will be entitled to a defence barrister if they deny the charges, however abhorrent their actions, chants and beliefs. Why? Because, as the Secret Barrister tweeted, when goaded by someone to say if they would act for Nigel Farage if Farage had been arrested:

> Easily. Because we don't judge our clients. Like doctors, we just help the person in front of us, no matter what they might have done. That's the job. That's what keeps the Rule of Law alive. That's what sets us apart from the politicians who denigrate us for cheap clicks.[5]

The energy and commitment of the principled and public-minded barristers who work at the coal face of the justice system are preyed upon by the state. Successive governments have relied on the Bar's

---

[4] Open letter to Suella Braverman signed by 140 academic lawyers calling for an end to public criticism of lawyers, see https://www.lawgazette.co.uk/news/academics-call-on-braverman-to-end-lawyer-attacks/5117156.article. The letter called on the government to condemn the compilation of dossiers on individual lawyers such as that of Ms Jacqueline McKenzie, partner at solicitor firm Leigh Day, and 'cease its unjustified criticism of immigration lawyers' for promoting the interests of their clients in ensuring the government acted legally. This request was met by silence from the then PM Johnson. Braverman's attack is one of many she has made upon legal aid lawyers.

[5] https://x.com/barristersecret/status/1820886980626088144?s=46&t=9nG-gQ2GZ97ZUFt3Tmw-Ew

willingness to do more for less money because we can't turn our faces against clients in need while the government, year on year, reduces its investment in and public support for the work we do. For years the legal aid Bar has been decried by the likes of politicians like Priti Patel, Suella Braverman and Kemi Badenoch. We are not defended from slurs levelled at us by politicians, or by press barons about the independence of the role when called upon to defend the 'enemies of the state' or its 'undeserving' criminals. We have few politicians who will publicly defend our principles, politics, ethics and pay, leaving it to us to take to the streets and strike, as my colleagues at the Criminal Bar did so effectively in 2022 when they refused to go to court in protest against stagnant fees. Almost 2,500 barristers participated after 94.4 per cent of CBA members voted to support a 'no returns' policy from 11 April 2022. The strike came to an end some six months later following a deal with the then Secretary of State for Justice Brandon Lewis. This episode taught me that we need to be better advocates on our own behalf – for the independent legal aid Bar can no longer shoulder the weight of a collapsing family and criminal 'justice' court system.

The likes of the Secret Barrister and my colleagues on social media such as Crime Girl, the author of 'Pink Tape' blogs Lucy Reed KC, Mary Aspinall-Miles, Mary Prior KC, and many others I discuss elsewhere in this book, have sought to break through much of the mystique and misunderstanding that suffocates the Bar to reveal its ethics, its workings and its struggles. As common law barristers we have different specialisms, we have different styles, but what we have in common is our work for and with the most disengaged and vulnerable members of society – those who face allegations of being unsafe parents, of committing crimes, of being unfit to live in our country. We live and breathe legal aid. We Set the Bar. We fight for equality, education, empowerment and change. We speak about the antisocial work hours, the lack of pay and pension, the dark places our work takes us to in terms of its violence and degradation; man to man, man to woman, adult to child. We read and watch things that expose us to the unimaginable cruelty that some humans (and the state) have the capacity to inflict upon others. We shout aloud about the racist, sexist and classist barriers placed in the way of recruitment, retention and advancement at the Bar that place a stranglehold on progression into the senior ranks of the judiciary. We call out ignorant comments by the press, public or politicians and hold our professional system to account when it fails our members (such as sexual harassment and abusive bullying behaviour). We write and speak not in competition with one another but in support of each other.

My colleagues strengthen my resolve to stay in this profession and fight for it and my clients. As they support me by being open about their struggles, I lean into that camaraderie and reach down to pull others up the survival ladder. When I first tried to become a barrister, I felt I needed a rule book, dictionary, map and translator to make sense of the Bar. I did not see or hear anyone that reflected any image I could see a part of myself in. I have not forgotten what being an outsider felt like. This book peels away the layers that shield the woman at the heart of Professor Jo Delahunty KC, for I was not, at the beginning of my career, very different from many a young person who wants to jump the groove and take a career path that their background and income might not have destined them for.

My story

According to my professional portfolio, I am an Emeritus Professor of Law of Gresham College,[6] a KC, a Recorder, a Bencher, a patron, a public speaker, alumnus of Oxford University and award celebrant. I was awarded the Freedom of the City of London and named as one of Middle Temple's 100 women of distinction in the last 100 years for my contribution to the law. I'm listed in *Who's Who* and a Wiki page has been created about me by Women in Red.[7]

---

[6] Established in 1597 by Sir Thomas Gresham to provide education of the highest order to the public (https://www.gresham.ac.uk/). Gresham lives up to its creed, 'For the Love of Learning', by providing free and freely accessible lectures to the national and international public by brilliant minds in their fields.

[7] https://en.wikipedia.org/wiki/Wikipedia:WikiProject_Women_in_Red. Women in Red is a WikiProject intended to address the current gender bias in Wikipedia content. The worldwide project focuses on creating content regarding women's biographies, women's works and women's issues.

I am now, also, an author. That list quite frankly shows why judging someone by their job titles or CV headlines is superficial at best, misleading at worst. I do not recognise myself. Why? Because it blurs (if not blots out) who I am in the parts that matter. The sharp corners now honed into sharp blades from early rejections remain, and I will use them to cut out a space to talk about that which is special about being a barrister and aspects that are toxic. I entered the Bar, not to emulate the barristers I could see and hear around me, but to be the best barrister *I* could be. Some 40 years later I can claim the accolades I have been given with pride, but they owe much to the family I come from and the people I have surrounded myself with. If this book is about showing how being an outsider can be an advantage; if it is about being willing to expose the parts of you that don't fit the mould; if it is about paying back the gifts we have been given by those who have loved and supported us (and this book deals with all these things) then it is right that I talk frankly about my own unorthodox journey to the Bar. My past is what informs my passion for diversity and inclusion at the Bar. To understand why I remain as outspoken in my seniority at the Bar as I was as an upstart aspiring entrant to this extraordinary profession then you need to know of my past and my family – for I am proud of each.

I was born in Whittington Hospital, Archway, London in 1963. My mum wasn't allowed to have anyone with her as she gave birth or as she cradled me as a newborn. We were taken to recover in the 'unmarried mothers' ward. The stigma for my mother that had begun when my father left us continued into this most life-changing, frightening, lonely moment. My nan and grandad had argued with staff, then begged, to be admitted to see us. They were denied admittance. Only husbands were allowed on the ward to await the birth, and my father was nowhere to be seen. My mum *was* married, and to my father, but he had left her when she was six months pregnant with me. He left Mum for his mistress. I have never seen him nor communicated with him, nor he with me. I do not have a 'father' worthy of that title. Outside the protective hub of her family, my mum was very aware that my birth was a matter of social embarrassment to the tight-knit East Finchley working-class community that my parents came from. This embarrassment was also fuelled by the fact that Mum was well known in the community as a 'Norris triplet'.[8] She was the new mother people crossed the road to avoid; they didn't know what to say when she walked the pram in the street to my nan and grandad's for day care. It was a twice-daily walk of shame made necessary so that Mum could start the first of three jobs that she held down simultaneously to support us.

An 'unmarried mothers ward'? I appreciate this sounds extraordinary now, but this was the 1960s, when a woman's social value was intrinsically attached to a man's: her father, her husband, even her brother. Women were expected to get married rather than have a career, to give up a job if they married, and to stay married whatever they had to deal with in terms of domestic abuse, infidelity, gambling or penury. Women had precious little financial independence or social status without a man. My mum had adored my father, whom she had married aged 21. They worked in the same factory. Her friends were his friends and vice versa. I had been a planned baby, but my father's plans had changed. My mum was devastated when he left. The choice was my father's alone, but the consequences were for my mother to bear. She had tried to commit suicide by putting her head into the gas oven, but the kicks within her womb pulled her out of that abyss.

---

[8] Triplets, and surviving triplets, were a rare phenomenon. Pre-IVF, pre the establishment of the NHS and its antenatal, obstetric and postnatal care, to be born and survive as triplets whose birth weight combined was 12lbs was a matter of local renown. Nan and Grandad had not known they were expecting three (no scan tech then). My mum was the first born just before midnight and came in at less than 5lbs, delivered by my great-grandma 'Ma' who was the neighbourhood birther and healer. While grandad was celebrating fatherhood in the local pub, the anticipated afterbirth turned out to be my auntie Pam, less than 4lbs, then a third child, my uncle Brian, was safely delivered. He was tinier still. They all survived, despite there being no incubators then, as did my Nan, at a time of high maternal mortality. The novelty was such that the local newspaper featured their births, their first days at school, passing their cycling proficiency tests, their 18th and 21st birthdays. The Norris triplets were well-known in East Finchley. My mum wasn't anonymous. As such, she had nowhere to hide when my father left her.

My mum was 24. She had grit. She was a natural as a mother. Almost as important as her own qualities were those of the family around her, and she had their unqualified support to do what she had to do to bring me up. And 'we' – the maternal family – the Norrises, the Edwardses, the Burkes – *we* were many. My nan was one of eight; six girls and two boys. They were a close-knit family and as they married and had children they didn't stray far from their Pop and Ma. They all rented and lived in flats in East Finchley within streets of one another. They were all regulars at the working men's club. They worked hard and played hard. They were loud and loyal and a force to be respected as well as reckoned with.[9] My mum was offered a room with me in a relative's flat, and that became our base. Mum would bundle me up for the day and take me to my nan and grandad's flat so she could do a char job;[10] they gave me breakfast and took me to school, while she came home to wash and change into her second role, a secretary. My nan or grandad picked me up (or one of my many great-aunts did) from school and gave me tea until Mum scooped me up for bed and bath. Once sung to and asleep my mum started her night-time piecework by my side. Pauline Alberta Delahunty was a hero – like many women of her era she had to mend and make do. Like many women of her generation, she also went on to achieve remarkable things. Not history-making things on a grand scale about people that authors write books about and are taught of in schools, but groundbreaking achievements by working-class people on a domestic scale born of the need to survive and thrive that can change outcomes for those they love.

My mum was clever. She had passed the 11+ but hadn't been permitted to take up her place at grammar school as her triplet brother and sister had failed the exam, and the school didn't want to waste a place on a girl who was likely to leave school to join her factory-destined siblings at 14 or 15. The difference in opportunities for state and grammar school kids was stark, especially for the

---

[9] My father's extended family, the Delahuntys were really lovely people who did stay in touch, albeit from an inevitable distance.

[10] An old-fashioned (not to me, though!) occupational term, referring to a paid part-time worker who visits a building to clean it for a few hours.

post-war generation. The school they went to dictated outcomes in adulthood. To get to grammar school for a working-class kid was one of the few routes out of class-imposed barriers to social and economic progression. Mum was denied that chance by class-driven bureaucratic assumptions about her independence and ambition. Deprived of the chance to become a teacher as she dreamed of becoming, Mum went to work in a factory, but she took Pitman's shorthand courses to 'better herself'. She left the factory floor to become a secretary. She then trained to specialise as a legal secretary and moved to Midland Bank,[11] where she was promoted until she worked in their head office in the heart of the wealth of the City as PA to their most senior solicitor. That vista expanded her ambitions.

Mum was one of the first women in the country to be approved to take out a mortgage in her own name on her own salary with no family money as collateral. She achieved that at a time when women couldn't take out their own bank cards or sign HP (hire purchase) agreements in their sole name. As a result, we three – my mum, nan and grandad – moved into a house to live together that Mum now owned. We had only lived in rented flats before. I didn't have a father, but I had my grandad (a very special man), my great-uncles and my second and third cousins for male company. My cousin Al was my go-to 'grown up' brother figure to seek out in our primary school playground and, as we shared our teens, we would take to the dancefloor at the East Finchley Working Men's Constitutional Club to show off our 'moves' to the hilarity of our family egging us on (Al remains close to my heart to this day). The Burkes, Norrises and Edwardses were a combined force of nature to be reckoned with and they knew it. At a time and in a place when a woman wasn't allowed to go to the bar to buy a round, I was allowed to watch the men play and banter in the smoke-filled snooker room of a Friday evening in the club, an inner sanctum from which women were

---

[11] Now HSBC. Mum's former Midland HQ is now 'The Ned' hotel in Poultry marking the fourth corner that completes the square of wealth and power of the City pegged out by Mansion House, the Royal Exchange and the Bank of England. She had her own office on the top floor accessed via a private lift street side to enter her domain. She soared.

banned and other girls avoided. From my earliest days I moved easily between male and female company – I simply didn't see the barriers that had been erected between them. I had a confidence created by the total adoration of my family. I was clever. I had my mum's brains and my father's 'gift of the gab'. I went to comprehensives. I learnt with ease, not just academically but playground skills – mixing was something I was good at. Having an opinion and fighting for the air space to voice it around a noisy kitchen table, a crowded, smoke-filled, whiskey-laced party in Kitchener Road, or a sticky, port- and beer-varnished table at the club was a skill honed from an early age.

At 16 my careers advisor told me I was '*bright enough to work in a bank, but not front of house, as I had too much attitude*'. University wasn't mentioned. My mum was unimpressed. I was enrolled for A levels at my comprehensive by her. I was the first one in our family to stay on at school past 16. Mum wanted better for me than she had been offered by state education. She did her homework – looking at the CVs of the senior (male) solicitors she now worked for she figured that they seemed to come from one of two places, Cambridge or Oxford. Oxford was nearer to us. My mum wrote to every single college at Oxford asking if they took state students. A handful answered and sent leaflets. Mum packed me into our Mini, drove us to Oxford, stopped at St Anne's College (the first we came to who had replied affirmatively) and pushed me out of the door, telling me '*Go on Jo; go and ask if they'll take you*'. I had just started my A levels. We had no idea what the obstacles to Oxford entry were. Mum had a blinding (and biased) faith in my brilliance, so we just rocked up.

When I walked to St Anne's Lodge, I asked the uniformed, bowler-hatted, severe-looking college porter if I could speak to someone about coming to study here, but I didn't have any appointment with anyone, and I didn't know who I should be asking. The porter could so easily have sent me away, but he didn't. He picked up the phone to talk to the admissions secretary. The admissions secretary could have sent me away – she didn't. The admissions secretary spoke to the Principal's secretary about what to do. The Principal's secretary could have sent me away – she didn't. When the Principal's secretary spoke to the then Principal, Nancy Trenaman,[12] the Principal could

---

[12] Nancy Trenaman (Principal of St Anne's, 1966–1984).

have sent me away – she didn't. All these wonderful people treated the unknown youngster standing alone outside their college gates with respect and good humour. Rather than turning me away, each one opened the door wider for me to pass through. Nancy Trenaman's talk with me was empowering and self-affirming – her independence, breadth of vision and keen intelligence was a powerful stimulant.[13] I had not met her like before. This experience at St Anne's was life-changing for me. Emboldened by my talk, mum and I drove back to school with one aim: to get there.[14]

After my impromptu meeting with Nancy Trenaman, I wrote to St Anne's asking for a place (I didn't know how to go about things) and was interviewed by Ruth Deech, the college's law admissions tutor. I owe a great deal to Ruth, now Baroness Deech KC (Hon). My mum, the ever-efficient secretary, had made a verbatim record of the call, which I still have. Ruth told my mum that based on the interview alone she couldn't offer me a place, but she was encouraging and explained how to go about applying through the exam process. Ruth was, and remains, a champion of equality in opportunity and education.[15]

Mum acted on that advice. She told my comp[16] to get in touch with the Oxford admissions office and book me in for the Oxbridge

---

[13] It was Nancy Trenaman that steered the implementation of the controversial decision to admit men to St Anne's in 1979 – hitherto St Anne's had proudly supported the right of women to receive education of the highest quality and in their own space. Nancy saw that students can be stronger together and achieve more when the widest range of talents and backgrounds are brought together.

[14] This experience continues to have a profound effect on me. It could so easily have been different at any one critical stage. It's one of the reasons I try so hard to be available and accessible to those who are thinking about taking up a career in law. Each talk takes time, but its mine and I can give it, and it may have more significance for the person I'm speaking to than I will ever know.

[15] Ruth is a groundbreaking educationalist and a woman of firsts in so many ways (https://www.st-annes.ox.ac.uk/this-is-st-annes/history/principals/ruth-deech/). I owe her a great deal. She has given me her unwavering support for decades.

[16] A 'comp' is a comprehensive school, a place you didn't need to pass any exam to enter and free to all, unlike grammar schools (entrance

exam. In those days one had the chance of doing an internal Oxford entrance exam either at 4th or 7th term (pre-A level results or after). The 4th term entry option was later abolished as it benefited public school applicants who had special tuition to pass. Ironically, I stood a better chance in taking a 'flight into fancy/free-thinking/adrenaline-fuelled' exam looking for potential than I did from an A level entry base that assessed results (the teaching at my school was erratic in quality and so was I). Mum paid for the exam. I remember being given some extra classes in English for myself and another girl, but it was all a bit experimental (for us and the school). I passed the exam and was offered an interview, with Ruth and the panel. I loved the experience and Ruth later made me an unconditional offer. I just needed to get two Es at A level (not including art) to take up the place and I got two As, a C and an E. With Oxford in the bag, I did enough to get by.[17]

It wasn't just that Ruth took *a* chance on me. She gave me *multiple* chances. Ruth was sensitive enough to my situation to know that an act of kindness and empathy at the right time with the right words of advice can make a difference to an outcome. She took the time, after my knock-back, to ring home to give my mum feedback and the information we needed for the journey to continue – not to end at that first rejection. She gave me my second chance when she selected me for interview and the third when she admitted me to St Anne's. Ruth was and remains a great believer in levelling up opportunities to higher education. Neither Ruth nor myself could ever have thought that she and I would develop as adults to become friends and especially not that I would go on to follow in her footsteps as Gresham's Professor of Law decades later, when, yet again, she opened up that window of opportunity by putting me forward. She has encouraged me to write this book. There is no end to her support.

---

    exam and proximity to school) or public schools (pay to enter). Comprehensive schools risked being the place kids went when they couldn't do 'better' – aspirations for pupils were set lower.

[17] The E was in maths. Lord knows how I got that. Maths was incomprehensible to me. Now it appears I have dyscalculia – it shows just how little we knew of neurodiversity back then.

I am not alone in having my life's potential opened up by the kindness of others. One of the themes running through the stories gifted to me by my colleagues of their route to the Bar is the pivotal role that one individual can make to their life choices. These stories will play out in the chapters that follow. I am not unique in my unorthodox route to becoming a barrister. A gift we share is the significant role a teacher, a family, a partner or a stranger has played in our lives to change its professional trajectory. The kindness of strangers is inestimable in its value. I try to repay it in kind to people who are strangers to me.

If I believe words can change outcomes, and I do, for that is what I seek to deploy for my clients every time I write a document or enter a courtroom on their behalf, then I would like to think there is a purpose that drives the words I use in this book. That purpose is to speak openly about what is healthy and what is not in the profession I have devoted my life to. I want to break down expectations that the Bar is only for middle-class, straight, white, public-school-educated men. If they are in the majority still in some specialisms that is something to be challenged and changed. I am passionate about the Bar and the public's right to have access to justice through legal representation of the highest order whatever their case or their income. I am a legal aid lawyer to the core of my professional being. But unless we do more to make our work better understood, accessible and better paid we risk draining the pool of practitioners to drought levels and that applies across all specialisms that serve the most vulnerable members of our society – child protection, crime, immigration, housing, mental health, special needs. Those candidates or junior barristers we lose will be precisely those we need to attract and retain to make the Bar and judiciary better reflect the diverse society we are privileged to represent and serve.

My working world

Of my 40 years as a practising barrister, I have been a child protection specialist for about 30 of them. That means I inherited a way of working that operated without mobiles, email, X, LinkedIn, and so on. Social media (a term not in use when I began) was more likely to mean picking up a scruffy paper in a pub over a pint or on the way home on the tube than the 24/7/52/365 explosion of information and views on matters great and small that we have in our internet-fuelled age now.

Social media has ripped through previously impregnable barriers to information, news and views on our family justice system. There is now a climate of open challenge to the correctness of a judicial decision, whether through headlines such as 'Enemies of the People' or through social media campaigns conducted by enraged groups such as 'Alfie's Army'.[18] As of December 2023, a judge was very seriously physically assaulted in court by an unrepresented litigant as the judge made an order restraining the man from assaulting his ex-partner.[19] When a parent gets involved in the child protection system they don't have to rely on their trained lawyers for guidance, they have millions of voices they can listen to at the click of a button on their mobiles: and those voices are not singing the praises of the family justice system.

The public deserves to have a more transparent system of decision making in the Family Court to see where the 'justice' lies in practice in a family 'justice' system (if in fact it can claim to be just). They deserve to know what evidence is called in court, how it is tested by cross-examination, who is actually in court and legally represented. By way of example, how many members of the public know that in 'public law'[20] child protection proceedings the child has their own legal team, however young they are, to argue a case independent of the state or the parents? The public have a right to know how

---

[18] https://en.wikipedia.org/wiki/Alfie_Evans_case
[19] https://www.bbc.co.uk/news/uk-67596824
[20] There is a difference between 'public' and 'private' family law that is likely to be unclear to all save those who practice in family law. In simple terms: think of a private law dispute as *between* family members (a dispute about which parent the child should live or spend time with, and so on), whereas in public law, the dispute goes wider than within the family – here the state intervenes in the private family life of the child because they think the child might have been significantly harmed by someone in its family or be at risk of harm from them (so a local authority might apply to remove the child from its family and place them in foster care, for example, and negative findings can lead to adoption of that child so they are permanently severed from their birth family).

hard the court staff and judges work outside of court hours to make the trial run. The public also has the right to know when things go wrong: when time and funding constraints mean that the right experts are denied them; when unqualified and unregulated 'experts' are chosen in private law cases because they seemingly offer a one-stop service of assessment and professional judgement that cuts corners; when lawyers are outclassed or underprepared and don't deliver the quality of service a client needs. The lack of press in family cases is a loss to the profession and the public, and sometimes to the legal case itself. January 2025 heralded a fundamental shift in thinking with the introduction of the Transparency Guidelines, designed to allow accredited journalists and bloggers into every family court without needing to ask permission to remain in court and to report on what they hear, subject to protecting the anonymity of the children and family members who are before the court, and confidentiality with respect to intimate details of their private lives.[21]

In later chapters of this book, I will talk about the contrast between the image of the Bar and the reality of practice. I will identify my heroes, including the young, the ambitious and the courageous. These are the men and women who have Set the Bar for change higher than they met it at. I stood on the shoulders of giants to get where I am now, but I now feel small and insignificant when I see the difference wrought already by the younger generation, some of whom have made advances in the Bar's culture before they had even set foot in a courtroom as a practitioner.

In Chapter 2, 'Wigs and Gowns', I explore the reality behind the stereotype: who we are, why we do it, and what shaped and energised me to come to the Bar. As I explain, I came to the Bar to serve a purpose. I wanted to tear down barricades erected by social constraint and politics that stood in the path of equality and justice. I was politicised by the Thatcher years, the IRA, the Miners'

---

[21] https://www.bbc.co.uk/news/articles/c5yvln142rdo#:~:text=Transparency%20will%20no%20longer%20be,provided%20they%20keep%20them%20anonymous; https://www.judiciary.uk/message-from-the-president-of-the-family-division-reporting-pilot-in-the-family-court/#:~:text=Reporting%20must%20be%20subject%20to,on%20the%20Reporting%20Pilot%20page

Strike, and the divide between those who had money and those who did not, the actions of those who were in power (the Tories, the police, the City) and those who were disenfranchised from the state, caught in the cogs of its engines of power. I wanted to explore my colleagues' experiences, to see if there was a thread running through the activist lawyers who inspired me in my youth, such as Mike Mansfield KC and Baroness Kennedy KC, to those who act as leaders now, such as Caoilfhionn Gallagher KC, Shona Jolly KC, Karon Monaghan KC, Kirsty Brimlow KC, Brie Stevens-Hoare KC and Mary Prior KC, among many others. In being gifted with stories by friends and colleagues I was struck by a number of themes common to all, despite our very different paths into the profession. Traits such as family aspirations, a drive for betterment, curiosity, sheer bloody-mindedness, a sense of social duty and a vocation to serve are all cited as drivers. Many I interviewed for this book also had the ability to shift gear or redirect their professional focus rather than being thrown off course by challenge or rejection, whether that be early parenthood, feeling like a square peg in a round hole, or the sheer financial burden of pursuing this career. They were adaptable and resilient. They could identify the person or people who had made a difference to their career paths by supporting them when they felt alone and incapable. They all describe a driving force that had enabled them to push through barriers that had been erected by class, race, educational gaps, lack of money and lack of professional contacts. Interestingly, like my path, some of that force was fuelled by ignorance as to the terrifying height and number of hurdles in their path. They all have the gift of communication. Their diverse, non-traditional backgrounds, far from being a weakness, was a strength, enabling them to tune into different voices and to be the better advocate for their clients through that life experience. Lastly, despite their success, all to some degree had experienced, and some still suffer from, 'imposter syndrome'. They all Set the Bar.

Chapter 3 explores what a life in the law looks like. In this chapter I will explain a little more about what my job entails. This might make you question, as do I sometimes, why it is worthwhile. I knew nothing about the types of work barristers did when I applied to study law at university. I had no intention of going to the Bar – that profession lay way outside my knowledge. I had no access to professionals in my family so had no idea about careers in medicine, architecture or finance, let alone law. It seems not much has changed. In 2022, a report published by the Private Education Policy Forum evidenced the power of patronage that gives public school students their slipstream access to professions closed to many state school students. Their CVs have 'value added' opportunities provided via professionals in their family, via friends or the school network. They are more likely to know where and how to direct their university and career ambitions and how to get the experience needed to enhance a CV to make them attractive candidates.[22] An educational and social framework, shaped by income, provides a healthy address and contact book and begats opportunities for that child to graduate seamlessly into a professional career. That situation perpetuates privilege and entitlement.

For too long the Bar has turned its face away from acknowledging the trauma our work involves and that it causes. The psychological toll my work takes on me is profound and I am not unique in that. You will hear from my colleagues in the front row of legal aid work talk honestly and openly about the impact of our work on our personal lives and those we love. When you read of the work undertaken by myself, my friends and colleagues, recalibrate your preconceptions of who a barrister is – think of the person *behind* the 'barrister' name tag because *who* they are, *where* they have come from and *why* they have chosen their respective specialisms so often informs *what* they do. If you are already at the Bar it might make you too look at your colleagues with fresh eyes, to acknowledge you may have made assumptions about their past and path to your side without ever having troubled yourself to ask questions because of their accent or assured confidence.

In Chapter 4, 'Power and Patronage', I argue that there is a problem. One of sexual harassment and abuse, a problem compounded by our industry regulators' incapacity to deal with it when it surfaces. In this chapter I explore how the independent Bar's culture of tuition by shadowing (a pupillage) and advancement

---

[22] Private Education Policy Forum stats from February 2022 state that around 87 per cent of pupils at private schools come from parents who are business owners or have professional and managerial backgrounds (https://www.pepf.co.uk/fact-finder/facts-and-figures/).

in chambers (patronage) can blight a promising career as well as nurture it. Getting into the Bar needs the applicant to get through a tough screening process. What if the person with the power to advance the application abuses the process and makes personal advances to the student? Once 'in' a set, advancement within chambers can be, and is very often, based on a system of recommendation by a senior colleague of a junior as to whether the pupil should advance to become a tenant. Once you get a tenancy a senior colleague can raise your profile or strike you down, recommending or blackballing cases and appointments. This power imbalance is compounded by the invisibility cloak worn at the Bar, where so much can happen behind closed doors and within insular communities. The Bar has had its #MeToo movement. In this chapter I highlight the stories of those who have been bruised and abused by this obscene abuse of power at the Bar; those who have been sexually harassed and assaulted and failed by their colleagues, their chambers and the regulatory bodies when they found the courage to declare their experiences. I've been one of them, and I am far from alone. From their first-hand accounts it's clear the fight isn't over. Professional silence makes us complicit in sexual harassment and abuse by others. I have spoken out publicly about the flaws in our system and our personal duty to act and how we can put that duty into practical action. Hear what I have to say. Add your voice to mine.

We need to have a frank conversation about how judicial bullying manifests itself, its destructive impact and why it is a poisonous canker that must be cut out. This is the subject of Chapter 5, 'Power Inside the Courtroom'. Imbalance of power isn't built into the system of pupillage and progression of one's career – it's a product of it – and for some it's constructive, while for others not so. This is in contrast to the dynamics in a courtroom, where imbalance of power *is built into* the operation of law. The judge is the person in charge. The judge is the physical embodiment of the state's power over the individual. The judge is the arbiter of what happens in court and what can and can't be said or done in court. With that power comes responsibility to act fairly, neutrally and without bias or intimidation. Judges can and do abuse the power invested in them. While this is only a small number, the impact can be immense on the practitioner, the client and the case. Until recently, the victim would have suffered in silence, been told to grow a thicker skin and to move on. I experienced it, and I was silent about it. I decided that as a senior silk, by which time I had built a platform of professional respect to speak from and had an audience willing to listen to what I said, I would no longer be complicit by silence. I will continue to speak up until the issue is addressed more rigorously by the judiciary. I know of colleagues who have been gratuitously shouted at and undermined, and have experienced this myself. I have received countless emails from members of the Bar at all levels who have experienced judicial bullying and who have felt deskilled and humiliated as a result. No one I know has made a complaint, ever. Judicial bullying is not gender-specific – either the abuser or abused. It affects us all, but some more than others. One can't ignore the higher incidence rate for our colleagues of colour, and within that group, of women of colour especially. As I sat at an evidence-gathering meeting of barristers from all specialisms and stages of their career as part of the Bar Council investigation into the prevalence of bullying in our workplace, I was withered by the visceral anger expressed by my colleagues at being asked, yet again, to say that which they had been shouting for decades with so little acknowledgement by their fellow barristers and the judiciary. Their testimony confronted the longevity of the abuse, its prevalence and the lack of support and redress they had experienced. I felt ashamed of what we had allowed to continue unchecked and unrecognised for so long. I give examples of how we, individually, can make a difference to incidences of bullying and what we are entitled to expect in terms of support by our colleagues and professional bodies. In this chapter I make the case for education, transparency, accountability, and call for a 'no tolerance' policy.

You might think that state oppression of women and the legal subjugation of their rights to those of men ended when women secured the right to vote over a hundred years ago. Not so. That was the start of the long fight to achieve equality in the eyes of the law. Before the Sex Discrimination (Removal) Act of 1919, women weren't recognised in law as a legal entity. One hundred years ago I would have been denied all those rights to professional and personal self-determination as a lawyer and as a woman in society for no reason other than I was born a woman. In the eyes of the law pre-1919, I simply did not exist as a legal 'person'. I could not have become a barrister because I could not claim my degree at university. I could not be called to the Bar, and I could not practise as a barrister because of my gender. In Chapter 6, 'Women at Work: Glass Ceilings and Sticky Floors', I name and celebrate the pioneering women of all class and colour who paved the way for us to become barristers. When we think of how far we have yet to go to achieve equality at the Bar and Bench it's important to keep the fire in our belly by paying homage to those who have done bigger and better things before us. We have battles yet to fight. We need heroes. We need to learn from our past to improve our future. Compared to their fights, the argument made to be able to wear trousers in court as a female barrister seems small fry but it is striking that it was not won until 1995. That marked the end of a time when women were required to reveal their legs to the gaze of the judge, clients and colleagues or face not being permitted into court to make their case. It wasn't until 28 March 2023 that the Thai Bar Association amended its ethical code permitting female lawyers the right to wear trousers in court. Even now, equality cannot be taken for granted. We have a serious issue with retention and progression of women at the Bar, with too few female silks and senior judges, and still fewer GEM women. In this chapter I argue that you can't have a justice system fit for purpose if it doesn't share power and patronage equally with 50 per cent of the barristerial population. I set out the stall for change. This fight isn't for others, it's for us all, and should be by us all, not just by those most affected.

In the penultimate chapter, 'Advocating for Change', I seek to hold a mirror up to the best of the Bar and celebrate what they are doing to make the profession healthier, kinder, more diverse and more equitable. I explore what injustices they faced and how they struggled through them. Their stories have value because I cannot say that the hurdles they describe (income, racism, sexism) are not as current now as in their past experience. We need to confront and expose ourselves to the professional and public gaze because the gulf between white privilege and open access to the profession still exists. It won't change without strident voices making it harder to be silent and inactive than to join the chorus of dissent and act to effect change. Through the involvement I have in charities like Bridging the Bar, Speakers for Schools or organisations such as Young Legal Aid Lawyers, I witness shoals of talent swimming in my direction. But they cannot travel without hope, and one has to be ready to lean in and scoop them out of the incurrent before it ebbs. In short, we can't change the past of the Bar, but we can, and should, do all we can to challenge, change and curate its future. I believe that is an individual responsibility and not one to be shirked. It is also a collective responsibility of the Bar to act – not a duty to be shouldered by legal aid sets, or those non-legal-aid colleagues who have a social conscience. In this chapter I argue for more transparency from the commercial sets about their recruitment policies and diversity and initiative drives. We have not done enough to hold non-diverse chambers to account. They have let sets with a social conscience and the Bar Council take the strain for them. They are allowed to get away with inaction, not exposed nor shamed into explanation for inaction. We have some incredible examples of positive affirmative action that demonstrate what can be done when the Bar is populated by people who care enough to make change happen. They inspire me. Let them inspire you. Diversity matters. Visibility matters. Voices matter. We need champions for change at the Bar to be visible, vocal and honest about obstacles placed in their path to seniority. We need more senior men and women to step up to the mark to become activists for change and to call it out when positive action doesn't follow fine words. The point is, we at the Bar have to set the standards we want for its future health. We Set the Bar, and we have to set it fairly. We have gone beyond the stage of wanting *equality* of opportunity. We need *equity* in terms of access, retention and promotion.

 The privilege of acting for the vulnerable and the chance to make a difference to their lives for the good of society is a powerful buzz. What we do in court to make that happen requires an art of performance that is intoxicating when it works and devastating when we fail to deliver. Even when we fail, we lose a case, we might even forget our lines, we pick ourselves up and carry on, learning, alive to challenge, hungry for success. It's the job. It's addictive. It's consuming. It feeds off us. In the final chapter, 'Is It Worth It?', I explore why, despite its many deficits and the despicable underfunding of legal aid work, the independent Bar is still worth fighting for and being part of. It should be a bloody brilliant career for those gifted with individuality, passion, persistence and intelligence. For some it is. Others are failed by it. That dichotomy is why it's worth writing a book about and asking the question: is it worth it?

This is my book about the Bar. One voice. One woman. One barrister passionate about legal aid. One barrister among many of like mind. We speak in court as individuals, but we roar when in a pack.

2

Wigs and Gowns

I went 'up'[1] to Oxford in 1982. The 1980s were a time of great division politically in Britain. Violence was all around us. There were race riots in Brixton, Liverpool and Birmingham in 1981. The IRA detonated bombs in Hyde Park, killing four soldiers, seven bandsmen, seven horses and wounding 47 people and animals. IRA bombs in Northern Island killed three RUC officers. We were at war with Argentina over the Falklands. The Israeli ambassador to the UK was shot in London, an event that provoked the 1982 Lebanon War. Sinn Fein won their first seats in the Northern Ireland Assembly with Gerry Adams winning Belfast West. The Irish National Liberation Army killed 17 people in a bomb attack at a pub in Ballykelly. A Provisional IRA bomb in Harrods killed six. Politics and violence seemed intermeshed, with calls for the death penalty to be reinstated. It's staggering to think the idea was so current as to lead MPs to hold a vote on it (they voted 361–245[2] against).

---

[1] I've used this word for decades because I heard it at Oxford, it sounded posh and I repeated it in my chameleon-like way, not actually knowing what it meant. I thought it was a geographical term but it's actually nothing to do with north or south and comes from an old hierarchy. The official terminology is that wherever you are coming from you go 'up' to Oxford at the start of term and you 'go down' from Oxford at the end of term. 'Sent down' means being expelled.

[2] Think on that: 245 MPs voted in favour. Their votes could have led to the death of the innocent Birmingham Six, the Guildford Four and the Maguire Seven.

In terms of social unrest, unemployment had reached over three million for the first time since the Great Depression. The Conservative government announced plans to sell off council houses. At Greenham Common, 30,000 women held hands to form a human chain around the nine-mile perimeter fence in protest at the siting of American nuclear weapons on British military bases. The British Nationality Act came into effect, creating five classes of British nationality. Thatcher had gained power in 1979 and thus began 18 years of Conservative government. Thatcher held beliefs that were an anathema to me and many others and had far-reaching implications for policy decisions she made when she was in power; even as late as 1998, for instance, commenting on the number of children born outside of marriage, she proclaimed 'It is far better to put these children in the hands of a very good religious organisation, and the mother as well, so that they will be brought up with family values'.[3] I railed against the unjust society I was growing up in, ruled by a government I hadn't voted for and despised.

When I first thought about coming to the Bar, I had little idea of the barriers I would have to break through. I had no barristers in my family and knew no one who did. I had a passing interest in being a law student from watching a TV programme in the 1970s called *The Paper Chase*,[4] which made me think of law students as puzzle-solvers

---

[3] This was a creed she held and promoted in her public life. Even as of 1998 Thatcher told the audience she 'deplored' the high rate of illegitimate births and continued: '[I]t is far better to put these children in the hands of a very good religious organisation and the mothers as well so that they will be brought up with family values', the spread of illegitimacy 'devalues our values, our community'. She proclaimed that previous governments had made things worse by providing social security benefits for single mothers. These words, more than any others, from a former prime minister, reveal what social stigma my mum and many others like her faced due to the ignorance and prejudice of their 'betters'. http://news.bbc.co.uk/1/hi/uk/197963.stm

[4] *The Paper Chase* is a 1978 American drama television series based on a 1970 novel by John Jay Osborn Jr. involving the story of law undergrads joining a Harvard-like university. The programme opens with Professor Kingsfield in class, saying: 'The study of law is something new and unfamiliar to most of you – unlike any other

on a quest for justice. Aside from that, the prospect of studying law or becoming a lawyer as a career was not part of my thinking. I'd taken the English paper for my entry exam for Oxford and would have liked to study philosophy, politics and economics (PPE) but that was a non-starter. My mum had supported me going to university on the basis that it would be my entry ticket to a career with social respectability and financial security – things she had fought hard to acquire in a hostile, misogynistic and classist society. Mum wanted me to study law as the first step towards to becoming a solicitor. I had next to no interest in studying the former or becoming the latter; for me, Oxford was the prize. I wanted to spread my wings, meet new people and play. For me, an interest in politics came before any real interest in my subject of study.

So I had little interest in reading law until I realised the practical application it had. I lived in a world where the divide between those with wealth and power and those with neither was unbridgeable. Civil liberties were at risk and racial tensions were high. Being gay was a 'sin' and being 'outed' by the press was a threat used to tame and control many a person in public life. I had discovered that politics mattered. I wanted the old guard out – they didn't respect me or represent me. I attended anti-racist and CND[5] rallies and realised that the law, and lawyers, had value. We acted as legal observers. We were sought out when problems were caused by arrests, detention or challenges to lawful peaceful protest. We had value and purpose.

Only by comparing the Bar as it was when I joined its ranks to the profession I see now can I assess if we have done as much as we should to make it an inclusive environment for the health of the future independent Bar, the betterment of its barristers and the public it serves. I feel more optimistic about the future of the Bar given who represents that future. I gave the welcome speech of congratulations to the Bridging the Bar graduates of 2025 in June (a charity I celebrate further on in this chapter) and it was uplifting to see so many faces of hope turned towards me, rightfully proud of

---

schooling you have ever known before. You teach yourselves the law, but I train your minds. You come in here with a skull full of mush, and, if you survive, you leave thinking like a lawyer.'

[5] Campaign for Nuclear Disarmament.

their religion, ethnicity, culture and achievements. That energy is needed to drive greater change but I can't ignore the reality of life and income at the Bar for legal aid practitioners. In an interview I gave for the Bar Council in June 2025,[6] when asked to talk about the emotional cost of legal aid work, my proposed title was 'I'm not mad, I'm f****** furious'. Unsurprisingly that was edited but my point was made. I was asked to sum up what legal aid lawyers do and why they do it. The Bar Council quotes me thus:

> We are the legal emergency rescue team. Civil legal aid cases cover the breadth of human experience, including homelessness, domestic abuse, children in care, immigration, discrimination and poor quality of health care. We come to the defence of people when they're most in need, when they're most frightened. We do it because we fundamentally believe in the principle that every person deserves representation at the highest calibre, and we do it because we know that if we don't, there's going to be more injustice in the world. We do it through vocation even though the pay is appalling by comparison with privately paid work.

In January 2025, the Ministry of Justice launched a consultation into increasing legal aid fees for housing and immigration work, proposing an increase that would equal a £20 million boost once fully implemented. Fees for other civil legal aid categories are also under consideration. Fees haven't been increased since 1996, yet in that time the consumer price index (CPI) has increased 96.8 per cent, meaning any proposed increases will still fall far short of bringing fees back to 1996 levels in real terms.

I was asked what it was like operating in a system that has been underfunded for decades. My reply: 'It's soul destroying.' 'We're angry, we're frustrated. We're fed up, we're being kept waiting. We want someone to fight for us in the way we're fighting for others.'

---

[6] https://www.barcouncil.org.uk/resource/the-emotional-cost-of-legal-aid-work-if-you-ask-me-what-needs-to-change-it-s-not-us.html

I made that point because on 16 April 2025 a significant cyber attack targeted the UK Legal Aid Agency (LAA), resulting in a major data breach. It forced the LAA to take its digital services offline and implement contingency measures for legal aid providers. Effectively our means of payment for work already done was cut off. While service was restored for criminal legal aid fees by the end of June (albeit taking longer to process), for civil and family legal aid the system remains offline. On 24 September 2025, the LAA announced that they would not be in a position to restore service by the end of September. We were told at the FLBA conference on 1 November 2025 that it is now promised mid-November. I harbour doubts as to whether the MOJ will deliver full restoration of all services, including access to our aged debt locked into the old system. In reality, even if a non-emergency payment system is restored, the backlog will be immense, and our historic aged debt (on which we pay tax) pushed further back in terms of recovery.[7]

I talked (in the same Bar Council interview) about the aftermath of the cyber strike:

> The issues caused from the cyber attack on the Legal Aid Agency has been insult upon injury. You've got mortgages to be paid, you have rent to be paid, you've got food bills to be paid, you've got children to be looked after and ongoing expense to get to court to represent vulnerable clients. The bills keep coming in yet payment we are due, for work we have done, isn't. This cyber-attack, which has crippled the payments system, will have a legacy that's going to take too long to resolve. Add to that the burden of taxation on aged debt then we magnify our financial jeopardy. That impact on someone's wellbeing is hard to quantify.

I was asked what changes did I want to see in the system to better protect the wellbeing of those who work within it? The article continues:

> Jo reports 'The issues are systemic. One of the reasons I talk about the legal aid Bar is because there's a qualitative difference in wellbeing between the hidden well-paid,

---

[7] https://www.barcouncil.org.uk/resource/legal-aid-cyber-incident-updates-for-the-bar.html

traditionally better-off commercial sector and privately paid family work compared, for example, to all legal aid sectors.' Jo adds: 'The burden of the work that we do is borne by those who are least well paid. And so we need to be paid for what we do, not for what we're prepared to tolerate. Our pay needs to be reviewed. If it's not we will not continue to do what we are trained to do and we cannot expect newcomers, with the burden of debt they carry from further education, to fill the gap when we leave. My colleagues are the reason I stay. Whether they are solicitors, juniors, silks, legal aid executives, court clerks, ushers or (the majority of) our judges. They are incredible people. They make the intolerable bearable.'

And finally – 'If you ask me what needs to change, it's not us. We are the solution, not the problem. We are fed up being taken for granted, that needs to change before irreversible disillusionment sets in – it may already have done.'

That interview tapped into a rich seam of discontent that warrants being openly debated at the Bar. The private messages I received want that. I said what I said in print because I and my legal aid colleagues are advocates for the people who don't have a voice that can be heard in court or in society. They matter. And because they do, so does the service we provide.

I see every trigger for the young, the future Bar, to feel the need to make a difference to the injustices they see around them. In 2020/2021, we saw the Black Lives Matter protests following the death of George Floyd. In 2021/2022, we saw women walk the streets to Reclaim the Night, highlighting the appalling number of rapes and sexual assaults suffered by women that go unprosecuted. Sarah Everard was raped and murdered by Wayne Couzens, a police officer, and the peaceful vigil on Clapham Common protesting male violence led to women being brutally handled by officers to appalled protests from onlookers. We have asked why it is that when Global Ethnic Majority (GEM) women disappear, are raped or murdered, there is less press coverage and public outrage than for their white sisters. We have seen the 'Pride and Justice' marches calling for an end to racism within the LGBTQIA+ community and for the inclusion of trans rights.[8] We have seen how national borders offer illusionary protection against a pandemic, terrorism, invasion and war. In August 2024 we saw vile hate spread by far-right activists and politicians through the internet that lit the self-righteous flame of racist, fascist, violent, ignorant thuggery that infected the cities – until it was met and smothered by the courage and integrity of the marchers who outnumbered them and proclaimed the streets a safe space for all. The year 2025 has seen a convicted felon take the highest office of the United States, as president of the largest 'free world' economy. Again, as of 2025, we now have 'ICE squads' in the United States taking their own action against people they perceive to be 'aliens'.[9] As a society we are as divided and fractured now as when I first started to question the use and abuse of power. We have fake news to challenge evidence-based real news and fake news being believed in preference to credible news. No one country's actions stay within their borders. We have groups of the disaffected who can write their own histories with internet echo chambers that confirm their rewritten narrative.

We were, and are not, 'Great' Britain. We are a small, isolated and divided island – in income, opportunity and ideology. In this abyss, then as now, we seek out like-minded people to see, support and celebrate us.

When I first became interested in politics, such a like-minded person came to me in the form of 'The Boyfriend', who was as enraged and engaged with the fight as I was at that point. I met him, Jonathan Light, as a fellow traveller on a life-changing trip to China in 1981 ('China Clipper', a competition run by a national bank aiming for the undergraduate market for A level students, had over 24,000 entrants and just 16 winner slots – Jonathan and I took two of them). Jonathan was pivotal in turning me from a *Daily Mail* reading

---

[8] https://www.reuters.com/article/world/lgbt-marches-from-lon don-to-new-york-call-for-end-to-racism-idUSKBN23Y0X4/. See also this powerful piece in *The Big Issue*: Oscar Sharples, 'At London Trans+ Pride, I March for a Future that Teenage Me Didn't Think I'd Have', *Big Issue*, 26 July 2025, https://www.bigissue.com/opin ion/trans-pride-london-lgbtq-oscar-sharples/

[9] https://www.ice.gov/mission

teenager (the only paper allowed in the house by my grandparents) to a left-wing thinker. We fell in love. 'The Boyfriend' became 'The Husband' in 1990. Jonathan was to be instrumental in me becoming a barrister, of which more later. Every career step has been fuelled by his faith in me. Jonathan has supported me with each step I have taken professionally and personally. When my courage falters, he fuels it. We were and are a team. Back then, when I was cutting my teeth on politics and protest, Jonathan was already an outsider in the conservative ranks of students at Imperial College, active in the UN society, anti-Apartheid movement and CND. He and I didn't think 'why speak up' about the prejudice and oppression we were witness to, only 'how to speak up'.

The law had purpose for me but not in the direction my mum had hoped for. It became clear at Oxford that I was not cut out for routine or being told what to do, however well-meaning the guidance. I railed against authority. I worked to deadlines, not to a timetable. I was a performance and adrenaline junkie. I had acquired a reputation of leading people and of not easily taking the lead from others. I was, as Jonathan pointed out, 'unemployable'. If I was to be a lawyer, to use law in the way I wanted, then I wanted the front-line role – for me that meant being the barrister, not the solicitor – despite having next to no idea about what that world required or making a living in it entailed.

Breaking the mould

Like many of the youth I speak to now in my outreach work,[10] I had no role models for a career at the Bar. Not only did I have no contacts at the Bar, I had no 'professionals' of any type in my family to ask for advice. My mum was by then a secretary, my nan a cleaner, my grandad a retired toolmaker, my extended family were factory floor workers, builders, labourers and some were a bit 'naughty'. No one had a 'career'. My family worked hard to play hard at the weekend, had a blast, and then the week began

---

[10] Primarily with Speakers for Schools, Bridging the Bar, the Association of Women Barristers or at events run by the Bar Council and Middle Temple.

again. I had been the first of my family to stay on at school beyond the age of 16 (my mum's generation had left school at 15,[11] my grandparents at 13 or 14), the first to take 'O' levels,[12] the first to stay on into sixth form to take A levels and the first to contemplate university. Every year I didn't go out to work marked a difference between me and my family.

I was not alone in being told that the Bar wasn't for the likes of me.

Mr Justice Sweeting is now a High Court judge, but he was Derek Sweeting KC, Chair of the Bar Council, when he joined me at Gresham in 2022 to talk about our journeys to the Bar from inauspicious starts. Derek recalled how he was *'at a big comprehensive school in Essex which was not, I suppose, the usual route in the 1970s to the Bar, which is more or less what I got told when I raised it with my teacher "Well, it's not really something that people from your background do." It wasn't that he was saying I couldn't do it, in fact he was very encouraging about many of the things I wanted to experiment with at school, public speaking and things like that. It was just "that this required money and a particular educational background, Oxford and so on, so you really ought to think of something else". I think he was trying to let me down gently and to say it was over-ambitious for someone from my background at that time'.*

So too for Brie Stevens-Hoare KC, who joined us in conversation – she talked of how, *'the deputy head of my school told my parents explicitly that they should tell me or persuade me to lower my ambitions because I was trying to fly too high and I would burn my wings'.*

---

[11] The decision to change the age from 15 to 16 was announced in 1964 (when I was 1!) after the Newsom Report was published (the government had been on notice of this since the Spens Report of 1938 – the Newsom Report gave steps for its implementation and led to vigorous debate, which was not uncontentious) but the government deferred making the change until 1972/3 because of the parlous financial state of the country. Think how many generations were impacted upon by that political decision to deprive a large swath of children of the chance to better themselves through education. Despicable. My mum was one of those kids sent out to work when her brain was still hungry to learn.

[12] The forerunner to GCSEs.

Remember, too, we didn't have the internet, the remote 'phone a friend' option[13] to look for role models or inspiration, let alone advice. There were no forums, Facebook groups, podcasts where far-flung people could form a community over common interests, sharing knowledge and advice. The nearest I had to any information outside of public libraries about careers and especially law was via my mum's work as a legal secretary. My nan was a cleaner for a family where the husband was a partner in a local firm of solicitors. The family had seen me grow up over the years as I'd gone to their home with Nan during the school holidays while she cleaned and had helped out. As of July 1983, I'd just finished my first year at Oxford. I got a summer job with the firm by writing to the husband during term to ask for some work experience. I was doing well there. In Mum's eyes I was on track and she was proud of me. When I told my mum I was thinking of becoming a barrister she was terrified at the prospect and incensed at Jonathan (who she adored), for 'putting ideas in my head'. She wanted me to read law because she had assumed I would use it to become a solicitor. She worked for solicitors. She knew what they did (divorce, contract, wills, commerce). She knew what they got paid. She knew how they were treated. She wanted me to have the stability of income and respectability that she had never had. Mum did not talk to me for months. I turned to Jonathan. He urged me to at least explore both options, the Bar and the solicitor route. I was encouraged and did. The partner was kind enough to see his cleaner's grandkid. I openly explored my reservations about becoming a solicitor and the attraction the Bar held for me. He sought to let me down gently. I reported back to Jonathan, who was enraged (as is evident from the letter he wrote to his parents from his work placement with ICI in Dumfries). He writes of how the partner had told me *'in order to get over the gap in her social standing and all that shit, as well as the gap in her finances, she'd have to get a First. ... I just think she should give each option an equal chance and try not to let pathetic creeps in the Inns dismiss her on the strength of her pedigree. I've told her that if she doesn't attempt it, I can't think of anyone else who is going to break through the Bar's prejudice and insularity'.*

---

[13] It wasn't until 6 August 1991 that the World Wide Web became publicly available. Twitter wasn't founded until 21 March 2006.

Figure 2.1: Letter from Jonathan dated 24 July 1983 to his parents. His confidence in me and indigation at the preconceptions I was facing shines through. He was (and is) my motivator and champion.

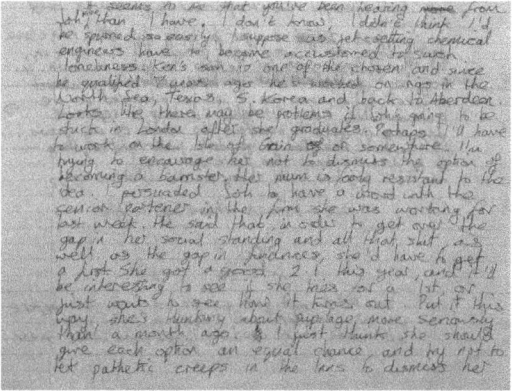

Note: All figures in the book are available in colour at: https://bristoluniversity press.co.uk/we-set-the-bar

Mum did request that her boss ask around to see if someone he instructed would be willing to see me, but with the aim that I would be made to see that it was not a career for me. Her boss obliged. I went for a 'chat' with a barrister at 3 Paper Buildings. It was kind of him to see me. For what was I to him? I was a stranger – the kid of a colleague's secretary – he didn't know me, he didn't know my family, he wasn't even a friend of a friend of the family.

Finding your way into the Inns is tricky for an outsider. The beautiful ancient walkways, cloisters and green spaces that form Middle and Inner Temple are hidden from the passing pedestrian's gaze. They offer an oasis of greenery, brick and cobbles fortified against the hustle and bustle of the Embankment and Fleet Street by vast formidable gates. Finding the gateway to enter this mini, fortified, hidden world of status and tradition was not straightforward (remember: no Google Maps back then). Working your way to your destination through narrow Victorian pathways, some with links back to the Middle Ages, was intimidating. The buildings are beautiful, unique, squished together to form a layer cake of British history. There was nothing, literally nothing, in the Inns that bore any similarity to anything I had seen before and there is nothing, even now, that anyone from a council estate, city street or suburb could look for to find a link with their home life. You might feel you were walking in a film set rather than a fully functioning working hub.[14] The Inns have their own gates, high walls, and are locked at night until dawn by their own system of wardens; it was a city within a city. The unique, historic layout of these two Inns marks the Bar out as a very special and privileged place indeed. It marked out territory that divided those 'in' positions of authority and the general public as outsiders.

---

[14] In fact, so heavy are the footprints of the past in Middle and Inner Temple that this special place often used as a film set for dramas that need a gothic Victorian setting or in fantastical films. I spent an evening of enchantment leaning out of the window of Garden Court Chambers looking into the grounds of Middle Temple watching the magic of the Night Bus run in *Harry Potter and the Prisoner of Azkaban* being created and unfolding before my eyes.

I felt like a fish out of water as I made my way to No 3. I was anxious. I wanted to impress. I'd dressed smartly. I didn't even mention politics as my reason for wanting to become a barrister but that was not enough to bridge the huge gap that divided us, which became abundantly obvious as the chat progressed. He (and there were few women around) very courteously enquired after my studies, my background, my plans. He was a kind man, and I think he did his best to try to understand me. He failed. There was no 'accommodation' between our two very different backgrounds.

In a letter I wrote to Jonathan's parents, I described how a tutor at St Anne's had told me I'd best *'tone down my colourful personality'* if I wanted to impress the conservative chambers that occupied the Inns. Looking back, I should have been cowed. But I was furious and appalled at the injustice of being excluded because of my background and attitude before I could even begin. I knew I wouldn't get a first. I was bright, not brilliant. I couldn't do anything about my lack of money or background. My 'attitude' and grit, generated by the belief that law was a route to challenge inequality, were my strengths. As I wrote at the time, '*I refuse to give up my ideals and act a lie this early on in my career*'. Supported by Jonathan, who was as incensed as I was, and with no insider knowledge to go on, I wrote to the Bar Council and asked for their pupillage handbook. They sent it back by post. It was a weighty tome listing every chambers in the UK and their contact details and pupillage process.

So it was that by 1983, my second year at Oxford, I had written to every single set in London that offered a funded pupillage to ask for a place. I want to pause to emphasise the sheer amount of effort involved in the process of applying to the Bar. This was all pre-internet, pre-laptop, pre-cut-and-paste. Every application had to be bespoke to the Chambers it was addressed to. This was pre any standardised pupillage process or criteria. There were no guidelines. Anything less than a personalised letter, neatly written or typed, no spelling mistakes (no auto-correct laptop check, no erase and rewrite a word – the whole page had to be rewritten or typed) would reveal a lack of effort and respect for the chambers I was writing to.

As of 1983, I was 20. I had no idea that the proper sequence of the application process was: (1) get a degree (2:1 minimum); (2) apply to and be accepted to study at Bar School for a year post-uni; (3) join an Inn; (4) pass Bar School exams (preferably with a distinction);

Figure 2.2: My letter dated 18 November 1984 to Jonathan's mum and dad. I'd started applying for pupillages while at Oxford in the second year of my degree, not knowing you were (1) meant to get your law degree and (2) get a place at Bar School and (3) be at Bar School before you tried to get a foothold at the Bar by way of pupillage. I was blissfully unaware of the 'proper way' to do things and blissfully arrogant about what space I intended to carve out for myself.

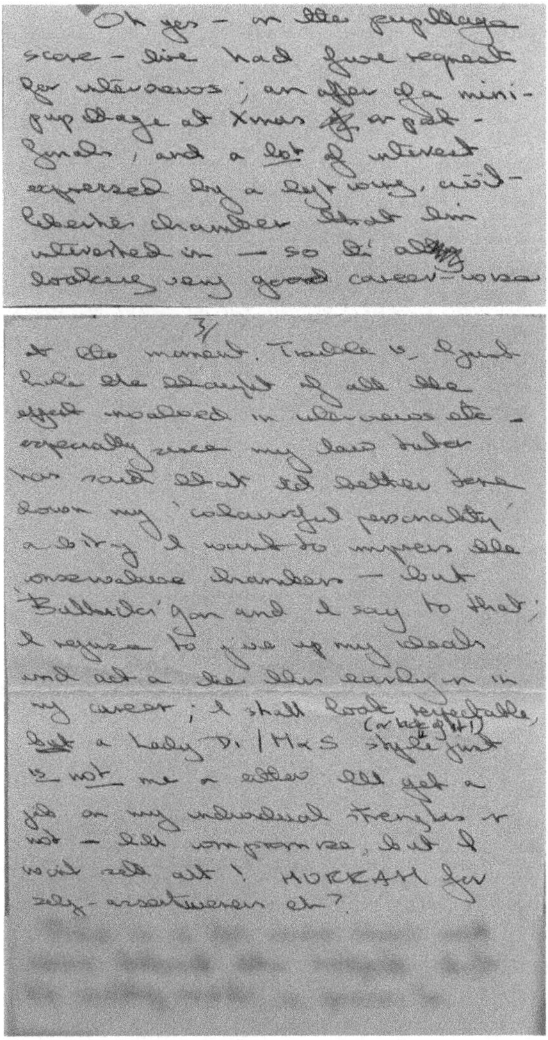

(5) apply for pupillages. I jumped the slow lane and raced to the finishing line out of sheer ignorance and chutzpah.

I received five interview offers and an offer of a mini pupillage. Just as with applying to Oxford, I didn't know enough about how unlikely I was to succeed at the Bar to be put off trying. Remarkably, after interview, I secured a 12-month funded pupillage at 8 New Square (a planning set – a subject about which I knew nothing and had no interest in) while in my second year at Oxford. Funding was more important than specialism as without it I could not take up the offer. I genuinely have no idea why No 8 took this chance on me. I only know I am more grateful now than I was at the time. I didn't know enough to appreciate what a chance they were taking on me.

Looking back

At the outset of this chapter I asked whether the fact I had been granted entry to it reflected a degree of inclusivism at the Bar I've overwritten since. The truth, as my story reveals, is that I came to this job through a combination of ambition, luck, doggedness and blissful ignorance. The Bar didn't welcome me – it erected barriers against me. But there are always weak points in any structure, and I found my way to break in via them. That wasn't because I was brilliant. I was the right person at the right time and place. In other words, 'chance and circumstance' played a huge part in my getting a pupillage, and that is the same now as it was then. I kick back when people say smugly 'isn't it funny – the harder I work, the luckier I get'.

Another link between my story and that of others celebrated in this book is the clear message that you need someone beside you to spur you on and believe in you when you feel overwhelmed. That person may change, as it did for me, from my mum to The Boyfriend. We need different people's energy at different times. Mum's work ethic and belief in me had shaped me into a confident woman. Mum saw the problems lying in wait in my chosen path and was fearful for and protective of me. She loved me. The Boyfriend, Jonathan, had the passion of youth and enough energy to galvanise my outrage into action. He loved me. I needed them both.

I've talked about luck playing its part in my route to the Bar. I can't say that the brightest of us always got the best breaks. Unless the young see the seniors in the job for who we are (as opposed to how we appear with initials after our name) we make our profession seem unattainable.

I did not get the first from Oxford that the solicitor had said I needed. Partying and politics had been my priority, not lectures. I got a second and was relieved that in 1983 Oxford didn't divide its degrees any further (I would have gotten a 2:2). I didn't cover myself with credit at Bar School either: I was still distracted. I was commuting to see Jonathan, who was by now a qualified chemical engineer employed by ICI in Runcorn. I had the safety net of a confirmed pupillage at 8 New Square, as unconditional as my place at St Anne's Oxford had been. That gave me the space to explore politics and the place of law in society. I was part of a group of left-wing lawyers active in the Haldane Society. I passed my Bar Finals, which is what I needed to do to take up my pupillage. I need to be clear – I *literally* passed. No distinction. Like most pupillage applicants, the dream of a tenancy was a long way away. The drop-off rate at each of the critical stages (getting a pupillage and being offered a tenancy) is breathtakingly high.

Today, when I look at the extraordinary CVs of the gifted young people applying for pupillage, I am shocked at my lack of skills and qualifications and the huge role faith and luck played in getting me a pupillage. Now I worry that the excess of demand over supply for pupillage places has set the entry level to the Bar so high (pun intended) that students think they have to mark themselves out for selection, not by simply being academically brilliant, but by having the time, contacts *and funds* to boost their CV with remarkable extracurricular activities. It discriminates against those who have to work to get by or don't have professional contacts.

Back then, what I had was attitude rather than achievement. A willingness to stand out from the crowd. I took a perverse pride in being a nonconformist. I was prepared to be awkward when I saw conflict between the 'way things have always been done' and the way they should be done.

In my application to join Middle Temple in 1985, there was a section on the form requiring me to insert my 'father's profession'. Lawrence Delahunty did not deserve a place on that form. More fundamentally, I couldn't see the relevance of any parent's 'profession', let alone a man's. My father wasn't applying to join an Inn – I was. Would having a 'professional' as a father mean I was a better candidate and more suited to the Bar? Without it, was I the 'wrong sort'? It made the application (and the institution), in my view, elitist, classist and sexist – and I told my Head of Chambers at 8 New Square, Graham Eyre QC, as much. That was a confident leap by a not-yet-barrister, confronting *the* most senior member of the set but ambition fuelled by outrage drove me to raise it (Jonathan was again as furious as I was – you only need one person to make you brave). Graham Eyre was persuaded. My form was submitted with the section crossed out, and with Graham Eyre's full support. He was an unlikely champion from the outside, but an honourable man to his core. He fought for me. I joined Middle Temple. The forms were subsequently changed.

From my early steps towards, and then at, the Bar I have believed that a lone voice can make itself heard when it matters. A principled stance, backed up by reason and grit and people who are willing to take on a challenge, can achieve change.

The way the Bar was

When I began my pupillage at 8 New Square, women were a distinct minority as barristers (though all the typists were female[15]). Of those that were there, no attempt was made to reach out to me. I did not have senior female role models. The barristers I saw around me were men, middle class, white and 'respectable'. I was a (dyed) blonde, with 50s flick eyeliner, red lipstick and a 50s fitted but severe black skirt suit.[16] I didn't sound like the Lady Di, Sloane

---

[15] Drafting was either dictated into a machine and handed over for typing or we handwrote the pleadings and gave them to the pool. Laptops de-sexed typing. Mum knew how being a typist marked her out as a worker not a decision-maker. She warned me against learning shorthand or typing (even for my own purposes, as if I was seen to have those skills, I'd be recording the meeting for others, not taking part in it. Spot on). Even now women are too quick to offer to minute take or given the task of minute taking. I make a point of swopping rotas for that duty in any meeting I am in.

[16] As mentioned in Chapter 1, a suit means skirt and jacket; women barristers weren't permitted to wear trousers until the Lord Chancellor's Practice Direction of 1995.

Ranger[17] types who were at Bar School, nor did I look like them with their uniform of pie-crust collars, pearl earrings and square-cut power suits. Nor did I look or sound like any barrister I saw in chambers, in courtrooms or in the planning inquiry rooms I attended as a pupil. Even my wig and gown didn't turn me into what I saw around me. If I spoke, I sounded 'common'. I wore my nonconformist look with a confidence I had no right to possess. But it had drawbacks. My look and accent fed into the perception by some that I wasn't a serious contender. It was thought I was the outdoor clerk and/or the mistress of my (always male) pupil supervisor. Too often to recount, a double room key was handed to my supervisor as we checked in for an out-of-London case. Too often, I had to protest and become a source of public attention and side-cast glances in order to be given a single room. It was humiliating. It was alienating.

Privilege surrounded me even in my peers – I became unlikely friends with some students whose life experiences were so unlike my own. This was starkly illustrated when Jonathan and I were invited over to one of the students' houses for 'tea'. We turned up at 5. There was no tea. There *had* been tea at 3 – 'afternoon tea'. In my home we had dinner at their 'lunch' time, my tea was their 'supper'. 'Tea' – same word, same substance – different meaning, different lives. As Jonathan said, '*you could take the girl out of East Finchley but not East Finchley out of the girl*'.

I was not alone in those experiences. I clung to the group of likeminded men and women I had met at Bar School. Friendships with wonderful, energising women like Freya (now HHJ Newbery) were created (and continue to this day). Back then we had to use

---

[17] I can say this now some of you will be familiar with Diana Spencer (as she was) and the Sloane set she embodied in terms of dress, given the drama series *The Crown* has aired and got to this period, along with a slew of films out in 2022. For anyone who succeeds in missing these cultural pastiche gems this wiki definition might help: 'a *Sloane Ranger*, or simply a *Sloane*, is a stereotypical upper-middle or upper class person, typically although not necessarily a young one, who embodies a very particular upbringing and outlook'. The Sloane Ranger style of upturned collars or pie-crust collars under round-necked jumpers, discreet pearl jewellery, and so, was a uniform – an effortless, although unambitious and unsophisticated, one.

landline phones and leave messages on answer machines. We played telephone tag. We had the Inn student rooms as common rooms, but time learning to be a barrister, and being at the beck and call of our supervisors or clerks, meant that meeting-up options were random.[18] It was by chance that we might meet someone we could talk to outside the set. I came from a comprehensive school where I was in the minority in my friendship group being white. That mix of ethnicities and backgrounds had changed when I went up to Oxford, but at least at St Anne's women were 50:50. Now, at the Bar, I was confronted by a sea of white male middle-class faces, young and old.

I don't remember that fazing me. It was as it was. It was a sign of what was to come. As you will read in Chapter 6, while then, as now, there's a 50:50 gender pass rate at Bar Finals, and 50:50 success rate at pupillage and at tenancy, the ratios become skewed at five-years-plus experience at the Bar, and especially around the time a second child is born. Not seeing women at No 8 or opposite my pupil master when in the 'Bear Garden'[19] or the corridors of the Masters' Chambers (let alone being the Master) of the Royal Courts of Justice was not unusual – it was the way things were.

It was clear to the set, barristers and clerks alike, that my interest in law lay outside of planning, with politics being my driving force. The conflict came to a head when I accompanied a member of No 8 to the Bear Garden, to challenge the legality of a strike ballot. I supported the strike. The experience highlighted how, for me, the law was a vocation, not simply a profession. I had come to the Bar to try to ply my skill for those whose liberties were oppressed

---

[18] Remember NO mobile phones! The original Motorola 'brick' phone was launched in 1984 weighing a kilo and with a price tag that meant that it was only for the wealthy. It was analogue. Digital generation mobiles were not created until the global network agreement was signed in 1987 and that created SMS (or texting).

[19] The Bear Garden is a hall next to the rooms of the Masters of the High Court. Lawyers often gather here to consider or discuss last-minute issues prior to appointments. In days gone by papers were lowered down to the lawyers in baskets from a gallery above. One day Queen Victoria visited the court and, hearing the noisy hubbub in this area, she remarked that it sounded like a garden full of bears.

by it. I will forever be grateful to the senior clerk of 8 New Square (Robin Soule – another supporter found in unexpected quarters) who pulled in favours among his network to get me an interview with John Hendy KC[20] at 15 Old Square; I ended up transferring the second half of my pupillage to them. I followed the fabulous work of Bill Birtles, Jeremy McMullen (not then a silk) and John as they worked for the miners during the Scargill/Thatcher power clash and national miners' strikes of 1984. John, Bill and Jeremy were men of character, principles and skill. John had charisma in spades. I had a hero in him. I didn't get a tenancy at No 15 though I applied. I started that process that will be familiar to many an aspiring pupil, namely doing a 'third six'[21] at a different set trying to fill experience gaps and getting my name known.[22]

That experience did introduce me to two remarkable women. Pauline Hendy was instrumental in getting me a pupillage at Cloisters, where she was a tenant. Cloisters was a politically active liberal set doing inspiring work in all matters civil. Through other radical young women, that shift in pupillage put me in the orbit of Barbara Calvert QC.

I celebrate this strong-minded, brilliant, outspoken and avowedly feminist woman in Chapter 6, but I just want to plant a flag against her name here. As an ambitious young woman, it can sometimes

---

[20] Lord Hendy as of 2019.

[21] Basically, another trial period of six months' work experience in a set of chambers. A pupil can expect to do a minimum 12-month pupillage before getting tenancy – the first six is training, where you are your pupil supervisor's shadow, following them at every stage of the cases they are instructed in. You watch, listen and learn but don't act in your own right. In your second six months you can start to take cases in your own name and go to court to act for clients, but you still have a pupil supervisor as your guide and teacher. After 12 months you might get offered a third six in the same set but it's more likely that, if you haven't been 'taken on' and offered a tenancy, then you will be expected to move on to make way for incoming tenants.

[22] I was rejected by Garden Court (a set that welcomed me with open arms as a tenant later on in my career in 2002 and where I took silk from in 2006) – an early lesson that setbacks aren't always the final word.

take just one strong-minded, brilliant, outspoken and avowedly feminist woman to make you feel there might be a place for you in her world. Barbara was that woman for me. I remember Barbara with clarity. She looked and dressed no different to the older women around me, terrifyingly a tad like Thatcher, who I abhorred, but her sense of humour was wicked and her laugh louder than a gang of a drunken Navvies. She was a radical fighter for justice and equality. Barbara had set up 4 Brick Court in 1974 to become known as 'The Monstrous Regimen of Women',[23] with the intention of taking on legal aid work, representing those who would otherwise be unable to afford access to the court. Barbara Calvert introduced me to the members of 3 Plowden Lane, Middle Temple, a young set who had set themselves up as a women-only chambers, given their frustration at not being given the same career opportunities as male colleagues. My network at the Bar was broadening to encompass older women who were proud to be awkward and outspoken, and actively sought.It wasn't until 1988 that I was taken on by Tooks Court, a set I longed to join, with Michael Mansfield at its head. Mike was (and remains) a charismatic leader.[24] The tenants of Tooks were a (then radical) mixture of men and women, straight and gay, GEM and white. Along with Wellington Street, Garden Court, Cloisters and that young dynamic feminist set of 3 Plowden Buildings, Tooks was a hub of political activism. We lived and breathed our work night and day, whether it be employment, housing, crime, immigration or family work. Fresh from the support for the miners and able to put that learning to good use, Tooks in association with the Haldane Society

---

[23] https://first100years.org.uk/barbara-calvert-qc-lady-lowry-the-pioneer-at-4-brick-court/
[24] Michael Mansfield KC (born 12 October 1941) is an English barrister. According to Wikipedia, he is 'described as "The king of human rights work" by The Legal 500 and as a Leading Silk in civil liberties and human rights (including actions against the police). A British republican, vegetarian, socialist and self-described "radical lawyer". He has participated in prominent and controversial court cases and inquests involving accused IRA bombers, the Birmingham Six, Bloody Sunday massacre, the Hillsborough disaster and the deaths of Jean Charles de Menezes and Dodi Al-Fayed and the McLibel case' (https://en.wikipedia.org/wiki/Michael_Mansfield).

of Socialist Lawyers set up the Seafarers' Legal Advice Centre, which welcomed fellow activist lawyers. For more months than I can recall now, we would travel to Dover for a pro bono legal drop-in centre we had set up to go through debt demands, social security entitlement and rent arrears of the seafarers. Our network of lawyers also formed the core of the Legal Observers, used to police the police during the era of the Poll tax. So plentiful were our numbers in my friendship group that Jonathan and I lost half the guests to our wedding on 31 March 1990 when the Trafalgar Square Poll Tax Riot kicked off and our friends rightly stayed to support the protesters in need and to record the evidence of the brutality of the protest shut down by Maggie's Army (as the police were nicknamed after the violent role they played against the miners in the 1980s pit strikes on behalf of Prime Minister Margaret Thatcher).

I was fortunate to have found a political and philosophical home. Tooks was vibrant, volatile and challenging. We were brazen in being the awkward squad and delighted in challenging 'the Establishment'.[25] In *this* place I found people who wore their wigs and gowns with grit and glamour. Mike became not just my colleague but my supporter. I met others who became lifelong friends – Patrick Roche and Peter Wilcock KC among them.

When I saw Mike in wig and gown striding into a courtroom, I was drawn forward in his wake. He was dashing, fun, engaging but, most importantly of all, he was a bloody brilliant barrister. He made the defence case come alive. He engaged the jury and enraged the judge. When I looked and listened to Mike, I saw what it meant to live and breathe a case and change minds and hearts as a result. Mike

---

[25] Some have joined it and still fight the fight. Vera Baird QC (as then) left the Bar to become Labour MP for Redcar then Commissioner for Domestic Violence, Emily Thornberry left to take Islington South for Labour, Patrick Roche (my best mate) was a Labour councillor and his ally in politics as in life, Barbara Roche, was Labour MP for Hornsea and Woodgreen, 1992–2005, Adrian Fulford QC (as then) took the Queen's shilling and went on to have a stellar career rising as far as Lord Justice of Appeal. He sentenced the rapist and murderer of Sarah Everard to a Whole Life Order. Adrian retired in 2022 having led the way for gay men to be out and proud at the Bar and in the judiciary.

Figure 2.3: June 1988: my first day as a tenant of Tooks Court and my tenancy announcement. Red lipstick is already a marker. No Lady Di 'frills'. I'm wearing the obligatory skirt (women were not allowed to wear trousers to court until 1995 when the Bar Council received permission to alter the dress code from the Lord Chief Justice) but it is long – no legs on show and no tottering in heels.

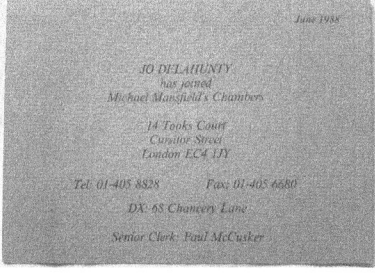

was the ultimate defence brief at the Old Bailey – he wore a wig with pride and panache, and his principles were plain to see on the sleeve of the gown he wore. That's what I wanted to do: challenge the establishment, as an employment lawyer acting for the unions and the workers. Now I don't wear a wig or gown save on appeal. But I'm still a barrister to the core of my being. A wig and gown don't define me as a barrister – my commitment to legal aid does.

I'm not alone in that drive – I will introduce you to people I admire, who are at different stages of practice and work in different disciplines, to let them explain why they choose to do the work they do and what it means to them. As my colleagues introduce themselves you will also note that they are not white, male, privileged and straight. That profile of a barrister is a legacy of the past that is loosening its hold on the Bar; more quickly in some areas of practice than others, perhaps, but nevertheless change is happening, they are gay, straight, GEM people, men, women, non-binary. They have children. They don't have children. They are single, they are married. They speak with different accents – Colin's East London accent is as sharp as his brain and cuts through artifice just as keenly, Ian McArdle has a Liverpool twang (the Bar is not all about London).[26]

As I said at the outset of this chapter, if I look around at the Bar as it is now, there is so much to admire and be proud of. The young Bar are doing things differently because they have different expectations. The people I talk about in this chapter are people who represent the society we seek to serve. THIS is the Bar as it should be. They Set the Bar.

Their diverse, non-traditional backgrounds, far from being a weakness, are a strength, enabling them to tune into different voices and to be the better advocate for their clients.

Reading their journeys to and through the Bar reveals just how much accident, and aptitude, played in their careers as it did for me. I'm older by decades, but their experiences bookend so many of mine. Like me, they have decided to talk about their journeys to and at the Bar, warts and all. Painful memories are exposed. That's brave and very trusting. Why gift that to me? Because they, like me, want you

---

[26] We have centres of excellence in major cities such as Liverpool, Birmingham, Manchester and Leeds.

to look further and deeper than the concept of 'wigs and gowns' as some 18th-century fancy dress worn by the privileged white elite. Each of them represents something magnificent about our profession.

They Set the Bar

The non-direct route

Ian McArdle was born and bred in Kirkby, Liverpool, which often features highly on tables for the most-deprived area in the country. If the law was a long way away from his school life, it was even further from his home experiences, which were neglectful and abusive. Home for Ian was the antithesis of anything that offered stability and safety, let alone encouragement. At school, when he told his careers advisor he had researched and wanted to be a lawyer, he can still vividly recall the meeting and the response: '*Are you sure? That doesn't sound very realistic but it's good to have dreams.*'

Ian was not to be deterred. A couple of weeks later, he accompanied his mother on a visit to her solicitor, as she sought a divorce: his dad was a heavy drinker and betting man. '*My mum and dad's relationship had become toxic and was punctuated by serious domestic violence (both being the perpetrator) which would often result in heavy make-up being applied or medical attention being sought by my mum.*' That trip to Kirkby town centre was pivotal. '*The solicitors' offices in Kirkby town centre remain etched in my memory. I was in awe. … I still remember that solicitor now. (She) left a mark and made me more determined than ever to have a career in law.*'

The kindness and professionalism of a stranger, the solicitor, had given Ian the inspiration to push on. Ian made it to university by his own efforts, to study law, and had to be self-supporting. But for Ian, like many others, his route to the Bar was as a second career. His was not a straightforward path to the Inns of Court and courtroom as a brief. Like so many from non-traditional backgrounds, he persisted, despite the vicissitudes of life.

For many of my colleagues, becoming a barrister was not on their radar – getting an education was a path to gaining status and empowerment.

For Srishti Suresh, education offered a passport to a different adulthood: '*Throughout my life, two of the three most abiding themes* have been duty and sacrifice. My parents ... sacrificed the familiarity of their home country to chase the promise of a wide-open future, and a better education for their children. There is a particular kind of courage they have in encouraging me to do things about which they have no knowledge, and no potential foresight.' Srishti ended up at Oxford, reading law, but 'hadn't quite shaken the feeling that I wasn't sure what I was supposed to do with my life. I remember being in the final weeks of my degree, the only person in my cohort of law students at my college that was graduating without a job having gotten through my law degree by the skin of my teeth. ... I was still a state-school-educated, second-generation immigrant woman, and if I hadn't been aware of it before Oxford, I certainly was now'. Srishti had faith in herself, buried deep within, but '[i]t was in the background when the trajectory of my life seemed inherently uncertain. It held me up when so much about the path I chose seemed daunting. And it sustains in my commitment to the work I do, and the belief I have in the importance of the family justice system'.

Brie Stevens-Hoare KC is now a senior silk in property and private client work, despite her state school origins. She now works in a world where she is acutely conscious of the privilege she sees around her. It wasn't where she had intended to end up: 'When I decided I wanted to be a barrister aged 13 it was all about fighting for truth and justice ... but I then realised it's much more complicated and nuanced than that and I also really enjoyed the more academic side of researching the law and explaining and unpacking property law for people to understand their disputes, the human interaction, the client handling and bizarrely the importance property can play in people's lives and histories.'

One of the key skills that each of us bring to the job is the ability to communicate, to gain trust to gather stories and defences. That is precisely why we need people from all walks of life being barristers, because real life doesn't end inside a courtroom or as soon as you go out, it's the body we inhabit to make sure that we can talk to people to find their story to best represent them.

Mary Aspinall-Miles' path to the bar was not straightforward. As a teenager, she 'besieged the local high street firms of solicitors with letters looking for work experience. Philip who was the partner at a local firm took me under his wing and was to change my life. He saw something in me that made him think that I could be a lawyer and then he did that thing the legal profession is famed for, he became enthused at the idea of inspiring and *mentoring me. So, he sent me off to do a mini pupillage at the set he instructed. And that was that: I fell in love with the nomadic lifestyle of the barrister.'*

Mary didn't have a place at the Bar in mind when she began. Nor did she join our profession *'by the straight path that is certain but rather a path that has meandered, looped and double backed on itself. I should add that there are no lawyers in my family at all, so I was taking the path with a blindfold on'*. Nor did she see her future in London nor in her now specialist field. Mary, like many of us, adapted and found a place at the Bar that was to become her natural home, just as mine was to be child protection law. As Mary recalls, *'the same values that drove my desire to be an employment lawyer were the same for crime: fairness, equality, protection of rights but most of all people. I like people. It has taken me a long time to realise this despite my protestations to the contrary or appearances which suggest otherwise. It is this alone above all else that probably makes me carry on doing the job'.*

Belonging and not-belonging

I've talked about a divide in culture and privilege between state and public schools, class and ethnicity – but that reduces a complex novel into a simplistic storyboard. It doesn't automatically separate the outsider from the insider. Shelly Glaister-Young attended a private school, but she had a complex home life. Her mum had serious mental health difficulties and she and her brother grew up exposed to its volatile, unpredictable consequences. A crisis point came and Shelly's mum was admitted to a psychiatric ward. *'Dad came home that weekend to a note which said, "Dinner's in the oven, the kids are in care". Dad told me that while my grandmother was able to retrieve my brother and me from care pretty quickly, I'd already changed and become withdrawn … my auntie told me recently she found me "destroyed". Not much later my parents divorced. Dad "lost" and mum "won".'* It was an acrimonious separation and aftermath. Following this, Shelly *'attended a private school and, for some time, boarding school. It was a huge stretch for my father, but there were two reasons for this extravagance. First, my father's wish to give me not just a good education but also the confidence and access to experiences and opportunities that a private school education provides. Second, my mother had (has) chronic mental health issues and after my father lost the battle for the children in the divorce, he wanted to make sure we were safe for as many hours of the day (and night) as he could afford'.*

For Shelly the sense of 'not belonging' was always a strong one. Shelly's clothes and those of her brother were often from the 'swap shop'. They were encouraged to eat well at school to save money at home. Shelly went through an adolescence with '*a belly full of insecurities, volatile emotions and general rage at the world*'. It was her economics teacher who saw Shelly's potential and had the patience to push her to fulfil it – despite Shelly's best efforts to sabotage her future. So, Shelly went to York University, an excellent university. She converted to law yet found '*life at Law School was a shock. I felt out of place from the moment I arrived. All but maybe two of my colleagues wanted to be solicitors. Some had already secured training contracts and were bound for magic or silver circle firms. Most were affluent, confident and well turned out. I didn't know it then, but the scene was set for how I would feel at every small group seminar, every exam, every dining session, every mini pupillage, every interview, every social networking event that followed. I didn't see anyone like me. I was a baggy-jeans wearing, pierced, ethnically ambiguous, angry product of divorce with a penchant for self-sabotage and a whole heap of attachment issues and defensiveness ready to be unleashed*'.

The people who Set the Bar for me were outsiders and yet they have carved a place out at the Bar for themselves – making it mould to them, not trying to straitjacket themselves into its restrictive practices. The point is there *is* a place for outsiders. Shelly persisted. Probably because she was then, as now, obstinate and (so she tells) truculent. During her pupillage, Shelly recalls that '*for the first time, I felt surrounded by people who were recognisable and approachable. Staple Inn Chambers was a wonderful and welcoming mix of characters, and the Bar soon looked like a place I could be relevant*'. Shelly is the best known pierced and tattooed woman in my working world. That takes an outward show of guts and confidence in oneself. Shelly is a nonconformist. She is also one of the best juniors I have ever had the privilege of working with and has become my lifelong friend.

Colin Wells, proud of his white working-class background, went to state schools and a polytechnic, and could only continue with his education through state funding and scholarships. Colin was acutely conscious of what divided him from others; I met him at the Haldane Society of Socialist Lawyers. But Colin did one thing I didn't – he kept his accent. Colin has a strong East London accent – he had and has the strength of character to retain it, but he's had to find a way to be heard. '*My first written piece was published in the late 1980s by the Haldane Society of Socialist Lawyers. It was my first opportunity to have a published piece and gave me great confidence to write more. The written word has no accent nor dialect.*' Colin says that '*writing was one avenue I chose to prove wrong to those who told me that if I wanted to "succeed" at the Bar I would have to change my accent. I am proud of coming from East London. I deliberately chose not to change my accent. I did not want to turn my back on my background for the so-called "success". One of my strengths is my background*'.

Ian McArdle had chosen to become a solicitor as a path that offered him a supportive working life alongside parenting his young children. As a young man in his early twenties, he had his first little boy with his young partner and then coped as a single parent to his two boys when, aged five and seven, their mother abandoned them to his care. Upon trying to transfer to the Bar, Ian found that being a parent was seen as an impediment by one set he applied to for tenancy: '*My first interview was horrendous. Interviewed by a senior male member of chambers, his first question was "You are a single father aren't you?" That set the scene for the rest of the interview. In fact, it wasn't really an interview. More of a lecture about how a single father cannot hope to have a successful career at the Bar as my focus would not be on my job and that I would take more from chambers than I would bring.*'

Parenthood can make you feel like an outsider. No aspiring pupil can tell if you, as a tenant, are a mother or father from your professional website. How exclusionary can that feel to a young mother or father thinking of coming to the Bar? Parenthood, especially young parenthood, as an aspiring barrister sets you apart – but why is it not evidence, not of your *inability* to come to the Bar, but the best demonstration of why you are *exactly* the type of candidate to cope at the Bar? The juggling of competing demands, the time management, the lack of sleep, the responsibility?

When speaking with Derek, Brie, Toby Coupe and I for a Gresham lecture on our routes to the Bar,[27] Mass Ndow-Njie shone a spotlight on the barriers that faced him coming to the Bar which resonated with many in the audience. Against the odds,

---

[27] 'How to become a Barrister', https://www.youtube.com/watch?v=uhQ48qRbUaQ

Mass secured the grades needed to apply to Oxford to read law but was ultimately unsuccessful in getting a place: '*I remember, at that moment, I felt almost like I had to start again because I saw Oxford as the only route to the Bar. When that was closed to me, I'd completely given up.*' He explains: '*I think there's still a narrative at the Bar in England and Wales that in order to become a practising barrister, you need to have gotten a first-class degree from Oxford and look in a certain way – essentially, be a certain colour, come from a wealthy background and talk with a specific accent.*'

Mass speaks honestly and without rancour about what it felt like to be so 'other' to the image of the Bar. He told us how '*like countless other aspiring barristers I find myself looking at a chambers website. Amongst other things, I scroll through the photographs of the members trying to find someone who might look like me. After scrolling top to bottom, and double-checking, twice, I cannot find a single Black person. I am also pretty sure that there are no people who grew up in my area. Next, I take a closer look at the profiles of some of the most junior members of the chambers, it becomes crystal clear what it takes to be a barrister here: you only need the ability to fly, publish a bestseller and have volunteered to save humanity at least once. In short, you need to have been a superhero in a previous life*'. Mass saw the competition out there and could not see someone like him who had made it. He wasn't being oversensitive. He was seeing the Bar as it was. Now he's seeking to change that through his charity, Bridging the Bar (BTB).

BTB[28] proclaims its belief with clarity and confidence: 'A Bar that represents society also benefits society.' BTB's vision for the future 'is a society where the Bar is accessible for everyone regardless of race, sex, class or other characteristics' and to that end it is committed to increasing the equality of access to opportunities within the legal profession across all under-represented groups.

BTB is the charity that Mass, then a pupil, founded in July 2020 to support aspiring barristers from a range of statistically under-represented groups at the Bar. Mass had much to celebrate. In July 2020, he became the first ever pupil barrister to be awarded 'Barrister of the Week' by *The Lawyer*. In January 2021, he was recognised as Advocate's 'Pro-bono Hero of the Month'

---

[28] https://bridgingthebar.org/

and commended as a Future Leader at the 2021 Chambers and Partners Awards. Recognising that his achievements in the law could inspire others, he dedicated himself to opening the doors of opportunity for people from non-traditional backgrounds. It is no accident that two of his colleagues on the board are Emma Hughes and Srishti who have also played such an important part in this book through their narratives. The rest of the team are equally committed and able but no mention of BTB is complete without referencing the energy and imagination of Eleanor Tack, in her role as programme coordinator. Eleanor, who was intrinsic to securing and developing the first ever UK Supreme Court internship programme, is now working with courts across the country to expand these projects.

Before going further I must declare an interest in BTB as I am one of BTB's triumvirate of Ambassadors, along with my friend and colleague Leslie Thomas KC and the esteemed Mr Justice Pushpinder Saini KC.[29] Leslie and I have been vocal supporters of this charity since its inception because, quite simply, we saw a man inspired to make a difference in Mass, and where he led, we wished to follow. Mass was and is a leader despite his youth.

BTB's home page proclaims its belief 'that for any organisation to reach its full potential, it must reflect the diverse society that we live in. We are working to create a Bar that benefits society by ensuring that the profession is open to individuals coming from all walks of life."BTB" is committed to increasing the equality of access to opportunities within the legal profession across all under-represented groups'.

The way it seeks to give effect to that mission offers lessons, I believe, for others at the Bar. The focus is on practical ways to level the playing field by 'up skilling' its students. It is also a collaborative organisation, making it clear it does not strive alone to improve access to the profession, it is part of a broader, emerging drive to improve access. Lastly, and I think significantly, it seeks to improve the transparency of the Bar in terms of those chambers who positively welcome candidates from non-traditional backgrounds.

---

[29] For a full list of the BTB team, see https://bridgingthebar.org/programmes/

BTB has clear goals with deliverable methodology to achieve them. It seeks out students whom, owing to their disability, ethnic background, socio-economic background, education, sexuality or other characteristic, belong to groups which are statistically under-represented in the profession. It works collaboratively, not in competition, with like-minded groups, and they can now claim to have joined with over 70 chambers, 26 sponsorship partners and over 300 barristers and members of the judiciary in support of their vision of a Bar accessible for everyone regardless of race, sex, class or other characteristic. BTB publishes directories which highlight chambers and other organisations which are leading the way towards equal access to opportunity at the Bar.

Impressively, in 2023 BTB set up an Academy for 100 students, where selection is through an open competitive process. I met and gave the opening speech at last year's graduation. I can see for myself what it has achieved. Every graduate is a success story, personally as well as professionally, because what they have achieved is against the odds and has been hard fought for. Whether successful in gaining pupillage or not first, second or multiple times around, they support each other and their camaraderie is humbling to witness. The number of graduates may be relatively small but its impact for each admitted student is high because, as they say, 'The hope is that by focusing our resources on a smaller group of candidates, we can maximise our impact that programme has.' To all its students it offers advocacy and training weekends, CV and confidence-building workshops, and so much more. It enables ten students of those 100, again, selected through competition, to have an internship at the Supreme Court.

The trainers who support the students give their time and expertise for free. Shelly is one of the many committed barristers who gives up her time to play a role in those sessions, as do Emma and Srishti. They are but three of the many generous men and women at the Bar at all levels of experience who give up their time to help others walk their path. I cannot name them all but they are each critical to the success of the Academy. For my part, I take part in training days and give workshops on subjects like 'What makes a good advocate during pupillage interviews'. I give talks on whatever BTB think I can best offer that year. I do one-to-ones with students and from this year onwards (2025) I have created and self-funded an essay competition with a cash prize.[30] The money helps a little but the win gives one person a chance to stand out and mark it down on their CV. It may be the first academic prize they have won. BTB wants to improve confidence and to challenge the perception that the Bar is not for us. We can all do more than simply clap from the sidelines.

Each of us who takes part in BTB gets so much more from it than we give. It is an empowering, inclusive organisation – it teaches its teachers to live up to the advice to 'be yourself'. It was a powerful moment at the graduation ceremony for the BTB graduates of 2024 when Mass chose to wear Gambian traditional dress and his hair in braids and, with pride, spoke about wanting to be 'seen' for who and what he is.

Alongside BTB (and one of BTB's partners) is the imaginative and effective '10KBI' initiative, part of the '1000 Black Interns Project',[31] which in just five years since its inception has created a community of 25,000 interns. Its homepage shouts out that 'Talent is everywhere, Opportunity is not' and then sets out to redress that imbalance through its programme of mentoring and supported internships across all sectors of British industry – including the Bar. My colleague, Andrew Powell, is on its steering committee and if the family Bar needed an ambassador to the young for what we do at the Bar (and especially the family Bar), and we want to hold out to them for advice and inspiration the best of us, then Andrew is that man.[32]

---

[30] This year the essay question was: 'Consider the legal framework and practice guidance that the UK has in place that seeks to accommodate the needs of neurodiverse individuals in legal proceedings. Does it achieve its aims? Discuss'. The prize was £500.

[31] https://10000internsfoundation.com/our-programmes/

[32] To see what I mean just dip into two of his podcasts ('Talking Law' with Dr Salli Penni MBE, https://podcasts.apple.com/gb/podcast/andrew-powell/id1446876356?i=1000497268704; and this one for Women in Law, https://www.facebook.com/watch/?v=1552887522106022). When Andrew won the LexisNexis award for International Family Lawyer of the Year in 2024 he received a hall-wide standing ovation.

All of this is a start, not a silver bullet. We need to see how the policies work out in practice: fine words don't change a culture. Some colleagues are further behind than others in grasping the concept of respectful challenge.

Why is it important to me that the next generation of potential lawyers see the Bar as a place where they could succeed? Because they need to be able to see the finish line and to be prepared to stumble and fall on their way to it. They need to know that others at the Bar have found a route to success after setbacks which they wouldn't know by looking at them as they are now. Hence the value of these narratives I share.

You may not have been to Oxford or Cambridge, you may not see faces at the Bar that represent you, your accent may distinguish you from those you hear in the Inns, people may anglicise your name because they can't pronounce it right and don't ask how to do so – any one of all of those factors can make you feel your ambition is hopeless and misplaced. Most importantly, that feeling, that you shouldn't actually have got this far, might still linger.

Personal champions

We all need someone who sees the potential in you and sticks with that faith to supports yours when it is crumbling under rejection. At the first stage it might be the person who sees past the failure to secure a pupillage to the potential that others have not yet. Later in our careers at the Bar it might be the person who suggests we apply for silk or public appointment. It might be the person who suggests you write an article or host a seminar with them or offers to make the introductions so you can start to be read, seen and heard. We all need personal champions at each stage of our careers, starting from the beginning: '*It was actually a middle-class white man who was my biggest champion. It was an openly gay white member of the Bar who mentored me for five years whilst I applied for pupillage; giving me interview practice and reviewing my application forms I submitted between 2005 and 2009 faithfully and patiently. The gift he really gave me was a constant reminder that I was good enough and that I shouldn't be put off by the double jeopardy in my head (at being mixed race and LGBT). I also learnt that your mentors don't always have to look like you.*' So says Stephen Lue of HHJ Lochrane who supported Stephen when others had walked away.[33]

Mass had given up on the Bar until he received a nudge from his former sixth-form teacher, who had entered him into the moot competition at school that triggered Mass's dream of becoming a barrister. That teacher wrote: ' *"Mass, are you a practising barrister yet?" (knowing full well I was not). I responded giving all the reasons why I had not pursued a career at the Bar, and he just said "Mass – someone I know just secured pupillage at the government legal department. I think they will still respect and value your experience even though they aren't in legal – put an application in.*' That's what Mass did. He started on the route that would redirect him back to the Bar. He now has a highly successful practice specialising in clinical negligence, inquests and inquiries, sports law and international cases.

Toby Coupe owes his dream of coming to the Bar to a barrister on his paper round, who he became curious about after seeing the pink ribbons on their desk. They always seemed to be working on a Sunday morning when he dropped their papers off. This barrister kindly offered him a week or two shadowing them at court. He went to Bradford Crown Court and *'absolutely loved it and thought "this is me, I'm sold"'*.[34]

As Emma says: '*The greatest obstacle is ourselves, our self-doubt and self-selecting out of opportunities due to imposter syndrome. I still suffer with low self-esteem at times but I encourage you to surround yourself by warm, kind, patient people who will go above and beyond to critique pupillage applications, do mock interviews, give you constructive feedback and have a true passion for the law and giving back to society.*'[35]

It can just take one person, perhaps different people at different stages in your life, to make a difference. Luck has a part to play, the kindness of strangers all the more so.

Srishti said she found a path to follow through following mine before we had even met: '*The stars (and Google) aligned, and I found*

---

[33] Stephen is now a specialist family barrister nationally ranked for excellence in our directories.
[34] Toby is a now a nationally ranked personal injury specialist.
[35] Emma is now a family specialist at 4 Brick Court.

Jo.[36] *I had met feedback throughout my academic career that my interests were too niche, too culturally specific, and ultimately, too unrealistic to ever lead to a real career. Yet here was a person whose profile was exactly what I wanted to do. It felt like the world had set into motion, and I finally had a clear idea of the work I could be doing, and the practice I could have, one day in the future.*[37]

For me, my supporters at the Bar came later in life. Mary Hogg J and James Munby J (as they were back in 2005 – now The Honourable Dame Mary Hogg and Sir James Munby) were the people who saw the potential in me. They supported me for silk and acted as my referees under the very first appointment process in 2006 that awarded silk as a result of open competition rather than the 'tap on the shoulder' by the chosen of the chosen. At each stage of my career henceforth they have been a constant in my professional life. They are the people I can turn to not just for wisdom but for kindness and companionship. I have much to thank each of them for. I was an outsider candidate. They took a chance on me and I have tried to live up to their expectations ever since. Their generosity warrants nothing less. Just as significant in terms of support and warm-heartedness were their respective clerks, Christine Hill and George Pitchley. The dynamic between a clerk and their judge is like no other. Very often, if you earn the trust of the former you are well on the way to gaining the latter's, for the judge's clerk is the eyes and ears of the judge outside court sitting times. The clerks see us as we really are, not always how we want to be perceived as in the corridors of power.

But let's be clear, we can't leave the future health of the Bar in terms of selection and promotion to random acts of kindness. The brutal truth is that 'fairness' is not part of the Bar playing field at entry or achievement level. As Brie honestly says: '*I have to be*

---

[36] I was shocked and humbled when I read this. I'm including it though it feels hideously embarrassing to do so, but this time, for Srishti it was me, for many others it could be Srishti herself, Mass or Leslie Thomas KC – it just takes one person to be more like the person you see yourself as.

[37] Srishti is a specialist family barrister – she won the Family Law Young Barrister of the Year 2021.

prepared to say that the Bar is not a perfect meritocracy. You can't run with this idea that the best talent will rise to the top, because whilst talent is a significant element, there are so many other things at play in terms of the opportunities, your understanding of the opportunities, and your ability to recognise them when they cross your path. You have the sort of strength and robustness within yourself to sustain constantly looking for them and trying to maximise on them.'

What next?

We need to grapple not just with the principle of 'equality' to have a more representative Bar but 'equity'. What do I mean by that? This analogy helps. Equality is giving everyone the same pair of shoes. Equity is giving everyone a pair of shoes that fits. Equity refers to the specific things each person needs to succeed. We don't start from a position of equivalence – think back to Mass's example of how someone might achieve the same grades at A levels but despite all the hurdles set in their path, lack of space or silence at home to study, lack of support, lack of money. Unless that imbalance is recognised, we aren't looking at the same thing in terms of potential or achievement.

Nowadays, I'd like to think aspiring lawyers, even barristers, can see and find support around them through the internet. There are more resources to seek out guidance and information, courtesy of the internet, and more chance of being reached out to by organisations such as BTB or the like.

Accessing those supports does however still require a young person to see the Bar as a possibility for them. How many even know it is a career? Whenever I go to schools for outreach work, I start by reciting the long list of titles I now have: Professor, KC, judge ... it alienates the students from me. I can see that distance widening as I roll out the CV, before I *then* I tell them, frankly, that at their age not only had I not flagged these as career points to aim for, I did not know enough about the law to even dream that I might be a barrister. I talk to the students about my mum, my grandparents, our rented flats, the kitchen that doubled as a bathroom by having a wooden plank over the bath to use as a worktop. I talk about the three jobs my mum held down simultaneously to support us while my nan and grandad looked after me. I talk about 'Johanne as I was, not Prof Jo DKC as I am now'. Then I put on all the gear – the wig, the silk waistcoat, the silk gown – and point out I'm still the same person underneath it, however unfamiliar and 'authoritative' I may now seem. I show them the signs that still (proudly) mark me out as a nonconformist – the tattoos across my forearms and ear, the multiple ear and nose piercings. I break down the barriers I have deliberately set up to make the point that I was more like them than they can imagine.

Figure 2.4: This is the regalia one wears when we attend Westminster Hall to be sworn in as a Queen's/King's Counsel by the Lord Chancellor. This is the Ceremonial Court Dress for 'silks' as QC/KC are colloquially called – a full bottomed wig, a silk, long-sleeved, black made-to-measure waistcoat, long black silk gown (with a silk rosette), white gloves, white neck and wrist lace, and bejewelled black patent leather shoes. Red lipstick optional for all but me. This is me in October 2006. I put it on when I go to academies to make the point that it disguises the reality of the person who wears it, and not to judge from the old trope of what a barrister looks like – for I'm very much not of its mould, yet I have a place at it. The second image depicts making the law accessible as a career to potential legal champions of the future, 'Bring your mum/dad to work day' at nursery circa 1997.

The feedback from one of my recent talks spoke volumes: 220 students turned up in their own time and this was what they reported back: '*I can't believe she came to our school just to talk to us. I suppose that was the point she was making, though, wasn't it?*'; '*She was so NICE, Miss – I feel like I could do anything if there are people like her out there*'; '*I could've listened to her all day, Miss; I'm going to binge her lectures like Netflix*'; '*She gave practical advice, not just "life-lessons"*'; '*I felt like she was talking to me at exactly the right time*'; '*She didn't talk down to us and treated us as equals*'; '*We liked that she took her time to answer questions. It felt like she valued us*'; '*I learned that your upbringing doesn't have to mean that you will be limited in life and future opportunities, and with determination you can do what you want*'; '*I liked how she spoke to us like adults and not children. This made her seem like she respected and connected with us*'; '*She was genuine and realistic about her experiences. I learned that in order to achieve you have to ask, whether that is asking experienced professionals or universities*'; '*Students and staff have been coming up to me all day; they are buzzing with hope.*'

Frankly, it's not hard to make a difference – you just have to put the effort in. The rewards are immense.

When giving ourselves a pat on the back for what we are doing, we have to be willing to see what we are missing. We have groups dedicated (quite rightly) to creating paths of opportunity for young GEM students (such as the aforementioned '10,000 Black Interns Foundation'), we have women ready to support young women in many programmes – but what of those who fall between the cracks? What of white, working-class, destined to be unemployed, young men from council estates? BTB aims to scoop up all those students with potential regardless of ethnicity and gender but where are those targeted programmes for such a large sector of our youth? We can't say they don't have the same potential as the young women from similar backgrounds nor need less encouragement to look beyond crime and drugs as career choices. This omission becomes all the more important to address when clever, disillusioned, bored, early-school-leaver young white men have ready access to the internet where they will find many 'role model' mavericks eager to harness their energy and disaffection and invite them to walk under misogynistic and racist banners. I don't have the knowledge to answer my own question as to why we don't do more for more. Maybe a reader has.

I want to know because doing my best not to leave anyone behind is important to me.

When I started at the bar as a pupil, I had a strong sense of not wanting to become what the image of the Bar was but wanting to come to it and *to be seen* as a different sort of person doing it – not have *the Bar change me*, not to be assimilated. I wanted to change it – because to thrive the Bar must be more openly representative of the society it serves.

My role models, those who Set the Bar for me, have been taken to the brink of their own pit of despair, more than once, but they have come out the other side to represent the best of the Bar. What they haven't done in that process is lose themselves and make themselves into an image of the Bar as they saw it to be. We have brought our whole selves to the Bar and claimed our place at it. As Shelly would tell her younger self, '*She'll open herself up to the world and show others there is more than one way to barrister.*'

Each of the people I admire have brought their true selves and their unique life experiences to the Bar. Ultimately their individual life stories have given them bespoke skills in the competitive world of the self-employed Bar.

As Shelly says: '*By far the greatest challenge for me at the Bar has always been my ability to see and accept that I belong here and have a contribution to make, partly because of what I saw the profession to be when I entered it and partly the result of my own feelings of worth and fear of rejection that stem from early experiences. Lowering my defences and allowing people in has led to a greater understanding of why others also struggle at the Bar, why they're here and what motivates them. I've learned to harness the experiences of my life to fuel my passion for helping my clients and, in turn, the research and learning I'm exposed to has provided some clarity about where my own impulsivity comes from.*'

So, what can you draw on from these stories? I think what they reveal is courage, independence, persistence and an ability to think creatively about their future – to gather forces and to understand that, supported though they might be by others, only they make that effort count. Being at the Bar is about being *the* investigator, *the* strategist, *the* person who others might entrust.

The Bar is not for the faint-hearted. Those of us at it know that. No one I know has had a straight pathway to the Bar. You will need deep reserves of resilience and an ability to cope with rejection if you aspire to be a barrister. The attrition rate after qualification to getting a pupillage is staggeringly high. In 2022/2023 there were 2,979 applicants for 638 pupillages,[38] in other words, around a one in five chance of securing pupillage. Many people apply for a number of years before being successful. Not getting in doesn't necessarily mean it's not for you or you for it – it might be that competition in one year is especially fierce or you have not yet acquired the skills or shaped your personality enough to sell yourself to the interview panel – yet. Barristers face a lot of rejection and failure over the course of their careers and building up resilience and re-engaging for the next battle is the key to survival and success. It's tough.

So why on earth do we do this job with all its challenges? Because we can make a difference to people's lives, as you will read in the next chapter. What drives us to legal aid work is the desire to use our education, our skills, our passion for justice for the better of the neediest in society. That is not to say the neediest are always the most virtuous but we are not there to judge, that is the judge's job, we are there to represent those who cannot speak for themselves. As advocates, we support, we enquire, we challenge, we learn – we start the next day, the next case, with reinforced grit to succeed – it's an addictive process.

As Mary says, '*the primrose path of my life has meant that crime has been a good fit in the end for me. My life has not been smooth or perfect or even organised but rather a constant pursuit of doing things that make me feel alive, connected and in service of others but all the while making my monkey brain leap from tree to tree*'.

And I think that's rather splendid.

---

[38] Bar Council, 'Pupillage Gateway Report', February 2024, https://www.barcouncil.org.uk/resource/pupillage-gateway-report-2024.html

3

A Life in the Law

To assume one knows what a barrister's life is like in all its permutations – from chancery law to care, from trusts to the court of protection – is to assume that just because many creatures live, eat and swim in the sea, they are all the same species. A barrister's working day will vary from specialism to specialism, case to case, and barrister to barrister. While we all passed our Bar finals, completed our Qualifying Sessions, sat our dinners in Hall and were called to the Bar wearing a wig and gown, our working lives thereafter will have diverged. Some will never have secured a pupillage, let alone a tenancy; others will have landed both. Some will rarely have picked up a wig and gown to wear again; others will don them with as little ceremony as they pull on a pair of trainers. The skills needed to be a successful civil practitioner – somebody working primarily in chambers (in an office) contemplating the construction and interpretation of contracts – will not be the same as those needed to survive and thrive in courtroom life as a trial advocate in crime or care.

Working life at the Bar is as varied as our barristerial DNA. That's the joy of the profession. It caters to the quiet and to the flamboyant; to those who work in a solitary way, and others who thrive on the banter of robing rooms and courtroom bravura. There are those who prefer a regulated working day and others who function on adrenaline, not knowing if their all-nighter prep will be deployed before a judge or jury or go unheard if the trial is adjourned or collapses. All practices carry stresses of their own, but our workloads will vary and suit different personalities and brain types.

In this chapter, I'll explain a little more of what my job entails. You will also hear from colleagues whose work overlaps with mine, alongside those who have different specialisms altogether. The Bar's ethical code underpins all we do. I confess that there will be a personal bias in the people you will hear from because I have chosen to surround myself with people who share some of my core principles – for those of us who have chosen to work in legal aid areas, we all believe in public service; we all believe in representing the public without fear or favour, even if our clients may be 'unpopular' with the tabloid press; we all have something about us that sets us apart from the traditional image of the Bar; we all see communication with and service for the vulnerable members of society as our vocation.

The common thread that joins the lives of most of our clients is poverty – poverty of education, of income, of expectations. Many are illiterate, have mental health problems, addictions, and act out against authority with resentment and violence. They may have disabilities, and my work with that client is often the most rewarding of all, especially those with learning disabilities. I tend to prefer acting for the individual rather than the state – I like acting for the client with most to lose by a case.

We have more in common as lawyers than our different areas of specialism might suggest. We are all proud to be legal aid lawyers, but our work takes its toll on us precisely because of the areas of law that legal aid touches. This isn't some type of therapeutic outpouring to cleanse my soul and lighten my load. We are not open enough with one another about the downsides of being legal aid lawyers, and the mental health issues so many of us struggle with. I'm not just speaking with my own voice about my area of family law. I am lucky to be part of the common law Bar: our working lives in law overlap and complement each other. As legal aid lawyers, we all struggle with the contents of our law lives and how it impacts on our personal lives. I can no longer go to students from non-traditional backgrounds and inspire them to follow in my path unless I am clear about what it entails, warts and all. I wish someone had told me of the dark side of a life in the law before I fell into its shadows. It wouldn't have stopped me taking that course, but I might have been better able to cushion myself from the pain before it became debilitating. When legal aid is attacked and undermined by ministers and the tabloid press, when 'difficult' cases generate glib sound bites, I want it to be clear that they are misleading the public. This is an unvarnished account of what my work, and that of my colleagues, entails. We do this job, we defend legal aid, we support our colleagues because we are passionate about our working lives, despite the many reasons we may struggle to do it.

The Code that governs the Bar

I work in child protection law – 'care' cases in the main. I use the word 'care', but the reason I'm called upon is because of serious allegations that a child has *not* been 'cared for' at all. The children in my cases have (allegedly) been emotionally neglected, manipulated, abused. Many have been physically brutalised, shaken, raped, even killed. However grim the case, however serious the allegations of harm, I take a brief and go to court because I have a responsibility to my client to do so. I test the evidence witness by witness, expert by expert. I challenge the case against my client. I don't 'judge' my client – not their lifestyle, not their history and not their right to a defence. As a barrister, to do so would be to breach a fundamental principle of the independent Bar – our core strength lies in our adherence to our Code of Ethics. It's something we still have to explain more often than I can recall.

So, what does that mean? Barristers have a Code of Ethics that governs our working relationship with the client, the court and colleagues.[1] If you are a barrister, you will be asked, at some point

---

[1] For a fuller review of the codes watch or read the lecture I gave for Gresham, 'Ethics In and Out of the Court Room' (https://www.gresham.ac.uk/watch-now/ethics-court-room), but as an at-a-glance guide, we have ten core principles we must abide by. I MUST (not may or might or perhaps):
  CD1: observe my duty to the Court in the administration of justice.
  [CD1 overrides any other core duty if and to the extent any other CD is inconsistent with it.]
  CD2: act in the best interests of each client.
  CD3: act with honesty and integrity.
  CD4: maintain my independence.
  CD5: not behave in a way which is likely to diminish the trust and confidence which the public places in me or the profession.

in your career, 'How can you live with yourself and act on behalf of someone who is guilty?' This is just one of the ethical questions the Bar has grappled with and responded to for decades. Should we form value judgements about our client's culpability? Does that affect how hard we fight their case? The answer to each of these questions should be an emphatic 'no'. Perhaps the alternate question to ask would be 'How can you live with yourself and prosecute someone who is innocent?' The point is that we, whether we prosecute or defend, don't have any right to judge guilt or innocence. That's not our job. That's not our role. That's the task of the judge or jury. Our job is to represent the client who instructs us, to act on their instructions and to do so to the best of our ability, even when our defence makes the judge's job harder or infuriates them, the public or the press upon hearing it. When in doubt about how hard it can be to stand up for the Rule of Law and the right of the opposed and presumed guilty to be represented fearlessly, remember the judicial distaste with which the defences of the Birmingham Six were met, as Mike Mansfield KC defended these innocent men with every fibre of his being, and sectors of the press called for the six to be found guilty and the death penalty brought back.[2] Fifty years on we

---

      CD6: keep the affairs of each client confidential.
      CD7: provide a competent standard of work and service to each client.
      CD8: not discriminate unlawfully against any person.
      CD9: be open and co-operative with your regulators.
      CD10: take reasonable steps to manage your practice, or carry out your role within your practice, competently and in such a way as to achieve compliance with your legal and regulatory obligations.

[2] In November 1974, two bombs, attributed to the IRA, exploded in two Birmingham pubs, killing 21 people. It was an atrocity that led to six innocent Irishmen spending 16 years behind bars before their names were finally cleared. Former Master of the Rolls Lord Denning's role came in 1980, with the still-incarcerated Birmingham Six's civil claim against the police. Dismissing the case, he said: 'Just consider the course of events if their action were to proceed to trial. … If the six men failed it would mean that much time and money and worry would have been expended by many people to no good purpose. If they won, it would mean that the police were guilty of perjury; that they were guilty of violence and threats; that the

still have lessons to be learnt from its injustices.³ Chris Mullin, the investigative journalist and former MP who played a pivotal role in exposing the wrongful convictions of innocent individuals, spoke about his involvement in the case. When asked to comment on the biggest risks to miscarriages of justice now, Mullin referred to the issues surrounding the handling of evidence and the process of disclosure, and to Andrew Malkinson's case as an example of this. Malkinson had been carrying out his sentence for nearly 20 years before the Court of Appeal quashed his conviction of two counts of rape and one count of attempting to choke with intent to commit an indictable offence. The conviction was quashed in 2023 on the basis of new DNA evidence and undisclosed material recovered from the police. It is clear that miscarriages of justice of the sort faced by the Birmingham Six are anything but gone. Malkinson's case brought to light several issues with the current criminal justice system, including non-disclosure of relevant material, the process by which the Criminal Cases Review Commission reviews the referral requests which come to them, and limitations to access to justice relating to costs and finances.

But remember that not all barristers fight on the side of the angels. We fight for the client we are instructed by.

Your duty to the court does not prevent you from putting forward your client's case simply because you do not believe that the facts are as your client states them to be. There is a distinction between your 'belief' and your 'knowledge'. Your belief is irrelevant, as is your view about the attractiveness of the case or the client. Belief is a subjective response. Your belief may be influenced by the facts of the case, the apparent strength of the evidence, the nature

---

confessions were involuntary and improperly admitted in evidence; and that the convictions were erroneous. ... That was such an appalling vista that every sensible person would say, "It cannot be right that these actions should go any further".' The convictions were quashed in 1991. The 'confessions' had been extorted from them by force and intimidation. The police had lied. In 2001 the men would go on to receive approximately £1 million in compensation each. The police have never brought the real culprits to court.

³ https://www.barcouncil.org.uk/resource/50-years-on-the-birmingham-six-miscarriages-of-justice-and-the-fight-for-truth.html

of the case or the client. None of those are relevant to your role as the instructed barrister. You weren't a witness to the event in question, and you don't have any direct knowledge of the primary facts. Most importantly, you are not the judge nor jury member. It is not for you to determine what a judge or jury may make of the case they are presented with. Your duty is to represent your client and act on their instructions, however foolish or loathsome the client may appear to be.

This principle lies at the heart of the Cab Rank Rule. In simple terms: the 'cab rank rule' is the obligation of a barrister to accept any work in a field in which they profess themselves competent to practice, at a court at which they normally appear and at their usual rates. Were it disrespected, those who face the most serious consequences for the crimes or acts they have allegedly committed would be deprived of representation. The rule derives its name from the tradition by which a hackney carriage driver at the head of a queue of taxi cabs is supposed to take the first passenger requesting a ride. That analogy is imperfect – a passenger must also take the first cab on the rank, whereas a client, through his solicitor, is at liberty to instruct whomever he wishes. This distinction illustrates a fundamental point about the Cab Rank Rule, namely that its purpose is to protect the interests of clients, not the interests of barristers. The Cab Rank Rule is to prevent any unjustified restrictions on the client's choice of barrister.

The Codes of Ethics set out not just what you are obliged to do, but how you are obliged to do it. Your duty is to:

- Promote fearlessly, and by all proper and lawful means, the client's best interests.
- Do so without regard to your own interests, or to any consequences for you.
- Do so without regard to the consequences for any other person.

Applying the Codes

Our rules tell us that you must not permit your professional client, employer or any other person to limit your discretion as to how the interests of the client can best be served. I think that the motto of my previous set of chambers, Garden Court, puts our principles into words in the most meaningful way possible: 'Do Right, Fear No One'.

That motto was and remains so fundamental to our work and Garden Court have been called to defend themselves from attacks on their ethics and professionalism.

As of May 2025 an article in *The Spectator* under the heading 'The Radical Barristers Who Really Lay Down the Law in Britain'[4] described Garden Court as the base from which 'there operates arguably the most radically effective cell of left-wing activists in Britain', with a front cover tagged 'A Chamber of Horrors'.

Joshua Rozenberg KC (Hon), one of most respected and read legal commentators, went into print identifying errors in the article's hypothesis.[5] He said:

> The word 'cell' suggests a small group of politically motivated individuals. But Garden Court, according to its website, has more than 190 members – including 29 KCs. It's perfectly true that some – I expect most – of those barristers could be described as left-wing. Members of Garden Court 'use the full extent of the law to tackle social injustice and inequalities, narrow the wealth gap and promote the ethical use of corporate power', their website says. But does that make them activists? All of them? And if it did, would it stop them acting in the best interests of their clients? Clark identifies individual barristers whose political views he does not share. I don't share their views either. But provided those barristers act lawfully and comply with their professional obligations it is not for me,

---

[4] https://www.spectator.co.uk/article/the-radical-barristers-who-really-lay-down-the-law-in-britain/?utm_source=substack&utm_medium=email

[5] https://rozenberg.substack.com/p/a-cell-of-left-wing-activists?utm_source=post-email-title&publication_id=79530&post_id=162566356&utm_campaign=email-post-title&isFreemail=true&r=ntmhw&triedRedirect=true

as a journalist, to tell them what to think. Still less would I argue that they should not do their best to represent clients charged with protest offences. Without criminal defence lawyers, there can be no trials and no convictions.

Rozenberg continues:

> The trap Clark falls into is to imply that Garden Court – named after the chambers' original location in Middle Temple – is some sort of entity rather than a group of freelancers who have agreed to share overheads. That was the mistake made by the Chinese government when it imposed sanctions on Essex Court Chambers in 2021 after four members had written an opinion about how China's Uyghur population were treated. Those chambers said at the time, 'Essex Court Chambers is not a law firm and has no collective or distinct legal identity of any kind. Members of chambers are self-employed sole practitioners each regulated in their own capacity as separate individuals by the Bar Standards Board. Members of chambers are commonly retained by opposing sides in the same dispute, both in litigation and arbitration, with protocols in place to safeguard confidentiality. No other member of Essex Court Chambers was involved in or responsible for the advice and analysis contained in the legal opinion or its publication. The same principle applies to all barristers' chambers.'

This established principle did not protect Garden Court from attack as it should have done. As Garden Court made explicit on their website:

> Garden Court Chambers is aware of one of its members being instructed to present an application to the Home Secretary, requesting that a proscribed organisation be de-proscribed and engaging in publicity surrounding that. All members of Garden Court Chambers are members of the independent Bar of England and Wales, are self-employed and are regulated by the Bar Standards Board.

> Professional conduct of members is not regulated by Garden Court Chambers. The barrister concerned has chosen to undertake this application and publicise it in his individual capacity. This in no way indicates that Garden Court Chambers supports his client. Garden Court Chambers is aware of threats to a member of Chambers. We want to make it abundantly clear that we condemn such threats. Members of Chambers must be able to carry out their work as lawyers without fear or risk of harm. Members of the independent Bar should not be identified or conflated with their clients, or their clients' interests or views, if they are acting in the course of discharging their professional function as their legal representatives.[6]

To give you an example – your duty as a barrister, to act in the best interests of each client, includes a duty to consider whether the client's best interests are served by different representation, and if so, to advise the client to that effect. Are you up to the job? Do you have the skills your client requires? Don't accept a brief that's good for your career if your lay client[7] needs someone more senior – unless you are open with them, and they make the informed choice to stick with you. What about your instructing solicitor (your professional client) – are they up to the mark? I have before, and I will again, on looking at the case conduct, advise my lay client that they have been poorly served by the solicitor who has instructed me to act for them. I've had to advise them that they need to sack our solicitor. I've had to replace junior barristers. I've had to say that the case requires someone other than me to do it. That's not going to make me popular with the client, solicitor or barrister! I may lose work as a result – and

---

[6] https://gardencourtchambers.co.uk/press-statement-garden-court-chambers-addresses-barristers-role-following-press-comment/

[7] Lay client is the member of the public. Professional client is the solicitor. Unless you are qualified and have the right to accept instructions directly from a member of the public (the Direct Access scheme) then you can only act for a member of the public through the instructions of their solicitor who instruct you on the client's behalf. In my cases, all my work is via solicitors. They are the essential go-between between me and the client.

it is certainly going to be an awkward situation for everyone – but the client's case comes first, and it is they who need protection, not the professional ties. The responsibility we take on for our clients is non-delegable and weighty. It keeps me awake at night.

Let's tackle the classic question: 'How can you act on behalf of someone who is guilty?' In my cases, that translates to 'How can you act on behalf of that "paedophile"/baby murderer?' That question presupposes that the person I am acting for *is* an abuser. Whether they are or are not is the very question the court is having a hearing to answer. It's not to be prejudged, as the questioner has done. I have been in many a case where the client (and I) are faced at the outset of the trial with evidence that looks like overwhelming guilt. That's not unusual for my work. The case has to be serious, the evidence heavy and the consequences for the client profound, for the legal aid agency to approve my instruction and the extra cost to the legal aid purse it entails. In my line of work, my client's profession of innocence is usually said in the face of expert and other evidence to the contrary. I have to take that client's denial on board and act on it. Day by day, hour by hour, I am inducted into the raw, grim details of my client's life through the portals of CCTV, thousands of social media mobile exchanges and laptop internet use. I peer into the shadows of their histories and see and read things they never thought any stranger would see, and often what I wish I could unsee.

But this is the only way to pull apart the jumbled jigsaw puzzle of presumed guilt, piece by piece. When I pick up the pieces, with that deep-dive preparation undertaken, the picture I make during cross-examination may not be the same as the one the prosecution saw on the box lid. This is why the responsibility placed on barristers is immense. You can't start the trial half-heartedly thinking it's all a waste of time, because the client is guilty as sin, only to spot a gap in the case, start to exploit it and think 'Why did I go soft on that previous witness, and not pick up that thread I saw dangling in their evidence? Now I want to pull it, and this case could unravel'. You can't ask for a witness to be recalled on the basis that 'I didn't try very hard for that one as it seemed like a lost cause'.

The Secret Barrister's answer to the question: 'What do you do if you're having to defend someone that you're pretty sure is guilty?' is as good as any I've heard:

Quite simply, I defend them to the best of my ability. My job isn't to make a judgment on whether my client is guilty – that's for the jury. If he tells me he's guilty, that's a different matter – I cannot mislead the court, so can't stand up and say, 'He didn't do X' if he's told me that he did. But if he says, 'I didn't do X', then my job is to advise him of the strength of the prosecution evidence and the likely outcome of a trial, and if he still says that the 50 witnesses, DNA experts and crystalline CCTV footage have all got it wrong, I put on my wig and go into battle for him. Because he may, contrary to how it appears, be innocent.[8]

I take to heart the powerful words of a titan of the Family Court: Hedley J (as he then was) reminds us that

> Society must be willing to tolerate very diverse standards of parenting, including the eccentric, the barely adequate and the inconsistent. It follows too that children will inevitably have both very different experiences of parenting and very unequal consequences flowing from it. It means that some children will experience disadvantage and harm, while others flourish in atmospheres of loving security and emotional stability. These are the consequences of our fallible humanity, and it is not the provenance of the state to spare children all the consequences of defective parenting. In any event, it simply could not be done.[9]

The common thread that unites all the decisions made in a Family Court is the welfare of the child. It is the court's paramount consideration. We no longer live in an age where a child can be treated as a chattel. From the point of its birth, the child has rights of its own, to live a life without being subjected to significant harm and abuse within its family. That 'right' matters more than the 'right'

---

[8] https://www.shortlist.com/news/the-secret-barrister-interview
[9] *Re L (Care: Threshold Criteria) [2007] 1 FLR 2050*, para 50.

of the parents to care for their child, if by so doing the child will suffer serious harm which may blight its healthy development. But the state only has a right to remove a child from its family if it has suffered, or is at risk of suffering, significant harm caused by them. And the word 'significant' is important. As Brenda Hale, Baroness Hale of Richmond has explained: a

> We are all frail human beings, with our fair share of unattractive character traits, which sometimes manifest themselves in bad behaviours which may be copied by our children. But the State does not and cannot take away the children of all the people who commit crimes, who abuse alcohol or drugs, who suffer from physical or mental illnesses or disabilities, or who espouse antisocial political or religious beliefs.[10]

When you tune into the massive bandwidth of humanity, it can be a shock. You see what poverty does to a family's life choices. My clients may well make poor choices of partners, because their own childhood may have given them a warped model of what 'good enough' care means for a child, with few positive reserves to call upon when they become parents. Anger, stress, tiredness and lack of life coping skills can combine to create an explosive and toxic mixture, when married with the exhaustion of coping 24/7 with a newborn. Add to this addiction or innate vulnerability, such as learning disabilities and poor mental health, and you have a potentially lethal dose of instability that can kill or injure a child. A single loss of control, a single shake of a baby can kill. But accidents can also happen through tiredness – dropping a baby, oversleeping on a baby. Sometimes the 'accident' that kills is a genetic one – a condition undetected in life, a ticking medical time bomb that in death mimics child abuse. Think then of being such a parent, unable to bury their child or to grieve in private because their baby's body parts have become postmortem exhibits in a criminal or family trial. The parent accused of ending the life of the being they loved

---

[10] *Re B (A Child) (Care Proceedings: Threshold Criteria) [2013] UKSC 33, [2013] 1 WLR 1911, [2013] 2 FLR 1075*, para 143.

the most. Protestations of innocence undermined and doubted by experts, police, health and social workers alike.

For these next paragraphs a trigger warning is warranted (you can jump to the section titled 'The killer buzz', or skip the text set between asterisks.

★★★

The basic introduction to this issue may appear shocking in its brevity and brutality. I'm inured to that. Others may not be. What I deal with as part of my working life *is* shocking to outsiders. And by 'outsiders' I mean anyone that doesn't do the work myself or my colleagues in crime, human rights and the front-line-like do, not just the general public.

A case in 2012 shook me to my core.[11] It centred around the tragic death of a baby called Jayden and his young parents. The mother was mourning her dead son, pregnant and facing a murder charge, and both parents had been accused of causing their baby's death by beating him over weeks, fracturing many bones in his body and then shaking him to death. Jayden had been dead for over two years by the time the Old Bailey judge, on 9 December 2011, directed the jury to acquit the parents due to conflicting expert evidence. The parents had never returned to the former home having been compelled to leave it as they left Jayden for the last time in hospital as it was 'the scene of the crime'. Their names and faces had been all over local and national media. They had had to ask one another if the police medical evidence was true: had the other hurt their son? They stayed together and had another child as the investigations rolled on. By the time the criminal trial collapsed Jayda, their second baby, was by then 14 months old. She had never lived with her parents and saw them only at restricted times under close supervision. Her future, with her parents or placed for adoption, was wholly contingent on the Family Court's findings as to how Jayden died, judged to a lower standard of proof than in the criminal proceedings.[12] It was perfectly possible

---

[11] https://www.gresham.ac.uk/watch-now/guilty-until-proven-innocent

[12] The prosecution case is decided in a criminal case 'beyond reasonable doubt' (in other words, whether the tribunal of fact can be sure of guilt [that is, 99 per cent]) but 'on a balance of probabilities' (that is, 51 per cent) in a Family Court.

for the family judge to rule that Jayden had been killed by his parents despite their acquittal in the Criminal Court. The case was heard by Mrs Justice Theis over six weeks, taking evidence from over 40 medical witnesses and specialist experts. It was an intensely fought contest of cross-examination skills. It was exhausting, gruelling. Everything but the case was put on hold, including my own young family. Theis J did not find the local authority case of inflicted abuse proven. She decided that the multiple fractures had been caused by the innate fragility of his bones because of severe rickets undetected in life. The court said there was a need for further research, particularly in relation to the different aspects of the non-accidental head injury triad and the impact of vitamin D deficiency and rickets in respect of babies under six months old.[13] Chana Al-Alas and Rohan Wray were reunited with the baby Jayda who, at 18 months old, had never lived with them. Their dead baby Jayden could at last be released to them for burial.

I, along with fellow barrister Kate Purkiss (now HHJ Purkiss), and our solicitor Ann Thompson represented Chana Al Alas in her family trial. In our family trial we worked closely and collaboratively with Chana's lawyers instructed in her criminal trial. We won the case. We won the right for Jayda to have a family life with her birth parents. This is what legal aid lawyers do. We represent our client to the best of our ability however serious the charges and apparently open and shut the case is.

As this case shows, for my part, however overwhelming the case against my client looks on paper, I tackle each witness as though I can 'win' them. I have perfected the art of looking confident when I feel I want to crumble from the stress, the exhaustion, the responsibility. When I cross-examine, each question matters. I try to part the Red Sea, charting a precarious passage through an ocean of evidence. There is no rewind button if I put my foot in it with a clumsy question, the answer to which undermines the foundations

---

[13] For the case report see https://www.judiciary.uk/wp-content/uploads/JCO/Documents/Judgments/london-borough-islington-al-alas-wray-judgment-19042012.pdf. For my lecture explaining how we secured that outcome watch https://www.gresham.ac.uk/watch-now/guilty-until-proven-innocent

for a defence I'm constructing. Witnesses are scheduled as to when they can give evidence in the trial timetable. We don't waste time in court – it's a costly process. When the witness takes the oath, I have to be ready to question them, and the next, and those witnesses who are called in at short notice. I don't have an option of pressing 'pause' to phone a friend or stop the court clock from ticking. Performance pressure is immense.

The overwhelming case requires no less of a defence than the one where you can easily see the flaws and gleefully anticipate how satisfied and superior you will feel in court as you pick them out and dispatch them. Written evidence served on you is not the same as the evidence tested in cross-examination. For a parent to face legal proceedings for alleged child abuse the court will have been satisfied by the local authority that there is case for them to answer. The parent can't walk away from court without, in effect, walking away from their child. We, their lawyers, must gain their respect and trust outside of court to give them the best representation in court. But we aren't our client's social workers, or their friends, and we don't decide on guilt or innocence. We consider the evidence, advise, and act on the instructions we receive. We may have to move between communicating with a client with profound disabilities outside of court, to using specialised language in court when we cross-examine the experts. The barrister seeks to become a mini expert in ophthalmology, pathology, neuropathology, osteo-pathology, radiology, genetics, burns and bites, psychiatry and psychology. Long may that continue, but we will have to fight for it as it is a right that some judges are prepared to sacrifice on the altar of speed and brevity of a case. We seek to cross-examine specialists who have made that subject their life's work and for whom it is a year-round occupation in clinic and in court. For us, it will be one case among a range of others, equally serious but of a different nature. How can we hope to pick apart an expert's conclusion? But we have to try, and sometimes succeed, because that is what our instructions require, and we have a duty to pursue their case to the best of our ability. It is a feat that can change the outcome of a case when performed by the best of our profession. It is both a burden and a privilege.

★★★

The killer buzz

As high-functioning court performers, we rerun lines of cross-examination, long ago completed, in our heads on a loop. We go over our oral submissions, wishing we had said more or less. We write and answer emails 24/7, and my 'out of office' auto-message is a family joke. My family has been known to confiscate my mobile, lock it in a safe and give me a cheap 'pay as you go' phone with just their and close friends' numbers pre-programmed into it, all to keep me from being sucked into work.

Our work takes a heavy emotional toll on us. Our sense of duty to the clients leads (sometimes) to warped priorities. Obviously, we aren't indispensable; we have just become programmed to think we are. That feeds our ego, our work ethic and serves the court process and the client. I know of many a barrister who has come to court having received devastating news about a family death or diagnosis. I came to court having discovered a large lump in my breast and chose not to tell my husband or contact a doctor. I had two experts to cross-examine that day, the junior wouldn't have prepared so as to be ready to step into my shoes, the experts were critical to the case for my client – and so I reasoned that the lump must have been there a while to be so sizeable, so what would another day or two matter to get it seen to? Barking mad in retrospect – and selfish – given its potential impact on me as a mum, wife and breadwinner. But at the time, this was a personal, non-negotiable decision.

It's not just me: I know of women who have come to court having suffered a miscarriage overnight. It's also not a gender thing: I have a very close male friend (a fellow silk) who put off going into hospital against the instructions of his specialist when his pacemaker started misfiring. We were in a multi-handed sex abuse trial out of London, and he couldn't see how he could get from north to south, from court to hospital and back, and be guaranteed to finish the case. Nothing I said made a difference. It wasn't the money for him that mattered, it was the responsibility he had taken on for his client to fight their corner. Just this year, this same friend, as he lay in his hospital bed waiting for a heart operation, was reading case papers and writing legal submissions justifying why the experts needed to be called to court for him to cross-examine on behalf of a parent facing allegations of child abuse in a serious NAI (Non Accidental Injury) case. His fury bled out through the paragraphs but at what cost to his health? Other barristers might go to work when they are ill because, as self-employed barristers, they simply can't afford not to.

When I give talks or speak to aspiring barristers, I am often asked what is needed to cut it. In asking that question, they might be thinking about how to do 'a' case, but to survive at the Bar, you need not one case but a steady stream of them, month after month, year on year. Getting a tenancy (and hence a place to ply your trade from) doesn't mean that you have secured a future at the Bar. You need to carve out a reputation to keep the flow of work coming. Moreover, we are in competition with others for the same work. Being self-employed has many advantages. Personally, I wouldn't cope well with being told what to do and how to do it, but being self-employed also means if I don't work, I do not earn. I won't have sick pay funded by an employer, because I don't have an employer. I won't have a pension unless I set one up privately and invest in my own old age. I am likely to have to wait months, or sometimes years, to be paid, and yet my expenses for doing the work (hotels, travel) have already been paid out and I will have been taxed on the (outstanding) billed fee. I may not know when the next payment will come in, yet I will still have to pay my rent/mortgage. I will have a good idea of what money will have to go out of my bank account, but I might not know how much will come into it. Whatever type of work you do, but particularly legal aid work, you only do it if it is your vocation. Your professional life is something that affects you intensely personally, regardless of physical barriers between the courtroom and your home, or purposeful boundaries, such as turning email notifications off while on holiday. I can only speak for the legal aid Bar here. It might well be that those working in shipping, trusts, corporate or banking law can work decent hours in chambers or their home office and earn a sufficient sum to take breaks and enjoy the healthy financial rewards of their labour. They may have gym membership and home gyms and trainers, they take time to unwind, travel, and so on. But the legal aid Bar I know is an unhealthy profession.

Why do I say that? Because while the thrill of delivering a cross-examination that shifts the axis of a trial is a 'legal high' like no other, to get there, and to cope when you come down, takes its toll. It's the cost of my advocacy and I trained for it. But no amount of training can prepare you for what you see and read as part of your job. It is that deep dive into the dark vaults of humanity's capacity for inhumanity that inflicts wounds I find it hard to heal from.

A trigger warning is warranted again before you read on. You may wish to skip the text between asterisks and read the next section: 'So why do we choose this work?'.

★★★

My work is the stuff of most people's nightmares – I specialise in cases involving the death of or catastrophic injuries to a child. Sex abuse cases. Female genital mutilation. Ritualised abuse. Starvation. Poisoning. The list goes on. The ways a child can be abused are only limited by someone's imagination. When that fails the internet can expand the imaginative range. These cases are the stuff of my working life. They are grim. I work for the client who faces those allegations – the parents or sibling accused of abuse against a sister or brother. I do not turn my face away from these people. They need legal representation. They are *accused* of something – they have *not been found guilty* of it. The odds are already stacked against them being believed over the weight of professional evidence.

When I have a conference with my client, accused of shaking their child and causing its death, I have to take them back to that day and make them relive it hour by hour, second by second, in case we have missed something that may explain the baby's collapse. The client is likely to be traumatised, de-sensitised, by the specificity of the detail I am asking them to recall and describe. So am I. When acting for a child victim of familial sex abuse, accused of sexually abusing his or her siblings, I have to plot a conversation line with that child carefully as I trespass on secret, shaming, horrifying details of their experiences at the hands of others and to others. I seek to peel back layers of deception and denial so as to try to get to the reality of his or her life. At what cost to the client do I do that? I am not a therapist, and in all likelihood there is no therapist on hand to pick up the pieces afterwards of the conversation I have with them. In one particularly difficult case, I remember my 14-year-old client explaining (after years of silence) to me in conference why he had mutilated his penis with a razor: it was because his mother couldn't stand the sight of blood. The self-harm protected him from sexual abuse for as long as he could make himself bleed and it allowed him to vent his self-hatred. He was telling me now not because he wanted to, but because he felt compelled to, because he was accused of sexually abusing his younger siblings. As I worked through the evidence against him he was driven to the point where he felt he had to stop protecting his mother and say what she (and his grandmother, grandfather, uncles and aunts) had done to him to explain why he had acted as he had to younger children. In that case I was fortunate to have as my junior Paul Murray, a barrister who came to the Bar having been a solicitor and prior to that a social worker: a man of warmth and wisdom with whom I could share the emotional responsibility of acting for this vulnerable client. His previous social work experience enabled him to track down support for our client before he left our company. But that degree of professionalism and support was an exception. Too often we shoulder this burden alone – and we don't do that well. We think we are 'fine' and carry on to another case, another client, another court.

I do not know of a single junior criminal barrister who could take time off to recover from the stress of the work that they do, already operating at below minimum wage because of the hours they work, much of which falls outside any payment structure but is essential case management and preparation (such a questions for medical experts, drafting of skeleton arguments and submissions). Far from taking time off between cases to recoup energy, they have to double up on case prep and work in back-to-back trials to keep any type of income going.

You cannot do the type of work my colleagues and I do and not be harmed by it. I would not have had to contemplate the reality of a baby's body placed on a pathology table, once whole, now reduced to its constituent parts of organ, blood, muscle and bone, to try to understand how it met its death. Were I not instructed in a child sex abuse case I wouldn't have to read and hear childish words being used to describe adult sexual actions. I see images that become permanently imprinted on my retina and read histories that lodge in my brain.

As Shelly says, '*The emotional burden is immense, as is the impact of constant exposure to written, audio and visual evidence of child neglect, injury and other abuse as well as domestic violence in its many insidious forms. I imagine there are few employed roles with the likelihood of vicarious trauma we experience that don't mandate therapy of some sort.*'

Sometimes I am required to look at images of child sex abuse, or of dead children. Under the watchful eyes of the anti-terrorism force,

I have read restricted ISIS material: seen photos, moving images of the dead and dying and tortured. In my cases I don't just read social work statements to understand a case. We have a far more intimate source of data filed we have to digest. I read intimate, angry, drunken texts never intended to be read and dissected by critical strangers in court in cross-examination. I see photos – not the happy snapshots at Christmas or on Mother's Day – but the ones that show a flat where deposits of dog faeces fight for space on the bare, stained floor with soiled nappies. I confront our client with parts of their lives they had thought hidden and expose sides of partners that they hadn't known existed.

My colleagues who work in crime will face mirror images of the cases I deal with in the Family Court, and more besides. Becky Owen, a fellow barrister, had this to say about the pressures she and criminal colleagues were placed under, describing what for her was a tipping point in her willingness and ability to put up with it: *'For me, it was the conditions, the sheer volume of work and the complete lack of respect for me as a human being … I got sick of arriving home dehydrated, starving and having not had time to go to the loo. It takes its toll. There aren't many people who have to watch videos of two-year-old boys being raped before going home to sleep – and at times for less than the minimum wage.'*

In the course of my work with families during the Hillsborough inquests, I, and my colleagues, had to look at footage of the crowd, trying to pick out a loved one from the grim press images of the many fans suffering; zooming in on a loved one's face to try to work out the moment of death, the point at which the crush overcame the body's resistance to the pressure of the crowd. We watched as they died. Over and over again. A task made no easier by the passage of time since the tragedy. The work that inquest lawyers did and do, such as Mike Mansfield KC, Leslie Thomas KC, Mark George KC[14] and Marcia Willis Smith KC (Hon), is nothing short of heroic.[15]

---

[14] Mark died in 2022 and with him we lost a warrior for truth and justice. His obituary is available at https://www.thetimes.com/uk/article/mark-george-kc-obituary-mcr0mfgdp

[15] It's impossible to name everyone who worked for the families on the inquests of their loved ones but I'd like to give a shout out to these

Those who work in immigration and human rights work will need to deal with sex and trafficking rings, rape, murder, political and LGBTQIA+ persecution and torture. It's part of our job. What's more, we are all wired to think that we are the last line of defence.

A life in law can feel like your life is ebbing away while you try to protect the life and wellbeing of others. And sometimes, for some barristers, life does end. Rachel Spearing KC experienced the loss of a close friend at the Bar through suicide and became a pioneer in promoting mental health within the legal profession. She co-founded the Wellbeing at the Bar initiative in 2012 and later established the Wellness for Law UK Network in 2017 to support best practice across the sector.[16] Rachel is a trauma-informed advocate with a long-standing commitment to equality, diversity and safeguarding. I applauded her in my lecture on mental health for Gresham[17] as I sought to build on Rachel's work of breaking down the continued taboo about mental health crisis.

Cyrus Larizadeh KC has been a long-standing campaigner for better recognition of stress at the Bar. He was part of the Wellbeing at the Bar Working Group back in 2016 which created the contents for the Bar Council's first wellbeing website. His lecture in 2017, 'Wellbeing and Being Hit by a Bus on the Way to Court',[18] launched the wellbeing movement at the family Bar. Cyrus has been open

---

people who helped me as much as the families we were privileged to act for: Patrick Roche, Peter Wilcock KC, Stephen Simblet KC, Sean Horstead and Professor Phil Scraton, for they were my saviours. Thanks chaps.

[16] https://www.serjeantsinn.com/barrister/rachel-spearing/. Rachel's work profile is too vast to be accurately summarised so here is what she does via her chambers. What the web profile doesn't convey is why Rachel was awarded 'Female Trailblazer of the Year' 2025 at the Clio Modern Law Awards. Rachel seeks to make a difference to our working world. She is one of the people one comes across at court (as I did) and a link of friendship is made that spans different specialisms. Rachel is also one of Brie's magnificent women as I discovered later into our friendship.

[17] https://www.gresham.ac.uk/watch-now/family-lawyer-stress-distress

[18] https://www.wellbeingatthebar.org.uk/2017/06/27/wellbeing-bar-blog-cyrus-larizadeh-qc-victoria-wilson/

about the impact on him, as a barrister, of his mother's suicide in 2006, and talks of it with heartbreaking and inspiring frankness. Cyrus knows whereof he speaks when he talks of grief, a professional crisis in confidence, and finding a route to recovery and emotional equilibrium. When he was Chair of the Family Law Barristers Association (FLBA) 2021–2 we could have had no better leader to guide the family Bar through COVID-19; cometh the hour, cometh the man. Cyrus was a leader among leaders. We owe a great debt to him for his authority allied with compassion.

We strive to have a life outside of the Bar, but we are often torn apart by conflicting demands. While I argue for my client's Article 8 rights to a private family life, I too often feel my own family is being sacrificed to the cause. Parenthood is a 24/7 responsibility, and it's a hard juggling act managing the prep, travel and unpredictability of a barrister's day.

The parental exhaustion and guilt are a killer. As Mary Aspinall-Miles says, '*Other mother-barristers will know that tug all too well and the sense that you're not "good enough" at either as you feel you do both (in mental terms) part-time. When my children were little, I would wait until after bedtime to start my work or wake up at 5 am to start and then trot off to court. This was a cycle of rinse and repeat for many years.*' Emma Hughes is very close to that tension as a young mother and junior barrister: '*Simultaneously working, caring for my child, and studying was a difficult balancing exercise. As a mother there is a constant worry of the cost of childcare, and you question whether you are investing enough time into your child's education as well as your own.*' As Marina Sergides says, '*I can't pretend that the bar has been an easy place to work. I continue to juggle children, late nights, voluntary work and caring responsibilities. Deadlines are unforgiving and when I'm working at weekends, I'm acutely aware that I could be earning significantly more, more for less work, in another profession. I'm rarely in a relaxed state – if it's not dropping children off to their afterschool activities, responding to emails, being late back from court, billing etc., then it's the worry that a vulnerable family might be rendered homeless.*'

It's not just the practicalities, the guilt and sense of personal failure as a parent that drives you down, it's the double life you lead where the professional seeps into the personal. For me the hardest part of doing sex abuse cases when I had a young family of my own was

Figure 3.1: 'Strong Not Silent' campaign. During the COVID-19 pandemic, while other systems shut down, the Family Courts kept going, radically transforming their centuries-old tradition of fully in-person hearings before a judge into remote online court access. Court staff, judges, barristers and solicitors changed their way of working so as not to abandon families and children in need. What we developed and gained in technical knowledge we lost in terms of maintaining a barrier between work content and our personal lives, a pain made more acute as under emergency powers we were working in isolation from home, seperated from our own loved ones. Mental health dived. I joined this media campaign to be visible and vocal about what I knew I and my colleagues were enduring. Stigma and shame have to be confronted. It is a raw image. I am haggard. I am exposed. But I was not, and am not, prepared to hide from the impact of poor mental health.

returning home to their uncorrupted innocence and not being able to erase the images of innocence abused from the running image loop in my brain.

★★★

So why do we choose this work?

When reaching out to friends and colleagues to give me their perspective on the Bar, I was struck once again by how many people I am in contact with who sought out legal aid work as their practice areas and act for the person, not the state, within the common law cases we do. I don't think that's an accident. We have had a taste of what it's like to feel distant from authority and judged by it. Nor was I surprised that in legal aid work, whether that be child protection, crime, immigration, human rights or housing, I saw a far more accurate spectrum of the people who make up the non-legal community than in other fields of law. As Stephen Lue points out, '*I have noticed that if you look at the legally aided areas of practice, namely immigration, family and crime, that is where you get the most GEM and possibly LGBTQIA+ practitioners. Is that because our lived experiences of discrimination make us want to make a positive difference? The legally aided areas of practice are the least remunerated areas of law. I wonder what choices we would make if no discrimination had been experienced in our formative years? More to the point, I wonder which areas would be open to us if our life experiences did not draw us towards areas of practice with a social justice element.*'

The pressure on us to 'perform' is high. Consider the seminal piece of work the Bar Council embarked upon when they started to compile data for their Working Lives Surveys. Taking the 2024 edition with 2023 data by way of example, the barrister wellbeing analysis confirmed that in general terms barristers reported higher levels of work satisfaction and wellbeing compared to 2021. Although, under one-third of respondents (32.2 per cent) continued to report they currently had low levels of overall wellbeing. A similar number reported that they were not coping well with their workload. More than two-thirds of respondents in both 2021 and 2023 responded that they were 'perfectionists' and could be critical of themselves. White, heterosexual, 'able' bodied and privately educated respondents all reported higher levels of satisfaction than GEM, LGBTQIA+,

Figure 3.2: Bar survey report

9.1 Descriptive Statistics for individual barrister wellbeing questions and comparison across Area of Practice and Survey year

% Agree by members within each Area of Practice

Question	All % Agree 2023	Criminal 2023	Criminal 2021	Civil 2023	Civil 2021	PI/PN 2023	PI/PN 2021	Commercial 2023	Commercial 2021	Family 2023	Family 2021	Other/Int 2023	Other/Int 2021
d1a: Within the environment in which I work, there is generally a sense of cooperation and collaboration	79	70	70	82	79	84	81	84	78	79	83	84	77
d1b: I have significant control over the content and pace of my work	52	29	26	61	49	58	46	66	54	55	44	70	61
d1c: I am able to integrate the things that are most important to life and work	47	26	28	57	48	59	48	63	54	43	40	74	59
d1d: I tend to feel down or low in spirits (-ve)	35	48	49	30	32	29	35	23	32	36	34	23	25
d1e: I experience little interest or pleasure in doing things (-ve)	20	30	32	15	19	13	21	14	19	20	20	14	16
d1f: A case going badly has an impact on my confidence (-ve)	73	77	75	75	77	72	81	71	74	70	76	68	61
d1g: Overall, I find my workload manageable	49	32	40	56	55	58	57	63	59	46	48	49	70
d1h: I tend to dwell on my mistakes (-ve)	62	64	64	61	60	61	64	58	60	65	64	62	45
d1i: My current mood is good	60	52	46	64	58	63	61	69	61	59	62	61	70
d1j: I tend to be very critical of myself	72	75	77	73	71	70	71	67	69	74	74	68	69
d1k: My relationships with other colleagues are as good as I would want them	67	63	51	68	52	69	51	67	49	72	55	63	67
d1l: Within the environment in which I work, I feel comfortable to express my opinions, thoughts and ideas	69	62	60	72	65	71	71	75	70	67	67	67	75
d1m: I am able to confide in work colleagues regarding challenges experienced with my cases	78	78	76	79	75	79	76	75	73	79	78	80	65
d1n: Overall, taking everything into consideration, I am satisfied with my job as a whole	61	41	43	69	68	70	67	76	73	60	63	72	70
N =	3191	865	921	711	776	375	420	523	571	653	699	64	77

Notes:
- %Agree scores are the average % respondents who agree or definitely agree with questions.
- Colour coding indicates differences compared to the overall %Agree average for this question: XX = 5% worse; XX = 10% worse; XX = 5% better; XX = 10% better.
- Note colour coding for 2021 is related to the average question scores for that year.
- (-ve) = This question is negatively phrased, so that a higher %Agree indicates lower wellbeing stress. NB this means scores higher than average are colour coded red, etc..
- N = Number of respondents answering this question.

Source: © The Bar Council 2024

'disabled' and state-educated respondents.[19] I make the point elsewhere in this book about the imbalance in terms of diversity between those who are attracted by/selected to undertake legal aid versus other fields such as commercial law. This survey spotlights the personal consequences to those who choose to serve the public good at the Bar. Barristers working in family law had significantly lower overall wellbeing compared to all other practice areas, except for the criminal Bar. Barristers practising in commercial law reported the highest average overall wellbeing. Women, barristers from an ethnic minority background, and those who are younger and more junior had lower overall wellbeing. One cannot look at job satisfaction and wellbeing, and the reasons why it varies between specialisms, without confronting intersectionality.

If one looks at the 'tags' that flag up the main findings on this important publication you may think, as I do, that the negative impact of our work is concerning: 'Addiction, Alcohol, Anxiety, Balance, Bereavement, Bullying, Change, Clerks, Communication, Coping techniques, Culture change, Depression disorder, Drugs, Eating disorder, Exercise, Exhaustion, Frustration, Mental illness, Thinking, Overworked, Perfectionism, Pressure prioritising, Recovery, Resources, Self-harm, Self-injury, Sleep, Stigma, Stress, Suggestions, Support, Tips, Unwell, Vicarious trauma, Work-life balance.'[20]

It was significant, I believe, that when giving his 'First View from the Presidents Chambers' in January 2019, our then new Head of Division, the Right Hon Mr Justice Andrew McFarlane, singled out as his number one priority the unprecedented and unsustainable volume of cases in the family justice system, and the impact of that on working conditions for professionals. He identified the problems caused by the rise in private law applications and the increase in unrepresented litigants. He acknowledged the negative impact on cases due to the lack of paediatric experts willing to take on work in public law child protection cases. That much

---

[19] Bar Council, 'Barristers' Working Lives Survey: Barrister Wellbeing Analysis', January 2024, https://www.barcouncil.org.uk/static/e46b9663-a851-485a-9f0bb18fe561df63/Wellbeing-at-the-Bar-report-2024.pdf
[20] https://www.wellbeingatthebar.org.uk/tag/mental-illness/

was not news to us: we see the consequences every day in every court when appearing or sitting. What was new, however, was the 'official' utterance that 'it is neither necessary nor healthy for the courts and the professionals to attempt to undertake "business as usual"'.[21] This was pre-COVID-19 note. Under COVID-19 the family Bar and Family Courts worked almost without a heartbeat's pause to keep cases in court and children protected. We moved to and embraced remote technology and took on more cases each day as a result to keep delays down. We led the way. We were thanked by the President for our efforts but those words of respect now ring as hollow. I am absolutely sure that's not intended to be the case but that is the harsh reality for many at the publicly funded family Bar as the consequences have played out on us and our clients in case after case, month after month, year on year.

From 2023 onwards, the focus has been on the cost and number of family cases in the system and demands (now no longer exhortations) that both be reduced. We see why that is so. Few would disagree. I don't. Families wait in limbo for outcomes to be decided, children taken into care under emergency orders as babies remain in foster care as toddlers, memories of events fade and social workers come and go. Contact may be denied by one parent to another. Delay is inimical to the welfare of the child, but the human cost of cuts, in terms of fairness of outcome for individual cases, is less often, if at all, acknowledged by our power masters. So too is the unspoken assumption that the Family Bar can and should shoulder the case burden to do what it takes, pro bono, to make this cut-down service work.

When our efforts to secure a listing for a complex, multi-handed medical case that is more than ten days are met by some judges with disdain and seen as attempting to milk the legal aid system (as a 11-day + listing moves the barrister from one system of outdated payment to another), rather than reflecting the trial prep we have done to get to grips with the disclosure, expert evidence and issues, then our confidence in our seniors falters. When our applications to instruct a specialist medical expert to advise in the case are met

---

[21] https://www.judiciary.uk/wp-content/uploads/2019/01/amcfview-1.pdf

with judicial rejection and we are signposted to a treating clinician in place of the independent expertise the case warrants, we jibe. When we argue for the right to have the expert attend court for cross-examination and are met with a blank stare of astonishment at our temerity, we rebel. We are, as a result, no longer seen as problem solvers but problem makers by some.

As of 2025 we had to confront a pilot (SIHIS, the Suspected Inflicted Head Injury Service) launched in 2024 without any consultation with the legal sector, intended to cut deep into the respected practice of seeking out expert medical evidence for cases involving allegations of inflicted injury. Though commissioned as a clinical trial its potential reach became wider, longer and deeper, cutting into the fabric of what holds together our frayed faith in the family 'justice' system. The President said in his subsequent Guidance that 'the clarity of presentation, content, and opinion that the Clinical Report will bring should assist in reducing the number of Part 25 experts the court considers it necessary to instruct'.[22] In one sentence he has potentially (and a number of us say controversially) broken through an essential divide in responsibilities between the clinician and the expert and expressly suggested the former's 'opinion' (acquired pre-proceedings with no court overview or legal input on behalf of the family) can stand in place of transparently instructed independent experts. This saves the legal aid and Ministry of Justice money and the court's time, but at the cost of justice, I and many believe, for the families that come before the court. We have fought back. John Vater KC and I went public, and many more were active behind the scenes to prevent its widespread adoption. We may have succeeded. Silence has descended on its application – but I've learnt never to assume a bad idea in law is buried – it may just be hibernating ready to be dusted off when memories of indignation fade.

January 2025 also brought new Guidance from the President of the Family Division on the use of intermediaries with the express intention of reducing their use in court and in pre-court work with a vulnerable client. The President's then Guidance

---

[22] https://www.judiciary.uk/guidance-and-resources/a-view-from-the-presidents-chambers-july-2024/

referred, at paragraph 12, to the wide spectrum of vulnerability. By reference to this spectrum it is said that 'only towards the far end' will an intermediary be 'necessary' for the giving of evidence, 'only at the far end of the spectrum' will an intermediary be 'required' for the whole of a hearing and 'only in the very rarest of cases' will an intermediary be 'necessary' to enable the party to give instructions in advance of a hearing or for conferences. The Intermediary Guidance took the President's exhortation to 'make cases smaller' into new realms by severely limiting safeguards in place that provided assistance to highly vulnerable clients through the support of a qualified intermediary. In addition to helping them give their oral evidence, the intermediary could (if judicially approved) assist the client in the preparation of their case (by attending legal conferences) and in the course of the trial by explaining the evidence being given by others. The President adopted and promoted dicta in cases given by Lieven J and Williams J that made this holistic intermediary service as rare as hen's teeth.

In their absence, who takes up the skill deficit and work load? Answer? None from the President in that Guidance but one from a legal aid practitioner who saw where the answer lay – it was on us, our colleagues in the legal aid Bar and legal aid law firms. That man with an answer was one of my colleagues I admire hugely at the Bar for being prepared to be outspoken about the hurdles we face, as family barristers, to do the job we are trained to do. It was the self-same colleague who had spoken alongside me in the SIHIS tussle – John Vater KC. In 2025, John wrote this and spoke for many of us in so doing:

> Practitioners are already routinely in conflict with the Court about time-estimates, witness requirements, and the necessity of oral evidence from experts. We are already struggling to discharge our professional responsibilities with imposed and clearly inadequate time estimates, sometimes deliberately imposed to prevent cases falling into the VHCC (Very High Cost Cases) regime (which has not been increased, even in line with inflation, for decades, and is, when analysed in terms of hourly rates, or what might be available in privately paying work, hardly a Golden Goose). One

could be forgiven for thinking, sometimes, that we are regarded (dispiritingly and wholly unjustifiably) as being 'on the make', and our honest, professional judgements on case management issues are routinely discarded (frequently with inevitable consequences: cases running over, the necessity of this or that expert becoming suddenly obvious in the course of a trial, the absence of this or that lay witness suddenly becoming a problem. 'We told you so' has become the silent refrain of the advocates all too often). The inevitably increased time-estimates for cases where there is to be more limited intermediary involvement is hardly likely to decrease that conflict. Make no mistake, that conflict is corrosive in a jurisdiction where collaboration, at all levels, is essential. We work better when we work together. I cannot, for myself, think of a time in my near 30 year career when that has seemed more difficult to achieve. The relationship between the Court's objectives and the advocate's absolute duty to represent their client to the best of their ability was, historically, truly symbiotic and sympathetic. It is less so now than I can ever remember; there is an increasing tension which, in my view, serves neither 'the system' nor the children and families caught in it.[23]

The Court of Appeal reaffirmed that the boundary between fairness and injustice lay in the application of the word 'necessary', in their decision of April 2025.[24] Lieven J's words, endorsed by the President through his then Guidance on the use of intermediaries were addressed head-on: 'there was no warrant for overlaying the test of necessity with concepts of rarity or exceptionality'.[25] To watch this appeal livestreamed was a joy. Darren Howe KC led it, acting for

---

[23] https://www.harcourtchambers.co.uk/john-vater-kc-gives-his-thoughts-on-the-recent-practice-guidance-on-the-use-of-intermediaries/; see also John Vater KC, 'Make Do and Mend: Practice Guidance on the Use of Intermediaries' [2025] Fam Law March.
[24] https://www.judiciary.uk/judgments/m-a-child-intermediaries/
[25] *M (A Child: Intermediaries) [2025] EWCA Civ 440*

the local authority. He was masterful. Fully on top of his brief. His principles shone as brightly as his oracy. He was the champion we, and our clients, needed when it mattered. The President has now issued amended Guidance reflecting the Court of Appeal's decision.

The sense of disillusionment we have in our leaders, the feeling of being undervalued and under attack for standing up for what we believe in, is a canker. Especially when, as John says, we do so much more for our clients than can ever be funded by legal aid.

Every day we face a mountain of unpaid work we must do to get the job done. As the FLBA pointed out in its written submissions to the Court of Appeal in Re M:

> The extent of unremunerated work routinely expected of counsel has grown steadily and significantly over the last decade, commensurate with the increased pressures upon the court system. Many tasks that counsel is expected to undertake simply did not exist (or exist to the same extent) when the relevant fee schemes were devised. The complexity of the tasks to be undertaken, for example, reviewing digital data and the frequent need to accommodate late disclosure – to enable the fixture to be retained – increases the pressures. In cases where legal representation is funded by legal aid, even where work undertaken by counsel is remunerated there has been no inflationary or other increase in the rates of remuneration for this work since 1996.

This represents a 48 per cent cut in fees, taking into account inflation: '[I]n real terms fees are now approximately half what they were 28 years ago.'[26]

Quoting John again:

> For years, now, every one of us has been working in an environment with ever dwindling resources, and with

---

[26] National Audit Office, 'Government's Management of Legal Aid', 9 February 2024, § 3, p 48, https://www.nao.org.uk/wp-content/uploads/2024/02/governments-management-of-legal-aid.pdf

ever increasing pressures, not only because of workload but also how the Courts demand we manage that workload. We have continued to provide representation at the highest levels despite all of that, and very often through our good-will, through our determination to work when we shouldn't be expected to work, by forcing hearings and meetings into our diaries when frankly we shouldn't, and by regularly working for free. Whilst undoubtedly cynical, it is not unreasonable for others to assume that putting us under yet more pressure by cutting back on intermediary assistance will make no difference to the quality of service we will provide, because we have always, despite the pressures, provided excellence without compromise, so often to our personal detriment. Perhaps we are perceived as the infantry, always ready cheerfully to do whatever is demanded of us, whatever odds are against us, at whatever cost to us, because we have a willingness to serve and a vocation for service. As ever these days, in the Family Justice System, there are so many elephants in the room that it is hard to breathe.[27]

Social media has exploded, which means cases are now suffocated by having to set unpaid days aside to read through literally tens of thousands of pages of entries by family members to see if they cast light on what happened to their child. I receive emails 24/7, seven days a week. There is only a slight decrease at weekends. I send emails at 3 or 4am, because that's when I am thinking and working (I now send them with a message that I don't expect them to be read: my way of working should not impose the strain of a reply on a recipient at an ungodly hour!). Note that we do not get paid for reading, writing or sending case management emails under the legal aid family fee structure – but they are vital to keep the trial afloat. We have to work the case up from first principles and the data. To receive a 'Counsel's Brief' informing us what the client's

---

[27] https://www.harcourtchambers.co.uk/john-vater-kc-gives-his-thoughts-on-the-recent-practice-guidance-on-the-use-of-intermediaries/

instructions are on the evidence is now a rarity. I try to insist on it, because I have the seniority and status to do so, but I'm giving up on asking. Junior members of the Bar often simply have evidence, served on the solicitor, passed on to them by email, akin to a post box service. Solicitors have so much to do to keep a legal aid practice going that the thing they train and specialise in, being the interface between the client and the case evidence, is sometimes (often) just too much to ask. They have to process a high volume of work just to create a viable profit margin.

A 'working day' for me begins at any point from midnight onwards, when I start strategising cross-examination, or mentally listing 'things to do' to get a case trial ready. Waking up with the opening lines of cross-examination in my head at 3am, getting up at 5am to sync the thoughts with the papers or sending off emails while leaning to one side of the bed (trying to keep the light on minimum and the keypad sounds light so as not to wake my recumbent husband) is 'normal' to me. 3am, or whatever random time I wake up, is simply the thinking start of a working day that will take me from the wee small hours to the courtroom, thence post-court client care and home to start the next day's cross prep: trial tasks interposed with 24/7 email accessibility covering work on pending cases and other parts of my professional life: the Gresham professorship, advice and support for colleagues, writing articles, giving talks, sitting (and don't forget the joys of commuting), and on it rolls.

My family know my way of working. They know that's not 'normal'. They also know that it comes at personal cost. So, having told them I was going to talk about my way of working, I was told in no uncertain terms that if I was going to describe it honestly, as an obsession with performance, then nothing I said should be used to fetishise my frankly ridiculous and unhealthy approach to work as a child protection silk.

Mental health issues should not be stigmatised. The list of issues the Bar Council has advice on tells you that these problems are real, they are not unusual, they are a consequence of our working lives and there is help available – alcohol addiction, bereavement, eating disorders, financial stress, lack of sleep, stress, perfectionism, bullying, drug addiction, excessive workload, gambling, panicking in court, possible professional error, self-harm and vicarious trauma.[28] I worry that too few people are willing to ask for help. I worry that 'wellbeing' has lost its meaning, and I recoil when it is trotted out by leaders who say it but act against it. We are at breaking point.

I think that the Bar's increasing willingness to talk about problems within the profession, such as sexual harassment and judicial abuse, has brought wellbeing out of the shadows and into the sunlight for discussion. But only by some. The stigma about saying you aren't coping is still there. It requires a good support network among family and colleagues – and faith in your clerk's room – to say that you need time out. That is easier for the more senior members of the Bar than the most junior.

I know I am not a good advert for 'wellbeing' at the Bar. Frankly few of the legal aid silks I know well are. 'Wellbeing' gets sacrificed on the altar of success (or striving for it). I am a competitive silk. I want to be top of the food chain when it comes to getting the most interesting briefs in. And I do. It takes skill and stamina to build up a 'leading silk' practice and reputations are easier to lose than to acquire. In the small specialist professional world of very serious child abuse that I practise in cases are often unreported because of potential criminal trials in the wings or they don't hit the news because the court wants to protect the child's privacy – word of competence spreads by word of mouth. You are as good as your last case, your last cross-examination.

This chapter has talked about the people who I think Set the Bar for a life in law and what it costs them to tread this professional path. What has to be remembered, to keep walking on, is why we do it. Marina Sergides sets it out so well. She fights on in her specialism of social housing law because she is not only passionate about fighting inequality but also passionate about changing the Bar and to be a driver for change: '*Vulnerable people need representation that is as good as that received by the powerful and wealthy – why shouldn't that be provided by a state educated woman.*' She says that she and our colleagues, like

---

[28] If you can't talk to friends or family and you want to talk to someone who knows something about the work pressures you are under, then the Bar Council support can help. Log onto https://www.wellbeingatthebar.org.uk/. It includes a wide range of resources for barristers/clerks and staff/pupils. It has a really easily navigable page.

all public servants, deserve better working conditions, *'starting with fewer attacks on a legal aid lawyer's right to work. But, that all being said, I love my job. Being an advocate, learning and seeking to apply the law and working with the people I represent, make it worthwhile. Following and understanding how our law and legal system is shaped by the society in which we live, whilst simultaneously helping to shape it, is a real vocation. Law is a living instrument after all'*.

And what of me – why do I put myself through this? What drives me into these dark recesses of the human experience? Because a child's life matters. I am driven to try to understand how a child's life has been lived to bring it to the court's attention. It's a common fallacy to say that in court the judge is there to determine the truth of what happened. That's not possible, though sometimes it might happen. The judge is there to make the best decision they can on the evidence they have before them. That is why what I and my colleagues do in court to influence the evidence that is heard and how it is interpreted is so critical. Colin Wells, speaking from the perspective of a criminal barrister, agrees: *'Helping to enforce legal rights for individuals, particularly against the state, is an important task.'*

Anyone that does this type of work does it as a vocation. It exposes you to graphic images and tales of abuse that you would not dream any person was capable of inflicting upon a vulnerable child. But remember the question 'how can you act for them' before you leap to conclusions, for while child abuse is the stuff of nightmares so is being falsely accused of harming your child. Sometimes I can play a part in helping my clients towards a better, supported, future with their child. Sometimes a parent is exonerated. A case that begins with legitimate professional suspicion (whether that be social work, police or expert advice) can shift as layers of miscommunication and presumed fact are peeled away, and the clients give their own account of the best of themselves to the court for evaluation.

That matters to me: I know that if I don't do my job to the best of my ability and give my client the best platform for giving their account to the court, the alternative for a child might well be adoption. There is no greater and irreversible act of intervention by the state in a family's life than taking their child and placing that child's future in the hands of a stranger, severing all physical contact and legal ties in perpetuity between them.

As Sir James Munby eloquently explained when President of the Family Division:

> I have said this many times in the past but it must never be forgotten that, with the state's abandonment of the right to impose capital sentences, orders of the kind which family judges are typically invited to make in public law proceedings are amongst the most drastic that any judge in any jurisdiction is ever empowered to make. When a family judge makes a placement order or an adoption order in relation to a twenty-year old mother's baby, the mother will have to live with the consequences of that decision for what may be upwards of 60 or even 70 years, and the baby for what may be upwards of 80 or even 90 years. We must be vigilant to guard against the risks.[29]

In any one week, in any Family Court in the land, these scenarios are being argued and explored by the tens of thousands.

To my clients, there is no case more important than theirs, no job that's more important than the one I do when I cross-examine on their behalf. They put their trust in me to know the papers, score the 'cross' points, win over the judge (not always one and the same thing). They have to live with my witness wins or losses long after I've left the courtroom, the case and their lives. So, I work. I plan. I plot. I don't sleep well. Because child abuse public law work matters. That's not an excuse. It's an explanation.

Our life in law: image and reality

The image of a barrister is defined by the wig and gown, but that's a uniform. We aren't 'at work' only when we don it. Some of us rarely wear that 18th-century garb at all. But we are all barristers to the core of our being, and we live and breathe our job for too many hours a day, often squeezing out our own lives into corners where our families find it hard to see us. Being a barrister and being entrusted with trying to make a difference to a case that may forever impact on a client's life is a privilege and a burden. Never think

---

[29] *Re J (A Child) [2013] EWHC 2694 (Fam)* [28].

that duty is not respected. Never think we don't strive to live by the highest ethical and professional standards. Never think a client's case is forgotten when we leave the conference room or the court building. We try to give our clients faith in a legal system most have no knowledge of or trust in. The job we do as barristers is the most dynamic, passionate, life-affirming, valuable, entertaining, energising and inspirational job one can possibly do.

And why legal aid? Because it is the ethical glue that holds our 'justice' system together. Because, despite the cuts to legal aid, the closing down of fair trial options for parents in proceedings, the closure of courts, the waiting lists, I have to believe in our justice system and the change we can deliver within it because it's the one we have to make work. The tough question I asked at the outset of this chapter is not 'how do you act on behalf of someone you know is guilty'. It's not even 'how do you *prosecute* someone who is innocent' – it is, to my mind, 'how do you *protect* someone who *might* be innocent' – and that is an ethical question for the judge to address as much as for the barrister to live up to.

I believe that every person is entitled to a fair trial and to proper representation – if you were accused, if you faced losing your liberty to the state or your child to care, wouldn't you demand the same?

4

Power and Patronage

Power is not equally shared at the Bar. It can be abused, and it is.[1] All those who start with smaller (or non-existent) professional networks, and who don't already have an 'in' to a chambers as a pupil, or as a tenant with a secure practice and reputation, are at risk. That description applies to many aspiring and practising barristers in marginalised communities, such as our GEM and LGBTQIA+ colleagues. But gender, sexuality, class and colour are not siloed qualities – when they combine, the person's vulnerability to powerplay is magnified. These problems are compounded by the cloak of patronage which shelters the Bar's power culture.

---

[1] The IBA published a global survey on bullying and sexual harassment in the legal profession in 2018. Of 6,980 respondents from 135 countries, 715 British legal professionals participated: 'The results ... are concerning. Overall, bullying and sexual harassment is a pervasive and complex issue in British legal workplaces, including barristers' chambers.' International Bar Association Survey, 'Bullying and Sexual Harassment 2019', https://www.iba net.org/ bullying-and-sexual-harassment#:~:text=In%202018%2C%20the%20IBA%20 and,chambers%2C%20government%20and%20the%20judiciary. 44 per cent of respondents to the Bar Council's 2023 Working Lives Survey (see https://www.barcouncil.org.uk/resource/bar-council-barristers--working-lives-report-2023-pdf.html) reported having experienced or witnessed bullying, harassment and discrimination while working (in person or online). This figure rises year on year.

Chambers can be a conversational and professional hub, especially around the clerk's room or tea/coffee station. We may hot-desk or have no space at all and simply think of chambers as a virtual anchor to the clerks' room and a conference base. However much or little time one spends in a chambers, it is important to choose a set where you like and respect the people in it, and vice versa. If you band together in chambers, you have to be prepared to play your role in that set, as if in an orchestra, aspiring to the solo spots, sometimes playing second fiddle while you watch the greats, but always knowing that the collective voice is stronger and louder than any one individual member. Chambers is meant to operate as a collective, but that does not necessarily translate to equality or inclusion: not in what you see in the set, not in what you see in your colleagues outside of chambers, not in who sits beside you at court.

Feeling 'different', being junior, or simply feeling at sea in the professional world and people around you, is isolating, and with isolation comes the potential for abuse.

Think back to a barrister's beginnings. Chambers, for many, is their professional calling card. It is a stamp of belonging, of having 'made it' this far, a junior barrister's foot on the first rung of a career at the Bar. As a chambers pupil, we are especially exposed. We undergo a unique form of apprenticeship where we, as the pupil, shadow a senior member of the Bar. In our 'first six', where one goes, the other follows. In our 'second six',[2] we continue to be supervised for support and quality checking. Whether in one's first or second six, supervisors have power – power over the pupil's movements, experiences and references. They have access to the pupil's calendar,

---

[2] A 'second six' reflects the second stage of a 12-month pupillage. Stage 1 (first six): the pupil is the pupil supervisor's shadow, reading the paperwork, doing research, attending conferences and court. They do not do any work in their own name – they are not permitted to do so. Their 'second six' is where they learn to fly as a barrister. The pupil can go to court alone and be briefed in their own name but they remain under a pupil supervisor's professional supervision for oversight, support and advice. If you don't get into your pupillage chambers after your 12 months you may then apply for a third six with them or another set to gain experience and keep your chances of a tenancy alive.

personal information and communication devices. Supervisors, being tenants, will have more status than a pupil. They will possess superior resources in income, influence and knowledge of life and the Bar than the pupil. That creates a power imbalance. Pupillage puts a pupil and their supervisor in close physical and professional proximity. Pupil supervision and inter-barrister business within chambers is conducted behind closed doors, within insular communities. Supervisors have the power of a reference in their hands – whether to chambers for a tenancy, to another chambers for a third six or a tenancy, to solicitors who could instruct you, or to the clerks who want to know if you've got potential to take a brief and serve the reputation of chambers well. When you are a beginner, the name of the chambers you work in will be better known than your own. Being in their stable gives you a quality hallmark.

Getting a pupillage or tenancy is a matter of intense competition after years of education, training and cost. By way of example, in 2024/5[3] there were 638 pupillages, 58 per cent of offers went to those with first class degrees, 38 per cent to 2:1 holders. In 2021/2022, of those 578 who gained a pupillage out of 2,782 applicants, only 347 secured a tenancy less than six months after their pupillage year.[4] Those figures do not give away the true picture. In each yearly pupil recruitment cycle, candidates who have been unsuccessful at securing pupillage in the year prior will re-apply. Chambers across all practice areas regularly receive upwards of 300 applications for one available pupillage. A lot rides on getting a tenancy after years of struggle. Becoming a tenant is a very public professional endorsement of your legal credentials. In the Inns, as an incoming tenant, your name would be painted on a wooden slat in black script and inserted, in order of seniority of call, into a framed list of tenants (almost like a menu), topped by the Head of Chambers and hung on the Inn entrance. Pupils don't have their names on the board – they haven't yet earned the right to be part of the set. Tenancy is not a guaranteed

---

[3] Pupillage Gateway Report 2024/5, https://www.barcouncil.org.uk/resource/pupillage-gateway-2024-25-pdf.html

[4] Bar Standards Board (BSB), 'Pupillage Statistics', https://www.barstandardsboard.org.uk/data-and-research/statistics-about-the-bar/pupillage.html

outcome of pupillage by any means, and competition doesn't end at pupillage. Throughout your entire professional career as a barrister, your advancement is influenced by the views *others* hold of you; whether they be your colleagues in chambers, your clerks, solicitors, or the judges who preside over your cases.

Safe working conditions can be distorted by many factors other than simply junior/senior status – coercive and controlling behaviour has many forms and targets.

In different ways, your colleagues hold an extraordinary degree of power over your development: they are able to lift you up or strike you down with just a sentence. They can recommend briefs or starve you of them. Put in a good word for you as a reference or refuse to give you one.

A Petri dish for bullying and harassment

Abuse of power can play out via bullying or sexual harassment, and there is an overlap between those facets, which women are especially vulnerable to. The reality of sexual harassment or bullying is that it describes, more often than not, behaviour by male members of the Bar, most likely senior, towards a female target. Of course, this isn't just a 'women's problem' at the Bar: it may be male–male or female–male, but the stark reality is that it affects women to a significantly higher degree than men, if statistics and anecdotal information are taken as reliable indicators. Around two in five (41 per cent) of the female barristers surveyed by the Bar Council in its 2023 bullying, harassment and discrimination report[5] reported having suffered harassment: a percentage indicating no visible change over the past 15 years.[6] Moreover, the 2025 Pupil Survey found that 17 per cent of pupils reported personal experience of bullying, harassment or

---

[5] Bar Council, 'Bullying, Harassment and Discrimination at the Bar', December 2023, https://www.barcouncil.org.uk/static/5a630b6a-8e91-473f-bfa0cca11b707e42/Bullying-harassment-and-discrimination-at-the-Bar-December-2023.pdf

[6] Looking back, in the BSB's 2016 Women at the Bar survey, 40.2 per cent of the female barristers surveyed reported experiencing harassment, however only one in five had reported it. Female legal professionals in the United Kingdom experience sexual harassment

discrimination.[7] Making a 'fuss' may affect their chances of getting a tenancy or rising up the ranks, labelling them a troublemaker, and making life more difficult for them, as opposed to their abuser, in their workplace. This data will no doubt be updated to be commented upon in the Harman Report expected to be published in autumn 2025. So watch that space.

Barbara Mills KC, the Chair of the Bar Council, has a clear agenda to prioritise tackling bullying and harassment at the Bar. At her inaugural address in January 2025, she said: 'Talking alone is not enough. The actions I will take will focus on what we know from the Wellbeing report about bullying and harassment, the Young Bar and the earnings disparity and finally the employed Bar.'[8]

So, what do we mean by 'harassment', and where does it cross the line into unlawful conduct? Harassment is not necessarily sexual. Unlawful harassment is defined by the Equality Act 2010 as: 'Unwanted conduct of a sexual nature or related to gender, sexual orientation, gender reassignment, race, religion/belief, age or disability, which has the purpose or effect of violating another's dignity or creating a degrading, offensive, humiliating, intimidating or hostile environment for them.'

Harassment and bullying are both abuses of power, aren't they? Power does not always mean being in a position of authority – one particular personality can exert power over another, there may be coercive or controlling behaviours such as tracking the victim, letting the victim know you know where they are, calling the victim at inappropriate times and other intimidatory, predatory behaviours. Examples of harassment may include:

---

at a far greater rate – 38 per cent of women reported being sexually harassed, compared with 6 per cent of men. This equates to almost one in three women and one in 17 men. See also the IBA survey October 2018, 'Us Too? Bullying and Sexual Harassment in the Legal Profession', https://www.ibanet.org/bullying-and-sexual-harassment#:~:text=In%202018%2C%20the%20IBA%20and,chambers%2C%20government%20and%20the%20judiciary

[7] Bar Council, 'Pupil Survey Report', June 2025, https://www.barcouncil.org.uk/static/07067935-8b90-4faf-a21d2bbb0ce564ca/5bfec97d-eed2-4333-b83b353281c4be8a/Pupil-Survey-2025.pdf

[8] Barbara Mills KC, 'Inaugural Address', January 2025, https://www.barcouncil.org.uk/resource/barbara-mills-kc-inaugural-address-8-january-2025.html

- Overly personal comments or over-familiar behaviour, including questions about someone's relationships, sex life or gender identity.
- Continued suggestions for social activity after it has been made clear that such suggestions are unwelcome.
- Racist, sexist, anti-LGBTQIA+ or ageist jokes.
- Derogatory or stereotypical remarks about an ethnic/religious group, gender identity or sexual orientation.
- Offensive or intimidating comments or gestures.
- Insensitive jokes or pranks.
- Staring or inappropriate/suggestive looks.
- Invading someone's personal space.
- Sexual or offensive gestures.
- Inappropriate sexual advances or repeated unwelcome sexual advances.
- Inappropriate or unwelcome physical contact.
- Displaying/sending sexually suggestive pictures or written material.

The most common types of sexual harassment in the UK include:[9]

- Sexual or sexually suggestive comments, remarks or sounds (68 per cent).
- Sexist comments, including inappropriate humour or jokes about sex or gender (65 per cent).
- Being looked at in an inappropriate manner which made the respondent feel uncomfortable (53 per cent).
- Inappropriate physical contact (53 per cent).
- Sexual propositions, invitations or other pressure for sex (27 per cent).

As I've said, it's not right to assume that sexual harassment only happens to women. It doesn't; 6 per cent of men working in law in the UK revealed experiences of sexual harassment in the International Bar Association (IBA) report[10] (and I have had two described to

---

[9] IBA survey 2018, https://www.ibanet.org/bullying-and-sexual-harassment#:~:text=In%202018%2C%20the%20IBA%20and,chambers%2C%20government%20and%20the%20judiciary

[10] Discussed further on in this chapter.

me). But that still leaves an alarming ratio of 38 per cent of women reporting being sexually harassed, compared with 6 per cent of men. This equates to almost one in three women, and one in 17 men. These surveys more than amply demonstrate the reality faced by members of the Bar. Like many women entering my profession, I suffered sexual harassment and never made a formal complaint. I don't drink coffee even now, some 30 years after the experience, because the smell of it takes me back to the chambers galley kitchen, my body stiffening as I endured the wandering hands of the incoming barrister, an assault signalled by the stench of stale coffee breath from the mouth pressed into the nape of my neck.

As a pupil, I was booked into a double hotel room, on the assumption that I would be sleeping with my senior male colleague on cases. Who had made the booking? Why was it left to me to challenge it at reception? Was there a hope and an expectation that I wouldn't? I made a point of never allowing my male colleague to go to reception to book us in without me alongside him. Think back to what it would have taken to say 'no' to plans that involved more than sharing a cab to court. I wasn't a tenant. I was a replaceable pupil. I was skint. I was working away from home. I couldn't pay for a hotel room myself. My expenses were paid by my colleague out of his fee. We had no mobiles. I could only contact mum or Jonathan via the hotel phone, and what could they do? We didn't have the internet to transfer funds. It was a game of cat and mouse for the opportunist abuser, and a constant test of endurance and strength for me. I said to the receptionist that there must have been a mistake and endured the disbelieving look given in response. Women were not always allies, I discovered, but persistence paid off, and a key to another room was handed over.

At dinner that night, conversation with my supervisor was strained but we were able to discuss the case. I just wanted to forget the whole tawdry episode. I was unprepared for a knock on the door at 7:30 the next morning, way earlier than we'd agreed to have breakfast and go through the day's witnesses. I was in my underwear and a long shirt, sans skirt, when I heard the knock. No voice accompanying it to identify the caller. I hadn't stayed in hotels; I didn't know the routine. Was I being given some towels? I opened the door, and my pupil supervisor walked straight in. What do you do when a man, in a position of influence and power over you, simply walks past you into your open-plan bedroom/lounge and sits down, all while you are partially undressed? It was all very polite, a cheery '*Hello; I thought we could run through the plans for today*', all perfectly normal – except it wasn't. In those moments I felt exposed and confused. I didn't challenge. I didn't ask him to leave. I didn't call it out for the affront to my privacy that it was. I may instead have apologised ('Sorry, I was running late') as I gathered up my clothes and dived into the bathroom to get ready, shaking, furious. I felt ashamed of myself and my reaction. I didn't have the confidence I have now to make a fuss. I was called a 'pocket Venus' when I felt like a hand grenade ready to detonate. But it didn't. The pin was never pulled. Like many women, I simply acted as though this was all OK, and I could cope.

These incidents did not begin and end with one man. Too often, there were unwelcome, uninvited, lecherous slobbering kisses to be wiped away, when post-court drinks left a gap in the company around me, or there were shadows in the corridors to the loos to be pulled into. Nor was humiliation always furtive. In another set, another group of men, in a conference room where the chairs were all taken, one client noticed that I had nowhere to sit, but said that was fine – because he had a space in his lap, and he spread his legs and pulled me down to sit on him. I was taken aback, not nearly so much by that opening comment as by the fact that the male barristers in the room simply laughed, as if the client had been a real wit. When I said 'no' and got up with a tumble of hands, I became the object of the joke. The male tenants were all good guys. They were kind. They were supportive. But in that moment, they didn't speak up for me. It was just all 'good sport', and I played up to the joke, reverting to the type of language I'd used in the holiday camps of my adolescence when someone got 'fresh' with me. I gave as good as I got with the banter, because I had been brought up to never be a wilting flower. Was it my own fault? I don't think so. I think it's because I was a young, pretty, blonde female pupil in the presence of senior men, who thought, first, why not have a try, and, second, if I didn't respond positively, it was always something to laugh over.

I told Jonathan about these experiences but forbade him from confronting the abusers because it would harm my career. There were more instances, but this book isn't the place to recount all of them – some things we bury. At the time, I talked to female friends, but we had all experienced pretty much the same things, so we normalised it and just worked on avoidant techniques. Listening to the phenomenal Baroness Heather Hallett of Rye on Radio 4, I was stunned to find that sexual harassment was something she too had experienced.[11] I looked at her as someone with such a powerful personality that she could have withered the advances of a man with a single dismissive glance – but no, she had been propositioned. She didn't say anything. I didn't say anything. My friends didn't say anything.

Being targeted doesn't mean to say you are weak, vulnerable, asking for it. I think being confident and apparently resilient can make you a target because of the desire to take you down a peg or two. Abuse isn't about the personality of the victim, it's about the personality of the abuser, a power bid. My abuse eased off as I grew more confident in my own space and professional reputation. But I also grew older. That's relevant. The stark reality is that I'm now in late middle age, and as an older woman, I am less likely to be subjected to unwelcome sexual attention and comment. I become invisible with age and perceived diminution of sexual attractiveness. And even if I were to generate the pull, I have acquired the maturity, status and confidence to call it out and deal with it robustly. If it's less of a problem for us as senior women, it becomes easy to slip into the belief that it is not a problem for others. But that's an illusion. The further up the profession we go and the more senior we become, the more remote we appear to aspiring pupils and tenants, and the less likely it is that we will be told if they have a problem with a particular member of the Bar.

I have tried to stop that tendency towards complacency and reverse it, because the culture of abuse is still strong within the Bar. It still goes on, much in the same way as I experienced it, and it is now, as it was then, dealt with alone, or with the support of friends and family. It might be raised by a member of the Bar, but only once trust is established. It is rarely reported. While the intimacy of the pupil–supervisor relationship can be the basis of a lifelong supportive professional and personal friendship, it can also be the recipe for this type of unwanted and inappropriate attention or comment.

---

[11] https://www.bbc.co.uk/programmes/m000wshk; and BBC Radio 4, *Desert Island Discs*, 'Heather Hallett, Former Judge and Crossbench Peer', 6 June 2021.

For decades we have tolerated too much for too many. We have, quite simply, failed to change this pernicious aspect of the Bar's culture. We have continued to add victims to the roll call of shame. Those of us who have been exposed to it can count its cost.

I was a pupil in the late 1980s. I didn't speak of my experiences until decades later, by which time I had a cohort of strong, outspoken women around me and a platform at Gresham to use to good effect. My colleagues, and the constant support of Jonathan, give me the courage to say what I didn't have the courage, or audience, to speak out about when I was young. I felt ashamed of my inaction when I was the victim of harassment, and I'm not alone in that. My friend and colleague Brie Stevens-Hoare KC supported me by giving me her own named experience to share when I delivered my Gresham lecture in 2018[12] and went public about the prevalence of sexual harassment at the Bar. It was striking that no other man or woman would go public alongside me. But Brie and I took the view that if senior women didn't say what had happened to them, then we could not expect younger women to do so.

This is Brie's story. She too came from a state school background. Culturally, the Bar was new and alien to her, and financially becoming a barrister was taking a big risk, but this was a career she had dreamed of and worked towards from the age of 13. It wasn't generally a world that felt welcoming to her as a young woman in the 1980s – teatime gatherings, where banter and 'naughty' jokes about tits and bums and such were part of the Bar's atmosphere. Chambers had a handful of women (more than many) yet there was a small number of men who thrived on the banter, and it was clear that was 'ok': *'it's just ' "X" being "X"'*. So, Brie took on the 'banter' and dealt with it by endeavouring to 'give as good as she got'. Brie was at a hotel, again purely for work-related reasons. She was a pupil away with her supervisor. She had her own room, but it had an adjoining door to another. The door opened, and her supervisor walked in to ask not '*Will you* sleep with me?' but '*When* will you sleep with me?'. The question had been asked many times before but in the relative safety of chambers when others were present. This time they were alone in a bedroom. She was sitting on a bed. Brie said '*No*'. He

---

[12] https://www.gresham.ac.uk/watch-now/sexual-harrassment-bar

approached her, started massaging her shoulders and asked whether he could relax her and help change her mind. Like me, she remembers the thoughts that went through her head, vivid now even decades later – thoughts about what to say, asking herself '*If I say no, does this mean the end of my career, the career I've longed and worked for nearly half of my life, the career I've fought so hard to get? If I say no, what will he say to others that could affect my chances of progressing in my profession?*' Brie said '*No*' again, loud and clear. Later when Brie was a junior tenant and against her former supervisor, before a judge in chambers, he, with a big smile on his face and a table to hide his actions, put his hand up her skirt to squeeze her thigh while she was in the middle of her submissions. All she felt able to do was remove his hand and act like nothing was happening and she was completely unaffected by it.

Neither Brie nor I had told anyone, save the closest of friends, about our experiences at the time. Now, 30-plus years later, a lecture brought together two senior silks who had been strangers to each other as pupils. Why had this culture been tolerated? There is no one answer. It was the chamber's culture of 'banter' and casual sexism which blurred public professional boundaries and enabled some men to overstep them in private and even in public spaces. It was about the physical proximity between the pupil and supervisor, the shared rooms in training which can be isolating and overpowering. We think it's age – the big imbalance in experience between the junior barrister and the senior barrister, not just because they know the ropes of the job, but they know so much about life, or appear to. Both Brie and I talked about being starstruck by the lifestyle, going to restaurants, the theatre, having wine with lunch or dinner, which we hadn't been accustomed to doing as young adults. Our shared working-class backgrounds meant we had a lot to learn in terms of social norms in addition to the practice of law. Looking back on why we said nothing to anyone in chambers who might have helped us, we are not surprised. As Brie said, '*from a position of agency now I can believe that other members of chambers would've wanted to help me, but at the time I questioned whether they would. I didn't tell another barrister in chambers because they were 'the other'. They were on the inside, I on the outside. I wanted to step into their profession and believed they would consider I was not up to it if I couldn't take the banter and all that came with it. Would telling my story divide me further from them and the career I was on the brink of? Would they believe me? Would they brush it off as just "X" being "X"? Would they think I was not tough enough for life at the Bar? Would it cause problems for me and my career?'*

Brie and I survived the encounters and got on with our jobs. Time passed. We got older, more confident. This wasn't an issue for discussion at the Bar. Brie and I buried our past.

I thought that what we had experienced was also 'the past' for the young, and that it had no place in their working lives. I was wrong.

There are still bastards out there

Through the interviews I have carried out and the research I have read, it has become clear to me that what I had thought were problems of the past are very much problems of our present: and if we don't speak out about them, they will continue to blight the healthy development of our profession, and the young who aspire to join it. That is not acceptable. We *have* to Set the Bar higher in terms of the standards we hold ourselves, and our colleagues, up to. Set against a damn low bar we are still failing.

Harassment is more likely to be experienced by the youngest and most junior members of our profession, and they are precisely the people who fear to speak out, because of their concern that it may blight their career prospects. The young do not speak about their experiences. It is an under-reported problem. That's not just my view, it is that of the Bar Council, arising from the 2017 research work it has carried out and reinforced by the results mentioned earlier from the 2018 survey conducted by the IBA published in 2019.[13] Data taken

---

[13] Harassment remains a contemporary issue – of those who were sexually harassed, 32 per cent of cases occurred within the last year.

- Sexual harassment is routinely 'never' reported (74 per cent), for reasons similar to the under-reporting of bullying.
- Of those who reported incidents of harassment, a notable proportion indicated that their employers' responses were insufficient (34 per cent) or negligible (37 per cent).
- In 71 per cent of reported incidences, the perpetrator was not sanctioned.
- As a result, 40 per cent of harassed respondents expressed an intention to leave their workplace.

from the most recent Bar Council Working Lives survey produced in 2025 from 2024 data continued to evidence a toxic culture at the Bar that is intolerable and unacceptable.[14] This included experiencing ridicule, demeaning language, overbearing supervision and misuse of power. Respondents practising at the commercial bar reported lower levels of these experiences but reported higher levels of wellbeing. There is a difference in our experiences. There is a difference in the way people behave in different sectors of our profession. That is extraordinary – and unacceptable

The fact that sexual harassment is not reported, for example to the Bar Standards Board, does not indicate that there is not a problem with harassment: rather, this illustrates the problem that the Bar has in confronting harassment. The Bar Council has acknowledged the need for the Bar to approach bullying, harassment and discrimination as a systemic issue requiring a culture shift.[15]

We now have *yet another attempt* to bottom it out. In 2024 the Bar Council appointed Baroness Harriet Harman, PC, KC to chair the independent bullying and harassment review. It secured a formidable reference team to assist her. We have, of course, supported it but I think there is a sense of déjà vu and disillusionment. How many times can we expect victims to relive their experiences and repeat them again, to yet another person? Why should they believe this time it will make a difference? The response from colleagues was 'What will this add?' We have the evidence of the problem; we have report after report providing the data and experiences and we know what we are told is under-reporting – when and how will we see proper action to eradicate it? We will see the product of this latest attempt to eradicate a toxic culture when the report is published in autumn 2025.

---

[14] Bar Council, 'Working Lives Survey 2025', October 2025, https://www.barcouncil.org.uk/static/4982d3c7-9ad4-4d03-9f9881e818817547/Bar-Councils-Wellbeing-at-the-Bar-Report-2025.pdf

[15] Bar Council, 'Bullying, Harassment and Discrimination at the Bar', December 2023, https://www.barcouncil.org.uk/static/5a630b6a-8e91-473f-bfa0cca11b707e42/Bullying-harassment-and-discrimination-at-the-Bar-December-2023.pdf

Bullying and sexual harassment is a pervasive and complex issue in the British legal workplace. The #MeToo movement was a moment of awakening for many of us. Elizabeth Prochaska had had enough of the silence and stigma surrounding sexual harassment at the Bar and set up 'Behind the Gown'. Behind the Gown was founded by Elizabeth and other committed women, initially anonymously, in 2017, at the height of the global #MeToo wave. It was formally launched in May 2018, with a commitment to tackling abuses of power in our profession. I spoke at the launch. It was a full hall, with press attendance, and a deeply inspiring evening to be a part of.

As Elizabeth has said:

> It is very difficult for individuals to raise their concerns at the Bar due to a culture of patronage. Of course, it's almost impossible to call out individuals who you rely on for work when they behave inappropriately or bully you. While we are all in theory equal members of chambers, the Bar hierarchy does not help. ... Isolation and lack of support networks contribute to this.[16]

This is why I raised the issue of sexual harassment for public attention and professional debate in my time at Gresham. Once you put yourself on this platform and you're prepared to talk about it, you single yourself out as someone who is willing to listen. And you are told things that have never been told before.

As I gave my Gresham lecture, young women I knew to be victims were sitting in front of me. I told their stories, anonymised, with their permission. For many I had been the first person they told. They trusted me to use their histories to help others avoid what they had experienced. They were selfless. Perhaps they were unprepared to hear their stories told by an outsider. It was a shock to hear what they had experienced, not recognising their feelings about it until it had been exposed for what it was – an outrageous and inexcusable assault. For some, it gave them permission to publicly express the anger they had sublimated for so long. Until they heard their stories

---

[16] https://www.counselmagazine.co.uk/articles/interview-behind-the-gown

emerge and merge as a prolonged and fierce cry of outrage, they did not know that they were not alone. It was not their shame to bear – they had been isolated by the abuse. After the lecture, many chose to 'own their stories'. There is strength in solidarity. As the phrase goes, 'sunlight is the best disinfectant'.

Read and weep – then get angry and act

Consider this: an application for a mini pupillage made in the last two years, so recent history. 'S' applies to a set of chambers seeking pupillage. Her CV is the only information they have as to her suitability. 12:30am: a WhatsApp message appears on her mobile: '*Didn't realize we are in the same area.*' S Googled the name attached to the WhatsApp message, and the chambers' website showed up. It was from a tenant. Pause to contemplate the process and the timing of the communication from this barrister. In order for that WhatsApp message to be sent, he would have had to access her applicant's CV, check out her address, extract a telephone number, and then decide it was perfectly OK to send, not an email, not a text, but an encrypted format message at just gone midnight, letting S know that he knew where she lived. Perhaps it was well meant. But on what level could that man have thought it was the appropriate professional thing to do? It's creepy. It's stalking. S withdrew her application. '*I wanted to apply to that set for a long time, but it held me back from applying for a pupillage with them when I got to that stage.*' S was a young woman of colour from a non-traditional Bar background. The barrister in question was a white male.

What about this example: a Bar School student (female) seeking a pupillage. She applied through Gateway, which is a CV-only link. She then received a private message, along with an invitation to connect with the applicant, through LinkedIn, which had not been put down on the CV. '*I wondered if you wanted to meet up to discuss.*' He said he was on the interviewing panel. She reflects, '*Well, I wasn't quite sure that that was the right thing to do, but I was applying for a pupillage. I had gone through the right channels. I did sort of assume the thing that would happen will be I'd be interviewed by the panel rather than receiving an individual message. But what do I do?*' She spoke to her friends. She didn't want to appear rude. LinkedIn is a professional network. She accepted the invitation to connect on LinkedIn, but didn't reply to the message itself. Response: '*Hello? I can see you've read my message.*' He viewed her profile every day for two weeks. It stopped for a while, and then it restarted. She was scared to block him, because he was a senior man at the Bar. She didn't get an interview. '*He was still reviewing my profile after I've been rejected.*' That's not acceptable. That's stalking. She too was a young woman of colour, from a non-traditional applicant background.

I am concerned to know whether there's a disproportionate impact upon young GEM candidates. Why? Because if we are talking about a type of behaviour which is targeted at those who are less likely to understand how the Bar operates, then it is candidates from non-traditional backgrounds who are the most likely to be targets. When Brie and I came to the Bar in the 1980s/1990s we were in a minority as working-class women, but we were white. Now it's not simply gender and class that divides the insiders from outsiders – it's also a question of colour and religion. We need more research on this so as to target support where it is most needed.

Eve's story

Eve Robinson was a junior barrister, sharing the same chambers as a male barrister, who sexually assaulted her several times at a social event. At the time of the assault, Eve had been in pupillage. The person who sexually assaulted Eve was a tenant. Between the reporting of the sexual assault and the disciplinary tribunal hearing, Eve was offered a tenancy, which she accepted. However, she was not supported by her chambers during their internal investigation, or the Bar Standards Board (BSB)'s, nor was she supported by the BSB or Bar Council.[17] Eve was effectively left to her own devices, with a significant expectation that she would engage with each request

---

[17] The BSB regulates barristers and specialised legal services businesses in England and Wales in the public interest. For barristers it sets standards of conduct in terms of the way we perform our professional obligations and our ethical code of conduct – it sets and monitors our fitness to practice in effect. It regulates us and holds us to account if complaint is made about our behaviour. It is, in essence, our regulatory body and has the authority to discipline, if we are found to be in breach our professional obligations, by financial penalty,

made by the BSB, without issue. Her chambers carried out their own inquiry and found serious misconduct proven. They merely fined the respondent barrister and allowed him to continue working. During their inquiry, they had clerked the two barristers separately, but once their inquiry had concluded, they clerked them together, with the result that they sent the abuser barrister and Eve to act for parties in the same case. This compounded Eve's distress and left her astounded at what she was experiencing. This decision was taken while the BSB investigation was still ongoing. The BSB made the decision to proceed to Disciplinary Tribunal and Eve now faced this second process. Eve found the BTAS[18] hearing to be an uncomfortable experience. Having been objectified and deeply humiliated in the most personal way by the man who attacked her, she was then excluded from the parts of the hearing where his personal mitigation was heard while he had been privy to everything Eve had said.

No one asked Eve what the impact on her had been at any stage. Eve was not invited to give evidence on the subject. The panel was left in complete ignorance of the true impact of the respondent's misconduct. Following a finding of serious sexual misconduct by the tribunal, the abusing barrister received a suspension of three months.[19] This was despite sexual misconduct being proved that would have significantly crossed the custody threshold had it been prosecuted at the Crown Court. The BSB did not apply for an interim suspension while awaiting the BTAS hearing, meaning that Eve, as a very junior barrister, was left (still) being clerked alongside the member of chambers who had assaulted her. Despite the misconduct finding, the offending barrister could (and did) work for the entire period leading up to the formal suspension commencing. Eve was left feeling powerless, and that she had no choice but to leave chambers. Meanwhile, the barrister subjected to the suspension was able to 'diary cram', picking up work to financially tide him over the suspension period, leaving it with less bite and reducing its punitive effect. He was left on the website

---

suspension or debarment. For more detail see https://www.barstandardsboard.org.uk/

[18] The Bar Tribunal and Adjudication Service.

[19] https://www.barstandardsboard.org.uk/disciplinary_finding/183583.html

for some time, and the suspension was so short that it was much the same as a sabbatical or a long holiday. He remained a tenant at his chambers. For this entire period, Eve was left to deal with the consequences of the abuse, then the investigation process, alone. It was only thanks to disclosing what was going on to senior members of the profession outside of Eve's chambers that any real moral and practical support was received, albeit unofficial, and she was assisted in making her escape to another set, totally outside of where she lived and her practice base, with the solicitors who had gotten to know her. At least she didn't leave the Bar, which was the only option she thought she had until she spoke to me, and my group of strong women silks refused to tolerate a situation where Eve, as the victim, was penalised twice, once through abuse and then again for speaking up about it.

I will tell Eve's story here in her own words. She has long waited for them to be heard. 'X', as is her wish, denotes Eve's abuser.

After a conversation with my supervisor at the time, I reported what happened in the first week of July 2019. I vividly remember being incredibly frightened that I was about to ruin everything I had worked so hard to achieve and wave goodbye to my career at the Bar. Thereafter, the ball began to roll in a direction I had never anticipated.

I had to write a statement and those I had told at the time about what had happened were asked to provide statements too, which they did. Following the then Head of Chambers reviewing these, they contacted X via letter, setting out the general 'gist' of the allegations. X replied, in writing, a couple of weeks later. He admitted to everything but on the basis that he was drunk and couldn't remember anything. I was given the opportunity to reply to that document, with my comments. X had also asked to contact me directly to apologise, which I didn't consent to, as any apology on the basis of 'I'm sorry, but I was really drunk and don't remember' felt wholly inadequate to me.

During this time, I made the decision to continue with my application for tenancy. I had thought that if I could 'ride out' Chambers' and the inevitable BSB investigations, he would then be made to leave for what he'd done to me … how wrong was I! I received my tenancy offer in September 2019 and became a full Member of Chambers from the October.

Things then went fairly quiet. I'd not heard anything about the progress of my complaint, prompting me to speak with my Supervisor to ask if she knew anything. She contacted the then Head of Chambers on my behalf and, in turn, I received an email from them. It was explained that a panel had been convened, which comprised of the then Head of Chambers, an ex-Member of Chambers and one current Member of Chambers who did not know me or the perpetrator.

It transpired that a 'hearing' had already been conducted, whereby X admitted the allegations, was abjectly sorry and provided written representations from an external Barrister whom he'd instructed to assist him. I later learned that part of those written representations was a suggestion that a way to deal with this would be to pay me compensation. Within this same email I was informed that having considered all of the evidence, the panel accepted that the admitted facts crossed the threshold for expulsion but that the panel had neither that, nor suspension, in mind at that stage. They had decided that a simple financial penalty also wasn't sufficient therefore the 'hearing' had been adjourned for further enquiries to be made as to courses or training available. I was told they would review matters and reach a final decision in mid-November.

Mid-November came and I received another email, during the working day and whilst at Court, with the outcome of Chambers' internal investigation. Once again, this email came from the then Head of Chambers and, quite frankly, was one of the hardest emails I have ever had to read. I was informed that a 'stiff financial penalty' had been imposed, X had been required to view various courses as well as a 'very enlightening (but disturbing) lecture by Professor Jo Delahunty QC' (emphasis added), which I was also invited to watch. Ultimately, and here was the real kicker, X was to remain a member of Chambers.

I was advised that despite having been clerked apart previously, that would no longer be happening, with 'normal service' resuming and that 'whilst we all have certain opponents whom we find irritating (or worse) we must still handle them with at least a minimum level of civility'. I was also made aware that the matter had been kept extremely confidential, with only a 'tight group in the know', which I was advised I should ensure continued.

Unfortunately, it transpired that that 'tight group' that the then Head of Chambers had kept in the know was in reality no more than the three individuals who had been on the panel, myself and X. Other members of the Management Committee and of Chambers had no idea about what had gone on until publication of the Disciplinary Tribunal's decision and even then, were still largely in the dark as to precisely how matters had been dealt with internally.

Thereafter, I was contacted by the ex-Member of Chambers, Y, who I had never met previously. They asked if I would be willing to meet with them as they would like to sit down and speak to me about the panel's decision. I agreed, in the hope that may help shed some light; although I made clear that I did not want to know how much they had fined him. I did meet with Y, who whilst trying to be supportive and asking how I was, did suggest they could facilitate a coffee between X and I to speak, as I would need to move past this eventually. Needless to say, I declined.

Normal service then definitely did resume. I turned up to court in January 2020, my second day back after the Christmas break, to find myself on a case with X. I didn't find out until we were at court. At this time, the BSB investigation was ongoing, and I was due to go to give my statement to them the following week. It was an entirely impossible situation to be in. I spent five minutes having a cry in the bathroom not feeling able to face him, but also feeling entirely unable to withdraw because to do so would have left my client entirely in the lurch; not to mention I would have struggled to have explained why I found myself in that position. It was a complete ethical nightmare, let alone a personal one.

It took nearly 18 months before a BSB Disciplinary Tribunal was held; it was convened on Microsoft Teams on 22 January 2021. X received a three-month suspension and was required to pay costs. It was during this hearing that I learned that the 'stiff financial penalty' Chambers had imposed was one of £2,000 and the 'various courses' X had been required to do were three online courses, completed by him in the space of a day. My stomach sank.

It was after this that things 'took off' somewhat, with the published BSB report having attracted a lot of attention on Twitter, Legal Cheek and even the Daily Mail. The report came at a time where there had been a run of sexual harassment cases having been dealt with (or not as the case may be) by the Bar Standards Board and mine was, in effect, 'three for three' in regard to wholly unsatisfactory sanctions having been imposed despite the seriousness of the misconduct.

Further to this, a 'Send to All' email was sent, with no forewarning to me, that X would be remaining a member of Chambers and having submitted to both sets of disciplinary proceedings, as well as having fully accepted and apologised for his behaviour, Chambers considered the matter closed. X had three weeks before his suspension would commence, and I was regularly being told that he was in court during that time. The impression was he was getting in as many cases as he could before, what then felt like, 'having 3 months off'. That was the turning point for me. With that, I knew I couldn't stay, albeit had no idea how I would go about leaving, nor how I would answer the very obvious question I was going to be asked … 'why are you wanting to move Chambers?'

Fortunately for me, serendipity struck, and mine and Jo's paths crossed, which led to me being where I am now.

A lot has happened since April 2021 when I moved Chambers and whilst the horribleness of going through what I did has very much informed it, what I have been able to achieve as a result and what I hope to achieve, is what I want to focus on moving forward.

I have been able to re-establish my career at 36 Family, incredibly successfully, thanks to the support of 'Team Eve', my Chambers as well as my family and friends.

In 2022, one year on from moving Chambers, I waived my anonymity with a Twitter thread to finally honestly answer the 'Why did you move?' question! Positive doesn't really adequately describe the response I received. I was completely and utterly overwhelmed by the support I was given but, what it also made me even more aware of was the sheer extent of this problem at the Bar and the secrecy surrounding it. I was, and remain, determined that no one else should have the experience that I did and if little ol' me can make even a tiny difference by talking about this issue, then I'm going to.

I have been able to support others who are contemplating making a report to the BSB. I've spoken to the Bar Council, I contributed to the BTAS Sanctions Review which was launched shortly after the derisory outcomes of cases such as mine, and I will also be providing a submission to Harriet Harman's Independent Review.

But of significant importance to me is that I have been able to have a dialogue with my previous Chambers and the now Head of Chambers, with them having reinvestigated how the matter had been handled. With that, X ceased to be a member of Chambers. Whilst I wish that is something that could have happened much sooner, that someone would have just spoken to me (rather than emailed) and supported me properly from the get-go, I am a believer in better late than never and I am grateful to Chambers for taking the action that they ultimately did.

The aftermath for Eve

I learnt of Eve's experiences because I happened to be her leader in a trial we were working on together. I had given my Gresham lecture (which we can now see was used as some type of awareness training!) and it wasn't until some months into our case that she asked if she could speak to me about something she was going through. She was thinking of leaving the Bar – an all too familiar story of the victim paying the consequences for the abuser's actions. As Eve said, this was a chance encounter: '*I was extremely fortunate to have been led by you Jo, I knew you had spoken out about this issue, particularly having watched your Gresham lecture and as such, our paths couldn't have crossed at a better time for me. To an extent, it was sheer luck that I was put into that situation with you, had I not been, I'm not entirely sure what I would have done, and I am under no illusion that others won't have been so lucky or felt so able to come forward and say something.*'

I phoned up my silk friends in and around London. We became her champions. We set aside chamber's standard rules to look for ways to give Eve a safe haven. Hannah Markham KC (family) and Mary Prior KC (crime) at No 36 (both heroes of mine) had enough sway to create space for Eve within their rules. We became 'Team Eve'. This is Eve's perspective: '*You picked me up, dusted me off and reminded me that I am not alone at a time when that is all I felt. You created a safe space in this profession where I can get on with what I always set out to do – carve myself out, and excel at, my career.*' Aside from this circle of trust we created around Eve, Eve found her experience to be isolating. At the time I first spoke to Eve, she felt trapped and depressed. She told me she '*vividly remember[s] when contemplating whether to report what had happened asking my supervisor if I was about to "fuck up everything I had worked so hard to achieve" and, for a significant period, I ended up feeling like I had, mainly owing to the response I had received from those I thought would be there to help me.*'

Just pause to think about being in that situation – I deplore the stance her chambers took at the time when they could have made a real difference to Eve's experience, and not least because it was so easy to do the right thing. As Eve said, being heard was all that was required '*You all changed that feeling in an instant, I no longer felt alone, I no longer felt like I was the one over-reacting in this situation, even in the face of knowing deep down/with my rational head on, that what happened to me, as well as the response it received, was inherently wrong.*'

This whole sordid episode (the abuse, the chamber's poor response and the inadequacy of the BSB process and sentence) only came to light when an astute reporter picked up the BSB decision and it hit the press in 2021. X ceased to be a member of chambers in 2022 after

Eve waived her anonymity and tweeted about her experience. This was long after Eve had left chambers, so it wasn't to protect her. It was a damage limitation exercise by the chambers in reaction to the disgust their conduct had triggered when exposed to the critical profession and public gaze. Eve and I spoke of her experience at length, and at the pace she set. Much is too raw to be successfully processed.

As Eve says, '*Often the crux of these disciplinary procedures is that the perpetrator of the sexual misconduct has been deemed to have diminished the trust and confidence that the public hold in our profession but in my mind, the sanctions we have seen, and the procedures I experienced for that matter, go a long way in doing the same. I watched plenty of people, from all walks of life react to my case (and specifically the sanction imposed) on social media and the one consistent response was "if that were me, I'd have been struck off". Which for me, begged the question, why as Barristers, do we hold ourselves to any less of a standard than that of our counterparts? If anything, given the work that we do, shouldn't we be holding ourselves to a higher standard than most? I think being a Barrister is an extreme honour and privilege, but to subject a fellow Barrister, or any individual for that matter, to not only abuse in this way but also to the experience that then flows from it, is neither. There's just no place for it.*

At the end of it all I was left with the feeling of if I had known what I know now about the way in which my complaint was to be handled, both by Chambers and the BSB/BTAS, I would seriously question whether to report it or not, I mean even more so than I already did as a Pupil in her Second Six contemplating tenancy! For me, being left to feel like that was one of the biggest problems arising out of all of this. On one hand, it has worried me that speaking out about my experience will deter others from feeling able to come forward but on the other, I am hopeful that in doing so, I can help to ensure that no one ever goes through what I did. I know that I did the right thing, and I do not regret reporting it, but I know that a whole lot more can be done to improve the experience for those that do.'

Eve was brave to do what she did, but bravery shouldn't be required, we can't all be brave when we feel weak and alone, it's asking too much. Eve and I speak with one voice when we say that members of the Bar should feel safe, that they should feel supported, that they should feel respected. Yet the systems in place which are meant to be the safety nets, such as chambers' policies and the BSB's disciplinary process, are full of gaping holes that victims of this behaviour are allowed to fall through.

Knowing Eve's story as I do, seeing what she went through, reading the derisory sanctions handed down to men who have been found by the BSB to have abused their power, I cannot contain my disdain for our disciplinary process. It is not fit for purpose. We could have lost a young talented woman in our profession. Instead, Eve's career has soared. She won the Family Law Young Barrister of the Year 2023. Brava Eve.

We have a duty to act – we have to Set the Bar

When I first asked the BSB, back in 2018, for an idea of the numbers of complaints they had dealt with that involved sexual harassment and inappropriate behaviour they said, '*Over the past five years, we have received two complaints of sexual harassment or inappropriate behaviour.*' I asked myself how could it be that the BSB had only two reports in five years leading up to 2018, yet the IBA, in that same year, conducted the global survey already mentioned on bullying and sexual harassment in the legal profession, with 715 British legal professionals participating? They published their report *Us Too? Bullying and Sexual Harassment in the Legal Profession* in May 2019. Approximately one in two female respondents and one in three male respondents had been bullied in connection with their employment. One in three female respondents had been sexually harassed in a workplace context, as had one in 14 male respondents. As the report warned, 'The results provide empirical confirmation that bullying and sexual harassment are rife in the legal profession.'

I spoke at its launch in May 2019 alongside luminaries such as Dame Laura Cox DBE and Baroness Helena Kennedy KC, we drew together solicitors and barristers from the UK and internationally. The audience was both invited and free attendance. The shock waves were palpable as Kieran Pender rolled out the results, and the panel dissected them. The reaction from men was one of, I think, genuine profound horror. The response from the women? This is the reality of our working lives and that of sisters and friends – why are you so shocked to hear it? It's been around you if you cared to see. The 2019 report sent a message that could not be ignored. Following the publication of *Us Too?* the IBA undertook an unprecedented global engagement campaign. During visits to 30 cities across six continents, they held public events and met with hundreds of stakeholders. The report was so powerful that it gained international attention at the highest levels of power: 'This important report is a clarion call for urgent action. I urge you to absorb its facts and findings and then make a difference.'[20]

The report hit the quality press. The problem was out there for all the world to see.[21] But being told what the problem is and stopping it are two very different things. In 2024 the BSB reported that there was a fall in the number of sexual harassment and misconduct cases from 16 cases between 2022 to 2023 to seven cases between 2023 and 2024.[22] I do not take comfort from those figures – the reverse. I fear that the rate of incidence has not decreased but rather the reluctance to report it to the BSB has increased. In my view, the lack of reporting to the BSB illustrates that the Bar has a problem with confronting and punishing harassment and the BSB is not the agency trusted to be the forum for doing so. I emphasise this is my view, but it is informed by those who have gone through the process and found it wanting.

Consider this example of a course of conduct reflecting the reality of power imbalance/sexual harassment at the Bar when one man abuses his position of trust – repeatedly – and was still able to practise up until December 2024.[23] As of autumn 2025 the BSB records his sentence as at 16 December 2024 as Disbarred (Sentence still to take effect) with Immediate Suspension of Mr Kearney's Practising Certificate, pending any appeal.[24] This process has taken years to reach even this stage, as this chronology shows.

---

[20] Comments by Julia Gillard AC, 27th Prime Minister of Australia.

[21] The IBA have been at the vanguard of research, following up the 2019 report with the 2022 report, 'Beyond Us Too? Regulatory Responses to Bullying and Sexual Harassment in the Legal Profession' and 'A Global Directory of Anti-Discrimination Rules Within the Legal Profession: Main Findings'.

[22] BSB, '2023–24 Regulatory Decisions Report', https://www.barstandardsboard.org.uk/static/3092876d-ed33-468d-a03bd55038b2ed87/Regulatory-Decision-Making-Statistical-Report-2023-24.pdf

[23] https://www.barstandardsboard.org.uk/barristers-register/7A2E76D8BFC75896A29FAEAEF6B50174.html

[24] https://www.barstandardsboard.org.uk/for-the-public/search-a-barristers-record/past-disciplinary-findings.html?q=kearney

In March 2021, Robert Kearney, a criminal barrister called in 1996, was found to have sat 'uncomfortably close' to a male pupil he had never met before and 'put an arm around him engaging in excessively physical and unwanted contact'. The decision continued: '[Kearney] directed an uncomfortable, hostile, intimidating question to the pupil, after first asking his age, namely whether he had "ever taken a woman from behind".' Robert Kearney was fined £1,000 for behaving in a way which was likely to diminish the trust and confidence which the public places in a barrister.

When this conduct and sanction became public another victim came forward. She had been Kearney's mini pupil in 2015.[25] She had told others of his behaviour towards her at the time but not reported it having discussed it with her family. She is Person A. These were the findings:[26]

> Robert Kearney made the following comments, or words to that effect:
> i. that he kept his nails short because you can't finger women with long nails.
> ii. asked Person A if she'd ever had sex in her parents' house and the details about it.
> iii. told Person A that eating pineapple makes semen taste better.
> iv. said to Person A she should wear skirts and heels instead of trousers and asked Person A what was her bra size.
> v. lent into Person A when the two were alone inside the lift, smelt her neck and asked Person A what perfume she was wearing.

---

[25] A mini pupil is someone who applies to chambers to see what life as a barrister is like if they are contemplating that as a career. This would generally be applied for before they invest time and money in going to Bar School or apply for pupillage. So, we are talking about a level of youth and inexperience even greater than a pupil who comes to the Bar post university and Bar School.

[26] https://www.barstandardsboard.org.uk/disciplinary_finding/183588.html

vi. B also spoke about sex with his wife and was physically too close to Person A.

Kearney was found to have brought the profession into disrepute. He had abused his position of trust. He was suspended from practice for six months, advised as to future conduct and ordered not to take any more mini pupils. Costs awarded against him of £3,000.

In 2020 his behaviour gave rise to complaint again. The alleged misconduct involving the pupils took place on consecutive days in February 2020, first at a social event organised by his then chambers, Lincoln House Chambers in Manchester, and then at a bar.

According to the subsequent findings of the Bar Tribunals & Adjudication Service, Kearney 'inappropriately commented on the appearance' of Pupils A and B while also making 'inappropriate contact and hand placement' with them over the course of the evening.

He asked Pupil A how many older men and how many senior members of the Bar she had slept with. Kearney then told her: 'You need to have sex with senior members of the Bar, then you will be successful. … You have not slept with a man until you have slept with an older man. You need a man with more experience.'

Further findings of misconduct by the tribunal were as follows: later that evening Kearney sat 'uncomfortably close' to Pupil B. He told her that she needed to have sex with an older man, that she needed someone more experienced to show her a good time, and that he was such a man. He asked Pupil B how many men she had slept with, the age of the oldest man she had slept with, and if she was in a relationship. The tribunal recorded too that Mr Kearney told Pupil B that she needed to go and have 'fucking sex', and that she was frigid.

In July 2023 the tribunal, having found the allegations proven as recited above, disbarred him.[27] Kearney successfully appealed the decision and sanction of the tribunal in March 2024 on the basis of

---

[27] https://www.legalfutures.co.uk/latest-news/male-barrister-disbarred-for-sexually-harassing-female-pupils#:~:text=A%20male%20barrister%20who%20told,conduct%20towards%20a%20mini%2Dpupil

perceived bias.[28] He remained in practice. The case was remitted to another tribunal and in December 2024 the BSB. A spokesperson for the BSB said: 'Mr Kearney's actions were unacceptable and repeated and constituted a breach of the BSB Handbook. This conduct is not compatible with the standards expected of the profession and this is reflected in the decision of the tribunal to disbar Mr Kearney.'[29] Kearney was found to have acted in a way that was likely to diminish trust and confidence in the profession and a sentence of disbarment passed (sentence still to take effect) with immediate suspension pending any appeal.

---

[28] The court heard that, during an adjournment, panel member His Honour Judge Carroll emailed the chair of Inns of Court and the director general of the BSB in his capacity as chair of the Bar Tribunal and Adjudication Service. The email, read out in court, stated that 'as the hearing has not reached resolution, I should not disclose confidential discussions'. However, it noted that Kearney had two previous BSB findings or sanctions against him for 'almost the exact same behaviour'. It said, 'current guidance points to disbarment', adding that the panel was 'unanimous of the view that he is likely to behave like this again' and the panel was 'dismayed to find we have no such power' in regard to temporary suspension. The judge said: 'I should say straight away the allegation of actual bias is not made out, but I must consider apparent bias in the context of that email.' '[The email] said the panel was unanimous of the view the appellant could continue to cause offences. It appears [to be] disclosure of panel discussions and that the panel had already formed a clear view.' Returning then to the legal test, would a fair-minded and informed observer conclude there was a real possibility the tribunal was biased. In my judgement, in the totality, they would. See also https://www.lawgazette.co.uk/news/barrister-wins-appeal-over-disbarment-for-sexual-harassment-of-pupils/5118922.article

[29] Bianca Castro, 'Barrister Disbarred for Professional Misconduct over Sexual Harassment of Pupils', *The Law Gazette*, 19 December 2024, https://www.lawgazette.co.uk/news/barrister-disbarred-over-sexual-harassment-of-pupils/5121859.article

Jo Sidhu KC, a high-profile criminal barrister, former Vice Chair of the Equality and Diversity Committee of the Bar Council, former President of the Society of Asian Lawyers, former Chair of the Criminal Bar Association, and Bencher at Lincolns Inn, was also found to have abused his position of power. In December 2024, Navjot 'Jo' Sidhu KC was found culpable under three charges of professional misconduct brought by the BSB. The charges relate to sexual conduct towards a female student undertaking a mini pupillage. The tribunal found that Mr Sidhu had acted in a way likely to diminish the trust and confidence which the public places in him or the profession, in that, on or around 26 November 2018, while in a position of trust, he invited the student (Person 2) to stay overnight in his hotel room and in his hotel bed, an invitation which was inappropriate and/or unwanted and initiated sexual contact which was found to be inappropriate. While he was cleared of 12 misconduct charges that covered allegations made by three women and those in relation to Persons 1 and 3 were not established that was not without the disciplinary tribunal commenting that the sexual content of some texts sent by Sidhu to a law student were 'reprehensible'. Person 2 was a female paralegal to whom Sidhu offered a mini pupillage. The tribunal found that Sidhu had:

- Invited Person 2 to stay overnight in his hotel room, despite her maintaining that she wanted to leave the room.
- While in the hotel room, Sidhu had changed out of his clothes into pyjamas, divided the bed with pillows as a barricade and insisted that Person 2 sleep in the bed with him, which was sexual in nature.
- Sidhu had initiated sexual contact with Person 2 which was unwanted.

Pending determination of sanction the panel issued a suspension order barring Sidhu from practising, the silk having relinquished his certificate voluntarily earlier in the year. On 19 March 2025 Navjot (Jo) Sidhu KC was ordered to be disbarred.[30] Sidhu ultimately chose not to appeal the findings made against him, focusing his appeal of punishment, arguing that suspension was a more proportionate

---

[30] https://www.barstandardsboard.org.uk/resources/barrister-navjot-jo-sidhu-kc-ordered-to-be-disbarred.html

penalty than disbarment.[31] What I want to flag is the tone of the press release issued by the BSB at the time they made their decision to disbar. It was strong as a statement of principle and struck a note not heard before. A spokesperson said:

> We are grateful to those individuals that made a report and gave evidence, without which the BSB could not have brought proceedings. The BSB recognises how hard it can be to come forward. Conduct of this nature has no place in the profession and the public should not expect this from members of the Bar and this is reflected in the decision of the tribunal to disbar Mr Sidhu. We are committed to eradicating this type of behaviour through taking enforcement action where appropriate. We have also undertaken outreach sessions with the profession on the resources and guidance on bullying and harassment and how to report concerns and we are looking at additional ways to provide support. We would encourage anybody who has experienced similar behaviour by barristers to report this to the BSB.

Would this have been made so condemnatory had Sidhu's case not already drawn significant media attention, with significant news outlets calling out Sidhu's sexually harassing conduct?[32] Now Person

---

[31] *The Law Society Gazette*, 'Former criminal bar chief Sidhu appeals disbarment', 2 December 2025, https://www.lawgazette.co.uk/news/former-criminal-bar-chief-sidhu-appeals-disbarment/5125310.article

[32] Notably, *The Times*, 'Former Law Chief Accused of Sexual Harassment', 12 September 2024, https://www.thetimes.com/uk/law/article/former-law-chief-accused-of-sexual-harassment-tbj22dmrd; Tortoise Media, 'Jo Sidhu KC Committed Sexual Misconduct, Says Tribunal', 10 December 2024, https://www.tortoisemedia.com/2024/12/10/jo-sidhu-kc-committed-sexual-misconduct-says-tribunal; and *The Guardian*, 'UK Barrister Made Aspiring Lawyer Have "Unwanted Sex" with Him, Tribunal Hears', 22 November 2024, https://www.theguardian.com/uk-news/2024/nov/22/leading-uk-barrister-had-unwanted-sex-with-aspiring-lawyer-tribunal-hears

2, who since December 2024 might have thought this experience was behind them, will have to wait until the appeal is heard to see its end point. If the appeal against the findings is successful will they have the stamina to relive the process? I wouldn't.

The then Chair of the Bar Council, Sam Townend KC, had already (and rightly in my view) criticised the length of time the women had to wait for the misconduct proceedings. Noting that the two-year wait was too long, Townend also commented that '*the type of behaviour described by the tribunal is completely unacceptable at the Bar. Even though the tribunal found some aspects did not constitute professional misconduct, they found the behaviours to be reprehensible.*[33] *This intense scrutiny has sparked discussions about the power dynamics in the legal field and the barriers faced by those who come forward with complaints. One wonders how many complainants can be expected to endure this process. They have careers to build and lives to lead.*'

This last comment is, I think, a clear message about the duty of support and to report. As Townend said, '*it is incumbent on others, particularly senior barristers, who witness these behaviours to step up and report serous misconduct they have observed*'. I quite agree. Silence makes us complicit in abuse and fuels the abuser's power to continue the abuse.

In February 2025 the BSB issued its decision in respect of charges brought against Alan Wheetman, a barrister called in 1995.[34] The BSB suspended Wheetman from practice for 24 months and ordered that if Wheetman returned to practice he would need to first undertake a BSB-recognised course on Equality, Diversity and Inclusion. I note again how long this matter had taken (the sanction related to offences committed in 2022) and it is subject to appeal. How long do the victims have to watch and wait and their experiences be held open for question under professional gaze? The

---

[33] Bar Council, 'Bar Council Response to Serious Misconduct Findings Against Jo Sidhu KC', 10 December 2024, https://www.barcouncil.org.uk/resource/bar-council-response-to-serious-misconduct-findings-against-jo-sidhu-kc.html

[34] https://www.barstandardsboard.org.uk/resources/barrister-alan-wheetman-ordered-to-be-suspended-from-practice-for-24-months.html

BSB had found that Wheetman had made 'inappropriate comments and behaviour of a sexual nature' toward Person A, a woman involved in a case he appeared in. Wheetman was found guilty of charges of professional misconduct for:

- Telling Person A that he had 'stalked' her Facebook profile.
- Showing Person A photographs of semi-nude women on his photography website and sending her the link.
- Offering to take photographs of Person A, with the suggestion that the modelling could be without clothing and saying 'You don't have to start with fanny or minge shots, we could do face pictures and then we could do a bit more if you want.'

A BSB spokesperson said: 'Inappropriate conduct of a sexualised nature is not something that the public should expect from members of the Bar and the decision to prevent Mr Wheetman from practising reflects the seriousness of his conduct.'[35] It is difficult to detect remorse or reflection on that statement by Wheetman given his photography website, published on PurplePort, responded to the BSB's findings, 'Please be very careful when engaging people in discussions about modelling or showing any images from your portfolio to anybody in the workplace. What may be viewed by some as an innocent discussion about your hobby or pastime, can so readily be interpreted by others as inappropriate comments and behaviour of a sexual nature.'[36]

Also in February 2025 the BSB's published its findings for sexual misconduct related to Mr Henry Charles William King, called in 2018. King was suspended from practice in light of his professional misconduct.[37] The charges related to conduct in December 2023.

---

[35] BSB, 'Barrister Alan Wheetman Ordered to be Suspended from Practice for 24 Months', February 2025, https://www.barstandardsboard.org.uk/resources/barrister-alan-wheetman-ordered-to-be-suspended-from-practice-for-24-months.html#:~:text=Commenting%20on%20the%20order%2C%20a,decision%20is%20open%20to%20appeal

[36] https://purpleport.com/portfolio/wheetmanphotography?_ga=2.21126136.2135080485.1741780011-1186495772.1741780010

[37] https://www.barstandardsboard.org.uk/disciplinary_finding/183703.html

The first related to Person A who he inappropriately touched under her skirt on the thigh/bottom and/or on her breast at a chambers Christmas party. The second related to King making inappropriate and unwanted comments towards Person A. The BSB suspended King from practice for three months and ordered him to pay £2,400 in costs. The BSB didn't issue any public statement re: his conduct being not part of the standards the public are entitled to expect from the Bar, even though there were two victims – and I note the limitations of the sanction. So was an example made of Sidhu – who was struck off, while King was merely suspended – and is the Sidhu sentence an outlier to the historical 'slap on the wrist' approach to those who abuse or harass? I'd argue it should be the expectation when charges are proven.

The Bar Council has long called for an overhaul of the BSB's approach to sanctions in sexual misconduct and harassment cases. Change has been a long time coming. It was flagged as necessary as far back as 12 March 2021, when the Chair of the Bar Council Derek Sweeting KC (as then), published his letter to the BSB and pointed out that

> there appears to be a trend indicative of a level of inconsistency in sanctions based on offence. For example, a case where a practising barrister was awarded a more severe sentence for failing to renew a practising certificate, compared to another barrister who sexually assaulted two women at a Bar related social event. Rather perversely and seemingly not reflective of the seriousness of offences, the practising certificate offence received a 4-month suspension as opposed to the sexual assaults receiving a 3-month suspension.[38]

On 26 March 2021, the BSB replied emphasising that they were 'committed to working with Bar Tribunal & Adjudication Service

---

[38] Derek Sweeting QC (as he then was), 'Letter to the BSB', March 2021, https://www.barcouncil.org.uk/static/051359e4-b92d-4d03-a01ff58903eb24ed/Letter-to-Baroness-Blackstone-re-Sanctions-Guidance.pdf

BTAS to update Sanctions Guidance'.[39] In April 2021, the BTAS published the first stage of its consultation on reviewing sanctions imposed related to sexual misconduct. The BTAS recognised that sanctions had 'been subject to public criticism for their leniency in themselves but also compared for other types of misconduct'.[40] The report also reported feedback that the starting point for sexual misconduct was too lenient and suggested that penalties for sexual misconduct should start at a suspension of over 12 months and finish at disbarment. The BTAS then published a second consultation in September 2021, proposing that suspension for sexual misconduct would be a suspension between 12 and 24 months for the lowest cases, 24–36 months for the medium cases and disbarment reserved for the worst behaviour.[41] The final report, published in December 2021, announced that revised sanctions for sexual misconduct would be implemented from January 2022.[42] The BTAS announced that the starting point for sexual misconduct in a professional context would change from a reprimand and medium level fine or short suspension to the recommendations outlined in its September 2021 report.[43]

---

[39] Tessa Blackstone, 'Letter to the Bar Council', March 2021, https://www.barcouncil.org.uk/static/e1c2de78-1246-42be-85fce014c65d3c44/BSB-sanctions-letter-to-Derek-Sweeting-QC.pdf

[40] The Bar Tribunals & Adjudication Service, 'Sanctions Guidance Review', April 2021, https://www.tbtas.org.uk/wp-content/uploads/2021/04/Sanctions-Guidance-review-Consultation-paper-April-21-FINAL.pdf

[41] The Bar Tribunals & Adjudication Service, 'Sanctions Guidance', September 2021, https://www.tbtas.org.uk/wp-content/uploads/2021/09/BTAS-Sanctions-Guidance-2022-Draft-for-Consultation-For-Publication.pdf

[42] The Bar Tribunals & Adjudication Service, 'BTAS Sanctions Guidance Review Response to the Second Consultation December 2021', December 2021, https://www.tbtas.org.uk/wp-content/uploads/2021/12/BTAS-Second-Sanctions-Consultation-Response-Paper.pdf

[43] You can read the guidance from the BSB here: https://www.barstandardsboard.org.uk/about-us/how-we-regulate/the-decisions-we-take/enforcement-decisions/guidance-for-participants-in-reports-of-harassment.html?utm_source=chatgpt.come-decisions-we-take/enforcement-decisions/guidance-for-participants-in-reports-of-harassment.html?utm_source=chatgpt.com

And yet, come 2025, just looking at the decisions I've quoted from December 2024 to March 2025, we still cannot see any transparency over its sentencing rationale nor consistent application of sanctions.

In my view the BSB's failures are systemic, plentiful and long-standing:

- The mandatory reporting rule regarding a barrister's duty to report serious misconduct by another[44] has inadvertently closed down the issue, and deterred victims from confiding in colleagues. It's akin to sending out one lifeboat to a sinking ship when 20 are needed.
- The format of its process is adversarial rather than inquisitorial, relegating the victim to a mere witness rather than equal participant in the process, disempowering them and hindering the provision of balanced information to the panel.
- Although a great deal is made in the sanctions guidance about the 'impact upon the victim', there is not, as a rule, the facility of the provision of a victim personal statement akin to that seen in criminal proceedings. The BSB's website says 'the disciplinary tribunal process does not usually include the admission of a separate victim impact statement, so we seek to ensure that any statement to be used as evidence in a harassment case includes a section that covers the impact on the alleged victim'. That is not, in my view, good enough. The BSB needs to offer the ability for witnesses to submit victim impact/personal statements in cases where there is a complainant who has been wronged. We need redress for complainants like Eve, who felt that she was rendered 'voiceless' by her BSB complaint experience. Eve also felt deprived of the chance to convey to the tribunal the lasting effects the incident had on her life. *'There isn't really any scope for considering the impact on the victim. … There's dealing with the impact it has on you personally, but also the position what happened puts you in professionally.'* Eve's abuser was fined £2,000 and asked to complete

---

[44] Save to an approved group of recipients who are allowed to hear the account in confidence and not be compelled by our Bar Standard rules to report it.

some online courses, which he finished 'in a day'. *'I tried to avoid knowing what the fine was, because it was like a price being put on my self-respect.'*
- The BSB make insufficient use of interim suspension orders. Eve's abuser didn't face any application to suspend – he was able to pick up work to financially tide him over the suspension period, taking the teeth from the disciplinary sanction and reducing its punitive bite.
- The abuser has the privilege of privacy which excludes the victim when the victim's experience has been laid bare in proceedings. Victims of sexual misconduct, dishonesty, harassment and assault should not be excluded from sections of hearings where 'personal' mitigation is delivered, whether or not it relates to the respondent's health. It can be subject to reporting restrictions in the usual way, but the exclusion of the victim is inappropriate.
- The BTAS disciplinary sanctions handed down when breaches have been found are insufficient to deter and prevent future misconduct and to mark the disapprobation with which the conduct is viewed.
- Specific kinds of misconduct do not result in removing the ability to occupy concomitant posts: for example, those involving abuse of power and/or authority should result in removing pupil supervisor status; sexual misconduct should result in removal of criminal barristers from the RASSO[45] CPS list.

Back to Eve again: *'The system as it stands goes a long way in perpetuating the power imbalance between perpetrator and victim. ... If I'd known then what I know now, I would question myself even more about coming forward. Something's wrong if people are feeling like this.'* Eve is right.

In my view, we need to give victims more confidence to come forward. We need to improve the alleged victim's ability to engage meaningfully in the disciplinary process on equal terms as the alleged abuser. We need to rebalance the process by which the tribunal considers the factors relevant to sanction by enabling the victim to

---

[45] RASSO refers to Rape and Serious Sexual Offences, a specialised area of law and practice focusing on investigating and prosecuting these types of crimes.

directly and equally engage in that part of the hearing. Finally, the tribunal needs to be aware, and to properly reflect in its sanction, the discredit that accrues to the whole of the Bar by the misconduct of one member of it.

We can't look solely to the BSB to change their approach when we need action now. They have been put on notice, by many of us, that the nature of the complaint process is part of the problem. I went into print for Gresham and to the Law Society Gazette among other publications to make plain that '*What I get told by women who have gone through this process (or have withdrawn from it) is that, despite the best intentions of the complaint advocates, they feel marginalised and objectified by the trial process.*' That in large part stems from the fact that although, thankfully, proceedings are now determined on the civil standard of proof, the civil trial process is not followed. As I've emphasised, there is no equality of arms. The complainant does not have the right of disclosure of the defendant's case or to equal participation in the hearing. Victims are left feeling out of control and disempowered. That compounds feelings of isolation and helplessness experienced during the acts of abuse.

I have given up expecting the BSB to revise their processes to make the disciplinary process more balanced in terms of participation of the alleged victim, or to hand out punishments that are more proportionate to the harm the victim has suffered, and the disrepute the conduct brings upon the Bar. The bottom line is that this is our Bar and I believe the responsibility is on all of us to help ensure that it is a Bar that we, and others, will want to be a part of now and in the future. These are some of the lessons we can take from Eve's experience and those of the other women who have been brave enough to seek help.

Good communication within and by chambers, as well as proactive planning, is essential. If Eve and her abuser were to 'mutually exist' in chambers, as her chambers contemplated, there was a duty, on them and the clerks' room, to contemplate how it would work in practice. Just thinking through the practicalities of making it work would have illustrated how wrong the decision to protect the abuser's tenancy was. What thought was given to practical practice management for the barristers and their clients? Would they be clerked to make sure they were not in a case together? What would happen if client choice made that impossible? How would friction points of contact in chambers and at court be managed?

As Eve found out all too well, *'language is extremely important and the words chosen in correspondence with me had a significant detrimental impact, to the extent that I didn't feel like I could say anything/make a clear request to be clerked apart for example'*. Eve isn't a victim anymore. She isn't invisible anymore. She isn't powerless anymore. She is a woman empowered to act. She intends to use her voice and experience to pay the good will she received forward: *'I will absolutely keep my promise to do the same for others wherever and whenever I can.'*

When I spoke out publicly about sexual harassment at the Bar, I wanted to speak with a voice that was my own, and to an audience that would be wider than the legal profession. I wanted to bring this issue to public and press attention. I chose to do so as a professor of law and as a silk, to show that there should be no stigma attached to being the victim of such unacceptable behaviour. The shame is to be borne exclusively by the abuser, and the profession that had enabled it to occur.

We can and must do better. We have a duty to stamp this out – it's down to every single one of us in the profession not to stand by when we see, hear or learn of abuses of power, and definitely not stand back from confronting it. We MUST Set the Bar higher. Our conduct must be better than good enough. Our tolerance level of abuse must be set at zero.

It can be tempting to brush past 'minor' offences, but this attitude towards crude jokes and awkward, 'everyday' sexism opens the door to further abuses of power, acting as a gateway to more extreme behaviours. Moreover, the brazenness of committing such misdeeds publicly may indicate that the perpetrator has the potential to commit more serious offences privately. We have the power to act, especially if we are senior members of the Bar. Silence makes us complicit. Call it out. I went public not to present the Bar as a toxic profession, because it is not, in the main. It is a challenging, vibrant, intellectually stimulating and highly rewarding sector to work in. I went public precisely because the Bar is an incredible profession to work in, which can and should welcome men and women from all ethnicities, classes and stations of life, and we owe it to them and the reputation of the Bar to confront the areas where improvement is warranted: doing so makes us stronger as a profession, not weaker.

Individually, we can make a difference to the health of our profession and those in it. We can all take the simple step of handing over our business cards to young men and women and acknowledging the reality that the Bar can sometimes be a tough place. Let somebody know that if it ever gets too much, they are not alone – say '*If you need someone to talk to outside of chambers, then pick up the phone or email.*'

The Bar Council is fortunate to have an unsung hero in charge of its equality, diversity and social mobility work. That person is Sam Mercer. Sam was in the audience when I gave my lecture at Gresham, just as she was at the launch of 'Behind the Gown'. Sam has been a pillar of strength and moral courage, as well as a source of practical advice. At the launch of 'Behind the Gown', an audience member mentioned the concept of anonymous reporting and recording via artificial intelligence – that was 'Spot'. Sam was a critical factor in making Spot happen. Spot was taken up by the Bar Council and has now been refined and applied to the Bar. 'Talk to Spot'[46] is a confidential helpline that pulls together histories of abuses of power at the Bar, sexual harassment or bullying based on three pillars:

- *Identify*: ensure inappropriate behaviours including sexual harassment and other forms of harassment and bullying are recognised.
- *Report*: ensure inappropriate behaviours are challenged, and/or reported either in chambers or in the Inn of Court, and if necessary to the BSB. Processes should be in place, fit for purpose and effectively implemented; and
- *Support*: ensure victims/witnesses are looked after and suffer no career detriment, and that chambers are advised on how to prevent and manage inappropriate behaviours and protect the careers of victims or witnesses.

The Bar Council explains that:

> To address reluctance to come forward, the Bar Council is working with Spot, an online tool, to give the

---

[46] https://www.barcouncil.org.uk/support-for-barristers/equality-diversity-and-inclusion/talk-to-spot.html

> profession a secure, constructive process for dealing with unacceptable behaviours. Spot will let you make a record of exactly what happened, who did it, who saw it, where it happened and when ... if you deem it necessary, you can use the record to support a complaint about the incident. A complaint can go to your chambers, employer and/or regulator. In the case of criminal behaviour, the record can be used to help report an incident to the police.

Spot offers us the chance to record and maintain control; but it also gives the Bar Council the chance to spot patterns of abuse and perpetrators of it by building a picture of harassment and discrimination at the Bar.

> If the Bar Council receives multiple anonymous reports about the same individual, Spot will make it possible for us to go back to the people who made the records and let them know there are others with the same experience. This could give them more confidence in pursuing a complaint or at the very least let them know they are not alone.

I have been challenged about speaking up about abuse of power. I have been told I am showing the Bar in a 'bad light'. But I'm not taking that. It is because we do things so well at the Bar for others that we can afford to be honest about those things that we don't do so well for ourselves. Because when we tackle them, we make the Bar a better profession for everyone, and we are able to provide a better service. I say again, the Bar is not a toxic environment, but it has some people operating in it that make it so for individuals, they're the ones we need to change. It is not tolerable; it cannot be tolerated. We have a duty to act and intervene.

We need a cultural shift in the attitudes we bring to our workplace. We need to be alert to the fact that challenging sexual harassment requires an intersectional mentality, seeing the aspiring and junior members of the Bar for the multi-faceted individuals they are. We need to be alert to the fact that colleagues from non-traditional backgrounds and cultures may be more vulnerable to abuse than their privileged peers.

It has felt necessary for me to take a stand, even when it's personally uncomfortable, because abuse of power in our profession is a problem we have buried for too long. That much is obvious not just from the data that the Bar Council and IBA have collated, but from the individual tales I receive that evidence the statistics in the surveys. Men and women contact me to ask if they can tell me their story, not always to get advice, but just to be able to speak frankly about their experiences, their shame, their fears. It's not easy making time to answer the calls or emails, but until there are more senior people who are prepared to do so, the burden falls on a small number of us: those that have made our protest visible.

My message is that 'If it happens to you, you won't be the first, you won't be the last. It's not your fault, speak to someone you trust about it. You are not alone.'

5

Power Inside the Courtroom

In the previous chapter, I discussed how the unique history of the Bar, with its system of professional education via pupillage, and camaraderie between tenants, can become toxic when boundaries between members are not respected and the power of patronage is abused. In that dynamic, the corrosive imbalance of power is a consequence of the continual influx of talent to the Bar, and the evolution from apprentice to junior and senior status. Imbalance of power is not built into the system – it is a byproduct of it.

Contrast that with the dynamics of the courtroom, where the power imbalance is built into the operation of law. The judge is the most senior person in court, regardless of their age, gender or years of experience in the law. The judge is the arbiter of law (and of fact also, in the civil courtroom[1]). The manifestation of that authority is symbolised by the way we behave in court: we do not enter court until our case is called on to be heard by the judge's clerk; we wait in court to receive the judge, we stand up and bow to the judge as they enter as a representative of the monarch in whose name they administer justice; we do not sit down again until after they do; the judge takes their place beneath the emblem of Royal Coat of Arms; the judge sits on a special seat, behind a bench separated and elevated from the parties before them; we rise when the judge rises to leaves court, and remain standing until they have left; save with permission, we do not leave the courtroom while they are in it; we call the judge by a title of rank, such as My Lord, My Lady, Your

---

[1] Save inquests.

Honour, while they address us with our given surname; we do not interrupt or speak over the judge (in theory); when the judge speaks, we fall silent. Some barristers still open a submission to the judge with the words 'If it please My Lord …'. We are respectful of the judge because they sit as the title holder and representative of justice. We respect the legal system in which we all practice, and the crucial office the judge holds. The judge has a duty to preside over the cases brought to them for resolution. It is remarkable that outbursts by the public in court are so rare. Rarer still by barristers. That can only be explained by the contract of social obedience we submit to.

Moreover, during the progression of the case in court, the judge has complete control over how the proceedings are managed. The judge determines the remit of the case to be argued, ruling that this issue be tried and that one be dropped. The judge decides the order in which witnesses are questioned, how long a witness will give evidence, and allots time for the advocates to question them. At any point, the judge can intervene and terminate questioning – or ask the witness questions of their own. Given that the witness won't be able to gauge what agenda motivates the question, in the way that they may do when being cross-examined by the opposing party's barrister, and given the judge's power over the case's resolution, the witness is likely to answer differently to the judge's question than they would if it had been asked by anybody else. The power a judge wields in court is final, subject only to appeal.

The judge can deploy their power over the proceedings and parties in front of them invisibly, constructively and neutrally. They can also abuse it. When that happens, the trajectory of the case can shift, and the consequences for the counsel, let alone the client, can be profound.

So, what are the professional parameters for judges we are considering in this chapter?

Judges in the UK, once appointed, are in their role until retirement. Yet to be a judge is a step into the unknown in many ways. Unlike, for example, in France, we do not train to be a judge. We train in careers such as the law to be a barrister or solicitor, and the ranks of the judiciary are (largely) drawn from the ranks of practising lawyers (with the notable exception of Baroness Hale who was a legal academic). But the skills required to be a successful lawyer are not necessarily the same as those required to hold office as a judge.

The Judicial Appointments Commission makes careful appointments, and the vast majority of our judges humble us by the quality of the work they do for the society they serve. Very few fail our high expectations of them. We have an able and committed judiciary, and the many who perform their task well have nothing to fear from feedback. However, there are a small minority who consistently fall below the minimum standard expected of them, and should be left in no doubt, by their paymasters and peers, that their reputation, and that of the law they were appointed to uphold and fairly administer, is suffering.

Becoming a full-time judge is becoming increasingly less attractive at the highest levels of court appointment. Morale has taken a dive, the pension no longer compensates for judicial salaries, which are lower than those earned in private practice. Vacancies in the High Court are going unfilled. The job doesn't automatically carry the same prestige it used to, yet the demands of the job have increased, and the risk of abusive backlash on social media from disgruntled parties only makes the job more difficult. The backlog of cases and the pressure to get through them is oppressive and ever-present. Rigorous trial management is needed, and robustness can come across as rudeness to the disaffected party. At what point does robust case management become abusive behaviour unbecoming of a judge?

Marking a line not to be crossed

Let's take two markers – first, what conduct is expected of a judge, and second, what behaviour might define the point at which a line is crossed.

All judges are subject to the Guide to Judicial Conduct: '3.1 A judge should strive to ensure that his or her conduct, both in and out of court, maintains and enhances the confidence of the public, the legal profession and litigants, in the impartiality of the judge and of the judiciary.'[2] ACAS, the Advisory, Conciliation and Arbitration Service, is an independent public body that receives funding from the government and represents millions of employers

---

[2] https://www.judiciary.uk/guidance-and-resources/guide-to-judicial-conduct-revised-july-2023/

and employees every year to improve workplace relationships. ACAS defines workplace bullying as 'offensive, intimidating, malicious or insulting behaviour, an abuse or misuse of power through means that undermine, humiliate, denigrate or injure the person being bullied'.[3] Between those two markers lie many shades of grey. Barristers don't tend to be shrinking violets, and we know how tough the courtroom working environment can be for all professionals in it. Sometimes those pressures take their toll.

Credit must go Mary Aspinall-Miles, companion in arms on many a professional podium, for putting her head above the parapet in a public message, posted to X (formerly Twitter) about wellbeing at the Bar directed at the Criminal Bar Association. Her message opened a Pandora's box and created a platform for colleagues to speak out in support. Mary spoke of being addressed in court by judges in a way which warranted *'having employment lawyers on speed dial'* and pointed out that *'advocacy and performance is not improved by undermining and belittling advocates'*. Mary was right. Judicial bullying might provide emotional release for an irritated judge, but it's not going to be an effective tool for case management. It's counterproductive.

Mary's post picked up momentum and got coverage in the legal press. It soon became clear that this wasn't an issue confined to criminal court. Lucy Reed KC, a barrister specialising in family law in her blog (Pink Tape) posted about the 'striking parallels' between the #MeToo campaign and judicial bullying. She wrote:

> Most obviously, sexual assault is about power as much as it is about sex. And film producers are to aspiring actors what judges are to lawyers. What they say goes. My experience of judicial bullying has helped appreciate why it is that women don't often call it out. Because they are powerless, paralysed, silenced.

Lucy continued:

> Both lawyers and judges are under increasing pressure, and just as we tell our children that bullying at school

---

[3] https://www.acas.org.uk/bullying-at-work

is often borne of the insecurities of the bully, I suspect that that issue is at least in part exacerbated by the immense pressure on our judges. It is a tough job, and judges are only human. ... But here I'm more interested in the impact than the cause. Because I also suspect that some judges do not realise that what they say and how they behave affects those who appear before them long after they leave the courtroom. I've experienced shouting judges, rude judges, very demanding judges (haven't we all). All of that I can withstand, it comes with the job and is water off the proverbial. But only once have I had an experience that I would call bullying ... I'm not going to tell that story here, because it is intimately bound up with the private details of my client's case, and because in my heart I hope the judge in question was acting out of character and regrets their behaviour and would be mortified to read of it. But also, because it is actually too hard a story to relive. Having done so earlier this week I was unexpectedly right back there, a gibbering wreck, wracked with guilt for breaking down at court, for failing a client (I didn't but at the time I felt that I had), humiliated at my inability to cope and the treatment of me in front of peers and clients, powerless to make it stop because the judge had complete control.[4]

Mary and Lucy were not alone in their experiences, they have simply been braver than most of us in speaking out about it publicly. So, were those who only complained in private 'snowflakes', who should just take it on the chin, as part of the cut and thrust of a challenging work environment? Were they pathetic for not calling it out publicly? No to both questions.

Judicial bullying is a sad fact of professional life. It's not perpetrated by the majority by any means, but the minority who do abuse their position of power need to have a mirror held up to their behaviour

---

[4] L. Reed, 'Me Too – Judicial Bullying', *Pink Tape*, 2017, http://www.pinktape.co.uk/rants/me-too-judicial-bullying/

and be held accountable for their conduct. What cannot be commanded through respect should not be demanded by bullying.

Judges have power. They have their judicial oath to live up to, even when they may feel sorely tried, rightly or wrongly, by the inadequacies of we who appear before them. It is no longer acceptable for judges to be put on pedestals: judges must be held to high standards and meet them. Of course, judges are not expected to be perfect in all their dealings with the parties, witnesses or advocates that come before them. Judges are not automatons. They are human beings doing a complex job under challenging, underfunded and overburdened working conditions. They will have personal and professional pressures outside the workplace to manage. They can make mistakes as much as anyone when tired, ill, frustrated and overworked. Every judge can have an 'off' day. While rare, it's not unheard of for a judge to walk out of court in frustration or anger or throw the Red or White Book at us – it has happened to me.[5] More likely is that a judge might look at counsel with barely concealed contempt and dissolve us with acid words. And to be fair, barristers can contribute to that breakdown of respect. We might be acting for a seemingly unreasonable client. We might seem underprepared and out of our depth with the case. Our solicitors may have messed up on the bundles for the court. But whatever we do wrong can be fixed by and in court, by hook or by crook. We can't fix the wrong done by a judge who abuses their power in court by debasing us.

One of my former family law colleagues, barrister Judith Trustman, had bravely spoken out on X (then Twitter) and later wrote for *Counsel* in 2018. She too made the link between the #MeToo movement and the proper scrutiny of professional misconduct, asking 'Who Judges the Judges?' Judith put her mind to what judicial 'bullying' might mean in our workplace: behaviours such as shouting at counsel, deliberately saying things to embarrass or humiliate them; asking them to justify themselves in circumstances that are unfair; unfairly calling into question their professionalism; accusing them of incompetence; using various facial expressions to demean or intimidate them; refusing to give them time to formulate

---

[5] These are weighty hard-backed tomes – they don't float on the air like feathers, they are missiles when thrown as bricks.

an argument or response in circumstances where it is unfair to them and their client to do so.

When a judge falls below the standard of behaviour we (and their Oath) expect of them, the consequences can be profoundly debilitating and persistent. Lucy Reed KC, when junior, spoke eloquently about the impact of bullying, which many of us recognise in our own experiences or those of a good friend. It is rare that this behaviour is brought to light or openly discussed. That's why I went public on the issue. I realised that the anecdotal evidence from my friends and colleagues, whether crime or civil, junior or senior, was that outrageous, abusive, behaviour from the Bench was not uncommon but I could see little reported about it, or case law that addressed it.

This was one of the few examples I could find recorded (and that is an important signal of itself[6]) when I went public on this issue as far back as 2017. *A (Children) [2015] EWCA Civ 133* on appeal from HHJ Robert Stephen Dodds was a successful appeal granted on the basis that a child had been denied a fair hearing arising from the judge's peremptory dismissal of her application for DNA testing (in a bid to discover the identity of her real father). The Court of Appeal accepted the appellant's submission that the judge's conduct in the hearing amounted to a serious procedural irregularity and criticised the 'unrestrained and immoderate language' he used, 'which can only leave advocates seeking to present, on instructions, their cases to the court feeling browbeaten and impotent'. They formed this view after reading the following exchanges:

> 'Can I tell you how bitterly resentful I am at how much of my Saturday I spent reading this codswallop?' HHJ Dodds warned the assembled lawyers, having read their respective clients' position statements, 'You may want to put your crash helmet on', before saying (loudly): 'If she told you that the moon is made of green cheese will you

---

[6] There is another potentially – I note that *Re C [2019] 10 WLUK 502* follows *A (Children)*, but in that case while the judge was found to have interrupted too much she was not unpleasant, rather 'she seems to have alienated even those who she sought to praise and encourage'.

say, "Yes, S, no, S, three bags full S?"' He continued: 'For heaven's sake, in this day and age especially, just because the lunatic says, "I want, I want", you do not have to respond by spoon-feeding their every wish.'

Lady Justice King called his 'unrestrained and immoderate bombast' both 'deplorable' and 'unacceptable'. This was not the only successful complaint made against HHJ Dodds. He features in the records of the Judicial Conduct Investigation Office (JCIO),[7] the JCIO[8] being the body that supports the Lord Chancellor and the Lady Chief Justice in their joint responsibility for judicial discipline, so, whereas the Bar Standards Board is the Bar's regulatory body with authority to investigate and discipline us if we fall foul of our professional duties, the JCIO has the power to investigate and punish members of the judiciary, whether full- or part-time and at all levels. The JCIO deals with misconduct[9] complaints against:

- Salaried and fee-paid courts judges.
- Judges and non-legal members of tribunals.
- Coroners.

HHJ Dodd's behaviour in court was the subject of complaint to this body. In one instance HHJ Dodds' extreme grouchiness meant that, in another family case, everyone in court 'crumbled under his caustically expressed views'. Dodds compounded this appalling behaviour by then blasting the mother for looking 'upset and bewildered' by his rant. The JCIO wrote that HHJ Dodds' behaviour amounted to 'serious misconduct' in relation to three cases. A similar charge about a fourth case was dropped. Then Lord Chancellor Michael Gove, and

---

[7] https://www.legalcheek.com/2015/11/hhj-dodds-dubbed-britains-rudest-judge-after-series-of-kevin-the-teenager-rants/; J. Hyde, ' "Gratuitously Rude" Judge Stays in Post after Conduct Probe', *Law Society Gazette*, 2017, https://www.lawgazette.co.uk/news/gratuitously-rude-judge-stays-in-post-after-conduct-probe/505244article

[8] https://www.complaints.judicialconduct.gov.uk/

[9] Misconduct means personal misbehaviour which is serious enough to require the Lord Chancellor and the Lady Chief Justice to take formal disciplinary action.

then Lord Chief Justice John Thomas, agreed that Dodds' actions in three of those cases amounted to 'serious misconduct'. But despite being disciplined, HHJ Dodds was still allowed to sit in family court sessions until he retired in 2019.

I chose to speak up. In fact, I didn't just speak out – I shouted from the rooftops about it. I spoke about it in my Gresham lecture, 'What Do Judges Do in the Family Court', in 2017.[10] I took to the platform at the launch of 'Behind the Gown' in May 2018 to make the link between sexual harassment and bullying as toxic behaviours arising from power and its abuse. I wrote about it for *Counsel* in 2018 in 'Judicial Conduct: When It All Goes Wrong',[11] and I was interviewed by *The World Tonight* on Radio 4 in 2019. I have kept on raising the issue. In 2019, when appearing in the longest running case in English legal care history in Manchester, I was asked by the Association of Women Judges to share a platform with Sir Ernest Ryder, then Senior President of Tribunals, on the issue of judicial bullying before the assembled ranks of the judiciary. I agreed. I knew Sir Ernest from my days appearing before him when he was a High Court Family Judge and knew he was a man I wanted to stand alongside on this important issue to the people who might get value from it. For so long as the Right Honourable Sir Ernest Ryder was alongside me, there was a respectful silence, as first he spoke, then I followed. He then had to leave for London business, and I remained on stage to complete the session.

The change in atmosphere once I stood alone before the judges was first palpable, then audible. A small but vocal, angry, agitated and, it appeared, embittered portion of the audience began to challenge and attack what I had said. They were strident and defensive. There was a marked lack of judicial restraint: the many against the one. They were in a minority, but the rest of the room remained silent. The judicial white gloves were off. They challenged me. I didn't back down. The irony of being asked to talk about lack of judicial control, while being faced with a direct exhibition of it, was striking.

---

[10] https://www.gresham.ac.uk/watch-now/what-do-judges-do-family-court

[11] https://www.counselmagazine.co.uk/articles/judicial-conduct-when-it-goes-wrong

The reality that their poor behaviour was not challenged by the other judges was salutary. Poor behaviour can intimidate and silence those who are not the objects of it – even fellow judges. I think they were embarrassed and shocked. The behaviour of this minority was fed back by some concerned observers to Sir Ernest and to the Bar Council, and I was contacted by both to review what had happened. I emphasised that while I was appalled and momentarily taken aback, I was not intimidated. It did not silence me. It empowered me. I felt uncomfortable but vindicated in speaking up. Their behaviour had been poor, public and was abundantly mis*judged*. I had many witnesses to it. I held my ground. I did not feel responsible for the inappropriate behaviour directed at me. I was not the problem – they were. It felt curiously freeing to recognise that.

My fantastically supportive colleague, Darren Howe KC, was in the audience during this encounter. He has always been someone I can rely on to stand up for common decency in our profession. With Darren, I revisited the issue of bullying both in a closed session for the Family Law Barristers Association (FLBA) members during COVID-19 in 2020/1 and then in two articles we co-authored for *Counsel* magazine, on 'Recognising and Managing Oppressive Behaviour' in 2022.[12] I also took the platform about it with my colleague, criminal silk Michelle Heeley KC, at the FLBA conference in 2023. They are just the headlines. Back then and to date I have talked to more groups and individuals than I can identify here. One has a duty to speak about it because it does not stop happening.

But saying it often doesn't help forget how hard it was to say the first time. When I broke the silence under the protection of Gresham as their Professor of Law in 2017 it caused waves throughout our profession and the judicial ranks. It was a seminal moment for me. I was asked by Baroness Harman KC to recall and recount what it was like to be among the first to speak out about judicial bullying back in 2017. The truth is I felt little anxiety as I prepared and as I took the stage (it needed to be said). But when the words left my

---

[12] https://www.counselmagazine.co.uk/articles/recognising-managing-oppressive-behaviour-in-court-out-part-1
https://www.counselmagazine.co.uk/articles/recognising-managing-oppressive-behaviour-in-court-out-part-2

control and entered the professional and public domain through the Gresham lecture I gave I felt very exposed and vulnerable. It was a lonely position to take, for while the lecture received nationwide coverage in the press, and I was interviewed by the BBC, the swell of the public outcry was matched by the echoing silence within my profession. I received many *private* messages of thanks and support, but in public, including in my own chambers, it was not spoken of. I felt isolated from my senior peers. I *was* isolated from my senior peers.

It was not until a chambers Christmas party months later, when a superb man of principle came up to me and expressed his admiration at the stance I had taken that the wall of silence around me broke. That man was Mr Justice Peter Jackson (as then, now Lord Justice Peter Jackson). So too said the power duo that are Henry Setright KC and Her Honour Judge Kharin Cox (now retired) at a professional party. Silence was then transformed into clusters of chatter. I'm sure no one in chambers (aside from my friends) had any idea the impact the lack of public support had on me at the time – especially given that more recent discussion around judicial bullying is commonplace rather than controversial. Now colleagues may be shocked to revisit that time and my perception of it. But then, when I would have valued support so much, the silence echoed. Perhaps it was because I appeared in control and unshaken that so few thought I might welcome some words of validation. Maybe. Perhaps it was just not thought comment-worthy. It wasn't relevant. Again, maybe. But I think for some the silence was also bred of fear of contamination by association with me, concern about the potential for damaged reputations and lost references. It was embarrassing. It was 'not done'. I got and get that, but when we are appointed as silk, we have an obligation to lead, and not just in court. We have a duty to speak out for others who don't have a platform to be heard as loudly (if at all). I know my stance didn't attract compliments from some judges. It was seen as gratuitous and attention-seeking – it was 'unnecessary', as I was memorably told disdainfully by one High Court judge (female, and now thankfully long since retired). That judge was one, by the way, who had the least self-awareness of their courtroom management deficiencies and the highest level of confidence in their capacities.

The test for me then was whether, in the face of that silence and hostility, I had the courage of my convictions to continue to speak out, and I did thanks to forward-thinking, creative, challenging senior judges such as Sir Ernest Ryder and Sir James Munby and leaders of the Bar Council. I wrote for *Counsel* magazine (we have champions in its editors Elsa Booth and Sarah Grainger) and it started a wave of discussion. I spoke at conferences. I was interviewed by many a professional publication and contacted by more men and woman privately and personally than I can now count. I have used up a lot of words. But now I realise that words are worthless – we have used up too many and achieved too little.

The JCIO publishes a list of its disciplinary statements,[13] and looking at the latest 2025/2026 published data the vast majority are Justices of the Peace (27), a smattering of recorders (2) (part-time judges) and then lower-ranking judges such as district judges (2) and deputy district judges (2), but only 2 County Court judges and no High Court judges. Yet it is the conduct of these two senior groups of full-time judges that we at the Bar discuss most frequently with concern in relation to gratuitous, disrespectful behaviour in court. Of equal concern is that the number of decisions reported in the 2025/2026 data is significantly lower than in previous years when research indicates an increase in abusive behaviours reported to trusted non-JCIO sources. That is why I say, historically, you would not get a true flavour of the extent of the problem of judicial abuse of power from a review of reported decisions made by the JCIO. There are so few at higher levels, not because this behaviour isn't happening (as we know from the Bar Council research gathered time and time again), but because so few complaints were (and are) made by members of the profession. The reasons are multiple.

The JCIO has a narrow remit: one can bring, for example, a complaint against the judiciary if the judge has used racist, sexist or offensive language, fallen asleep in court, been late with judgment. That is easier to identify. Whereas bullying is more subjective, harder to define and prove. But it happens. It happens a lot. I know of colleagues who have been shouted at and undermined. It has happened to me. I have seen it in the High Court, and I have been told of it in the County Court. I have received a number of emails from members of the Bar, at all levels of call, who have experienced judicial bullying and felt deskilled and humiliated as a result. No one has made a complaint, ever.

---

[13] https://www.complaints.judicialconduct.gov.uk/disciplinarystatements/

Let me make it plain – it is not the uncharacteristic outburst of an otherwise good judge that is of concern to the Bar. It's the judges who routinely take on the role of 'bully' in their court. Those judges demean their office. *They* are the judges we have good reason to think poorly of, and they are larger in number than we might think. That was why I spoke out. I wanted to give a voice to a number of silent victims who had confided in me. When I did, it made the mainstream press headlines, breaking out from the legal community to reach the general public.

An isolated example by one judge may well be accounted for by the enormous stress of the role they perform, or personal issues they are labouring under. But the impact of their behaviour, especially if a reputation is gained for repeat offences, has consequences for the advocate far beyond the confines of the courtroom. Despite this, complaints are not often formally raised. Instead, they are left in the air, wounds salved over a drink with colleagues, or by crying on the shoulder of a supportive partner at home.

Why does this matter? Collateral damage – the case

This issue is important not just because of its impact on the targeted barrister, but because bullying has ramifications for the entire hearing and possibly the case. Imagine you are a barrister, putting forward your case on your client's instructions. The judge interrupts you before you get a chance to finish your sentence. They throw down their pen, or dramatically place it to one side, or close their laptop, ostentatiously taking no note of the points you are trying to make. They refuse to give you time to formulate your argument in response to a question they have posed, speaking over you when you try to address them. They walk out of court when you are mid-sentence. These things happen too often. It affects both the dynamics and the outcome of the case. Judicial aggression towards one person can embolden the opposing advocate to take points they would otherwise not have taken, because they scent blood. The harassed barrister may hesitate to take a point that should have been taken in their client's interests, because they have become tentative and nervous of their own judgement. There is a ripple effect felt beyond the row where counsel sits in the front line direct to the client who sits behind them. From the client's perspective, what they have seen and heard directed at their barrister in court can affect the evidence they give in the witness box. They might move into appeasement mode, saying things they think will 'please' or mollify the judge. Judicial bullying is embarrassing to witness for an opponent, and it is humiliating for the barrister concerned. Judicial bullying undermines not just the barrister's confidence in themselves but the client's confidence in the barrister. There is, quite simply, no excuse for judicial bullying. It undermines the impartiality of the judge, and it can taint the process for all and change the outcome of a case. Those of us who work in the family courts know that the temperament of a judge affects the dynamic of the case just as much as their skill. We can all name what judge we would want to appear before, and those we would wish to avoid, or hope retire from service.

The judge's power does not stop once a barrister steps outside the courtroom doors. A judge holds the power of patronage or reputational damage and can wield it as a weapon.

In one of my cases decades ago, soon after I had taken silk, it was revealed on the morning of the trial that the High Court judge had, when herself a silk, acted for a local authority against my client. As counsel then the judge had cross-examined my client, and my client still remembered her and the experience. My client felt prejudged. We discussed an application for the judge to recuse herself. I advised against it. I was acutely conscious of the long period of time that had elapsed between my client's encounter with the judge and the unlikelihood of one case of so many sticking in the judge's mind. However, the client had had just one case in her life, and it had impacted on her greatly. She remembered the judge as the advocate who had made her feel disbelieved through the tone and type of cross-examination. The client wanted to think about her options. I applied to the judge for time for her to do so and explained the context. This judge had a very mixed reputation among the Bar. She had clear favourites and targets. I was not the former. I was about to become the latter.

At the time the judge was clearly very put out that I would even contemplate recusal. After a short adjournment we resumed the case before the same judge. I had made a request for time precisely so that I could gain the trust of my client (who I had met for the first time that morning) and talk through the *un*likelihood of judicial bias. I was able to assuage the client's fear. No application to recuse was made. The client had just needed time and focused advice to put the past behind her. The case moved on. So did I. I didn't realise that the judge had a reduced capacity to do so. The judge held onto her grievance for years. It came to light when I had to see her to find out why I had been rejected for a Deputy High Court ticket some five years on. She brought this incident up as an example of my poor judgement. She remembered it as an application to recuse, not a request for time, needed in order to explain the options to a vulnerable client facing serious allegations. It still clearly rankled. Her outrage, now exposed to me years after the event, explained why I had had such a tricky time before her, in that and later cases. I now know that in her mind, I was being put in place for my 'presumptuous' and 'disrespectful' conduct. I hadn't realised how obvious the judge's distaste for me had been, until a silk in a current case some 16 years after my first clash with the judge, remarked how it had felt to him, as a bystander, watching battle lines drawn up between me and the judge each time I rose to my feet, and him thinking I had nerves of steel to keep on going. I had long put it behind me – part of the mental armour we acquire to move on to the next case – but I now know it became a power game I was never going to win for a judge holds the best cards and they can lay them in public, or in private when time for references arises, as they think fit. We can't give feedback to a judge. They can about us. That matters.

Many of us have had experiences where the imbalance of power and lack of mutual respect between Bench and Bar has consequences that linger outwith the courtroom. The Hillsborough inquests, for example, came to represent a dark period in my professional life because of the courtroom conduct of the trial judge, made bearable only because of the need to do good for the amazing, brave families I was privileged to work for and by the support of fierce friends and colleague from Tooks and Garden Court Chambers who literally stood by me in public and supported me in private when I crumbled.

Another judge, now retired, at the family High Court Bench was made vicious to many of us in court through some deep well of private dissatisfaction with the world that flooded out in court. It tumbled out in waves, not just in her treatment of me, but to many of my most level-headed and kindly of colleagues, Kate Brannigan KC, for one, Darren Howe KC for another. This judge's appalling courtroom conduct was a matter of widespread knowledge. To me, having successfully appealed her, it would take the form of the judge entering the courtroom to open the day's hearing by telling me she intended to have a transcript of each of my cross-examinations to review overnight and then placing her pen down ostentatiously and looking bored and disinterested as I questioned the witnesses, occasionally flicking through various law books. The next morning, she would place the visibly marked transcript papers down with a flourish on the Bench before I rose to question the next witness. No one else's cross-examination was transcribed. She was literally showing me she was marking my card. I carried on. No one said anything in court – better not to be the target, especially if it made their case prospects of success easier. Support came later in the hotel or waiting rooms. Why did they stay silent? Reason might be found in the Bar Council analysis: 'This suggests that a culture in which bullying, harassment or discrimination is present can become toxic for everyone, not just the individual on the receiving end of the negative treatment.'[14]

There are so many examples of poor behaviour we give one another in private. So few become public. Why? The reality of life at the Bar is that judges have a lot of control over your working lives and your career progression. As a barrister, the judges that you appear before will later be asked to comment on your suitability to become a silk, or to sit as a judge. My experience is a striking example of how, if you offend a judge in the course of doing your job, the impact on your reputation can be profound. And yet, it is unchallengeable and the impact of it unquantifiable. Did it cost me a positive reference for promotion? I had never sought one from her, so I do not know. Did she share her negative opinion of me with other judges in positions of influence? Quite probably. Did it affect my career progression? I do not know. But I do know I have a practice and reputation that owes nothing to her.

---

[14] Barristers' Working Lives report 2021, 29 September 2021, https://www.barcouncil.org.uk/resource/barristers-working-lives-report-2021.html

We are not all equal at the Bar and before the Bench

In the Barristers' Working Lives Survey 2024,[15] based on data in 2023, the Bar Council conducted a review and analysed the data received in a more granular way. Stark differences were revealed in the experiences of working life as a barrister, particularly in terms of intersectionality of sex and race, when it came to experiencing bullying, harassment and discrimination at work. The survey revealed that 44 per cent of all participating barristers had experienced or observed bullying, harassment or discrimination while in practice; an alarming figure approaching half of all respondent practitioners.

Breaking this figure down, 35.2 per cent said that they had experienced bullying or harassment in person or online. Barristers who had experienced or observed any type of workplace bullying or harassment also reported significantly lower wellbeing than those who had no experience of this. Concerningly, each and every one of those statistics had increased from those gathered during the 2021 Working Lives Survey.

The Barristers Working Lives Survey, 2023,[16] previously looked at whether these experiences were equally felt by all sectors of the Bar. Not so. Experiences of bullying and harassment varied widely between barristers with different personal and social characteristics. More than twice as many female barristers had experienced bullying or harassment in the last two years compared with their male counterparts; one third more of LGBTQIA+ barristers compared with heterosexual barristers; two-thirds more barristers with a disability compared with those without; over 50 per cent more of GEM barristers experienced bullying and harassment compared with white barristers.[17]

---

[15] https://www.barcouncil.org.uk/static/e46b9663-a851-485a-9f0bb18fe561df63/Wellbeing-at-the-Bar-report-2024.pdf

[16] https://www.barcouncil.org.uk/static/1d1fe11c-d6c3-4db3-af3f5b25e0ece36d/Bar-Council-Barristers-Working-Lives-report-2023.pdf

[17] The 2024 report does not update these figures, in the sense it does not differentiate between experiences of bullying and harassment from barristers with different personal and social characteristics.

The differences are stark and impossible to deny. This comes as no surprise to me. It is not news to the Bar Council either.[18]

In 2021, I sat at round table meetings held by the Bar Council, alongside my GEM colleagues, to listen and learn about what had been invisible to me because I am white. It was a visceral experience, hearing their stories of harassment and abuse at the hands of the judiciary. Some of these stories were reproduced in the Bar Council's 'Race at the Bar: A Snapshot Report 2021 – the Impact of Bar Culture on Ethnic Minority Students, Pupils and Barristers'.[19] The differentiation in treatment begins at recruitment and continues into practice. I quote some stories from the report here:

> I was very conscious of how I look during interviews. There is a need to tone down your blackness. I wear the straightest bob for interviews. I wish I could be bold enough to go to interviews in my afro or braids.

> At Court, junior barristers of ethnic minorities are treated poorly. I have been asked if I am a social worker. I have been in a room with the mum's barrister, and I have been asked if I am a social worker even though the social worker would not be in the room with the mum's barrister. We need to draft policies for chambers

---

[18] Bar Council, 'Race at the Bar: A Snapshot Report', 2021. Rates of bullying and harassment at work are far higher for Black and Asian barristers than for white barristers. Nearly six in ten (58 per cent) female, Black and minority ethnic barristers have personally experienced bullying and harassment at work or online compared to 15 per cent of white men ... almost four times the likelihood. More than a half (53 per cent) of all barristers with Black/Black British, African and Caribbean backgrounds report that they have personally experienced bullying, harassment or discrimination while working at the Bar. The equivalent figures for Asian/Asian British, mixed origin and white respondents are 47 per cent, 46 per cent and 26 per cent.

[19] Bar Council, 'Race at the Bar: A Snapshot Report', November 2021, https://www.barcouncil.org.uk/static/d821c952-ec38-41b2-a41eb eea362b28e5/Race-at-the-Bar-Report-2021.pdf

> to know how to deal with these things. You have a stressful practice and people assume that you are a cleaner wearing a suit. I do not have the energy to feedback to chambers.

> One black young barrister over introduced himself to many, many clerks in courts so he would not be thought to be the defendant. He would over dress deliberately so they would know he was the barrister. People are getting wrongly labelled – more so online.

> I have anxiety going to a new court centre and being so visible. I now go to 4–5 court centres, that anxiety remains. I feel like this when I go, knowing I will be the only Brown face in that place.

And let this final comment sink in: 'There are issues about being your authentic self and inclusion.'

The Bar Council's Pupil Survey 2024 reported that of the pupils who experienced or observed bullying, harassment or discrimination within their workplace, 32 per cent reported that it was linked to race.[20]

The inequalities in treatment between white pupils and GEM pupils were further highlighted in the Bar Council's 'Race at the Bar: Three Years On'.[21] The report sought feedback from young barristers and pupils, and their feedback emphasised the challenges of pupillage for barristers from GEM backgrounds. Concerning being the first GEM barrister in their chambers, focus group attendees reported:

> There are those [in my set] who act like they have rarely interacted with those who look and sound like me.

---

[20] https://www.barcouncil.org.uk/static/c5fd7261-a586-40ad-b26a61ebd083cf49/Pupil-Survey-2024.pdf

[21] Bar Council, 'Race at the Bar: Three Years On', December 2024, https://www.barcouncil.org.uk/asset/F1DA4B31%2D7ADB%2D475B%2D900B6A0F20CF1530/

> They couldn't work out what to make of me, but they had low expectations of me.

Participants also reported a difference in treatment, where they perceived receiving worse treatment than their white peers:

> The support received from my pupil supervisor is not the same as other pupils.
>
> I was called another Black person's name.

As these reports spell out, aspiring or practising GEM barristers can feel hyper-visible, bullied, harassed and marginalised at work, especially at court. The sense of being hyper-visible when there is a problem has been reinforced by complaints data which indicated GEM barristers were more likely to be referred for disciplinary action in comparison to white barristers. Since 2017, analysis of complaints by ethnicity suggests this pattern has weakened but this has undoubtedly had a negative impact on practising GEM barristers. Perpetrators of bullying behaviours fall mainly into two categories – judges and barristers – though others are cited, including solicitors and clerks. Of course, what is and is not acceptable is inevitably subject to debate, context and the power dynamic between the perpetrator and victim. What might be said and intended to be robust advocacy or tactics to undermine an opponent in an adversarial setting may be received as bullying. But what is undeniable is that the targets for this behaviour are predominantly women and those with GEM backgrounds.

I have long regarded Leslie Thomas KC as a man unafraid to speak Truth to Power. He speaks for many who do not feel heard and seen and is entrusted with their stories as a result, such as one barrister who described to him how

> a white immigration judge, having heard an appeal by a Somali appellant, commented on how refreshing it was to see a Somali family working. The same barrister, who is herself black, was told by a different judge that it was nice to see her 'sitting on this side of the table', pointing to the side of the table where counsel sit. Another judge

told her at a training event that she did not have 'negroid features'.[22]

I want to drive this point home – bullying is targeted behaviour, and its targets are too often my GEM colleagues. I have quoted the Bar Council report, Leslie, and now I am ruling out any counter-arguments about self-bias by the Bar by nailing it with the conclusions of the independent study conducted by academics at the University of Manchester.[23] This study investigated the behaviour of judicial office-holders, and the responses raised profound questions about racial attitudes, procedures and practices in the English and Welsh justice system. Consider these accounts:

- Here, we again see a judge making the racist assumption that a GEM pupil is the defendant in court: 'I have witnessed so much, but for me the worst was a young pupil who was standing on her feet for the first time. I was prosecuting. DJ told her to move from the Bar into the dock. She ran from the court in tears.'
- Another response reads: 'The most frequent incidents I have seen are judges cutting across the submissions made by a barrister of colour, being dismissive and appearing not to afford the same time and space for submissions to be heard and developed.'
- Discrimination against GEM colleagues is also observed by white respondents: 'As I am of the same ethnic background as most judges, their bias is never directed towards me. I have seen judges treat advocates from Black backgrounds differently from the other advocates (I typically act in cases where there are multiple parties). I have seen Black advocates shouted at and treated dismissively by judges in circumstances where I thought the advocates' ethnicity was a factor.'

---

[22] Leslie Thomas, 'Racial Diversity at the Bar Matters', *Counsel*, 11 June 2020, https://www.counselmagazine.co.uk/articles/racial-diversity-at-the-bar-matters

[23] 'The University of Manchester Racial Bias and the Bench: A Response to the Judicial Diversity and Inclusion Strategy (2020–2025)', https://documents.manchester.ac.uk/display.aspx?DocID=64125

A year on from the University of Manchester's report, a hybrid event took place to mark its anniversary. Keir Monteith KC, the report's co-author, noted that 'this should have happened decades ago'. Aimbola Johnson, another barrister in attendance and Chair of the Independent Scrutiny and Oversight Board, supported Keir's words and noted that 'institutional change' was now needed.[24]

The situation was described as 'urgent' in the launch of this work in 2022, but few (if any) signs that the situation had moved were present in the Bar Council's research discussed in its report '2024 Race at the Bar: Three Years On'. According to that report 'the work to shift the cultural dial, is only just beginning'.[25] It found that overall the Bar was more ethnically diverse (16.9 per cent of barristers were from a GEM background, increasing by 0.5 per cent per annum). Focus groups also reported that the Bar was starting to feel more inclusive. Despite this slight increase, progress in the last three years for Black barristers has been limited. There have not been significant increases in the success rates of applicants for pupillage or silk and judicial appointments. Moreover, the Bar Council highlight that GEM barristers continue to experience higher levels of bullying and harassment. Laurie-Anne Power KC, the co-chair of the race panel, said in December 2024:

> As this report demonstrates, the most useful action is often in the most difficult areas – in ensuring everyone's experience of the Bar is positive, irrespective of background. We would like to see a profession where the chance of being taken on is not linked to race. Where the amount earned is not linked to ethnic origin. And

---

[24] The Legal Action Group, 'A Year On From *Racial Bias and the Bench*, Has Any Progress Been Made?', 28 November 2023, https://lag.org.uk/article/214860/a-year-on-from-racial-bias-and-the-bench-has-any-progress-been-made-

[25] Bar Council, 'Race at the Bar: Three Years On', December 2024, https://www.barcouncil.org.uk/static/f1da4b31-7adb-475b-900b6a0f20cf1530/cc0b3548-a8ac-4bf8-af795ded9e11a5d4/Race-at-the-Bar-three-years-on.pdf

where we all recognise tackling racial inequality requires sustained commitment.[26]

The report makes a series of recommendations, including:

- Mandatory Equality, Diversity and Inclusion (EDI) training and specialist race training for all members and chambers' employees.
- Monitoring work distribution and income by ethnicity and formalising practice review.
- Supporting equality and diversity officers (EDOs) to build an inclusive culture.
- Enhancing data collection and analysis across the board – by chambers, the Bar Council, Kings Counsel Appointments and the Judicial Appointments Commission.
- Supporting networks for Black and minority ethnic barristers.

The impact of this behaviour is profound. It is no wonder that GEM barristers reported significantly lower wellbeing than white colleagues. It is no wonder that we have such a high rate of attrition among my GEM colleagues. And what of the impact of that loss of talent on applicants for silk and sitting? Bullying has ramifications for the future health of the Bar and Bench.

Further guidance was also given in the *Equal Treatment Bench Book* published in 2024 and updated in 2025.[27] Within a section that explores race it touches on 'Black perspectives' and notes:

- It is necessary to understand the experiences and perspectives that many people from Black backgrounds bring with them to the courts. Distrust amongst many has roots in many decades of social disadvantage and discrimination.

---

[26] Bar Council, 'Race at the Bar: Time to Double Down on Race Equality Work', December 2024, https://www.barcouncil.org.uk/resource/race-at-the-bar-time-to-double-down-on-race-equality-work.html

[27] Judicial College, *Equal Treatment Bench Book*, https://www.judiciary.uk/wp-content/uploads/2025/05/ETBB-July-2024-May-2025-update.pdf

- In his report, David Lammy, now the Minister for Justice, concluded that there would 'continue to be a pervasive sense of "them and us" without a step change in diversity among the judiciary itself.'
- This is not simply a perception issue. People from Black backgrounds experience some of the highest levels of racism in all areas of life and some of the worst outcomes. There is concern that racial bias plays a role in the justice system.

To read about life as a person of colour at the Bar I recommend you buy the superb book by Alexandra Wilson, *In Black and White: A Young Barrister's Story of Race and Class in a Broken Justice System*.[28] I am not going to over speak Alex. Get the book, devour it, be outraged by it, learn from it. Alex is a role model for many, myself included, for her perception, wit, grit and brilliance.

Judicial guidance

We had judicial guidance issued in 2025.[29] It further educates on the issues of principles at stake and sets out practical ways in which judicial office holders should behave in a manner consistent with the expectations of court staff, as well as towards their colleagues and anyone else with whom they interact in the workplace. The Statement of Expected Behaviour published in January 2023 proclaims:

> We are one judiciary; no-one should feel that they are perceived as 'less than' because of their differences, personal or professional background, judicial office or jurisdiction. Therefore, we should all:
>
> - treat others fairly and respectfully;
> - be mindful of the authority we have and be careful not to abuse it;

---

[28] https://www.amazon.co.uk/Black-White-Barristers-Broken-Justice/dp/1913068285

[29] Courts and Tribunals Judiciary, 'Equal Treatment Bench Book: May 2025 update', May 2025, https://www.judiciary.uk/guidance-and-resources/equal-treatment-bench-book-may-2025-update//

- be aware of how our words and behaviour can affect others;
- remain patient and tolerant when encountering difficult situations'
- act professionally and courteously, including under pressure, and avoid shouting or snapping;
- aim to ensure that no one in a hearing room is exposed to any display of bias or prejudice;
- build effective working relationships with and support judicial colleagues and staff;
- welcome and support new colleagues; and
- be open to feedback if we have done something that may have caused discomfort or offence.[30]

Can one really say this is hard-hitting enough? Would I be reassured reading it? No. Would my colleagues who feature so highly in the statistics feel their experiences to recognised and supported? I think most would consider themselves failed.

Significantly for me, the Guidance is 'based on the principle that responsibility for deciding whether or not a particular activity or course of conduct is appropriate *rests with each individual judicial office holder*'. The problem lies with the words I have italicised here. Self-reflection and self-control are not going to stamp out the problem. The offenders are those who do not see their conduct as problematic.

The judge's role extends beyond the courtroom. They are part of a team and they are its senior member in terms of status. Therein lies a power imbalance. This fresh Guidance clearly wasn't enough to prevent the one senior member of the judiciary from behaving inappropriately to a junior member of staff. On 9 August 2024, Mr Justice Marcus Smith was found to have caused distress after writing a letter to the member of staff expressing his romantic feelings. The JCIO also found that Smith J had abused his position and a spokesperson for the JCIO said:

---

[30] Courts and Tribunals Judiciary, 'Statement of Expected Behaviour', January 2023, https://www.judiciary.uk/guidance-and-resources/statement-of-expected-behaviour/

His actions were part of a course of escalating conduct towards a junior member of staff who was in a very vulnerable position in relation to him. He had abused his position and crossed lines which should not be crossed. It was unsurprising that the member of staff had been distressed. The impact on the member of staff was likely to be lasting.

Mr Justice Marcus Smith was subject to a reprimand for serious misconduct by the JCIO.[31]

Nor was the Guidance enough to prevent His Honour Judge Davis from overstepping the mark with a female member of court staff. The member of staff made a formal complaint that HHJ Davis had made overfamiliar and inappropriate comments while they worked together, which made her uncomfortable. HHJ Davis denied the allegations, alleging that the staff member had misremembered or misrepresented his words. The JCIO found that HHJ Davis was not sufficiently mindful of his position of authority and did not treat the complainant with respect. While HHJ Davis showed insight into his actions, he did not offer an apology. Accordingly, the Lady Chief Justice and Lord Chancellor issued a sanction of formal advice for the judge's conduct.[32]

So, what can we do?

It's not as though we haven't been trying. Back in 2021, Darren and I gave a Zoom talk to members of the FLBA, who wanted to join us and share their experiences of judicial abuse. Our talk fed into two initiatives, working with colleagues across all specialisms at the Bar, and (again) with the redoubtable Sam Mercer of the Bar Council, to draw up guidelines. The Bar Council partnered with Spot.com to support members of profession who are victims

---

[31] The Statement from the Judicial Conduct Investigations Office, August 2024, https://www.complaints.judicialconduct.gov.uk/disciplinarystatements/Statement4124/

[32] The Statement from the Judicial Conduct Investigations Office, October 2024, https://www.complaints.judicialconduct.gov.uk/disciplinarystatements/Statement5224/

of, or witnesses to, discrimination, harassment or bullying – either by other members of the profession, solicitors, judges or others. Subsequently, with the support of two successive proactive Chairs of the FLBA, Cyrus Larizadeh KC and Hannah Markham KC, Darren drew up a blueprint for good practice drawing on our work. This is the 'FLBA Respectful Working Policy' intended to give practical advice to those who are the object of bullying, or those who witness it: 'To achieve the best outcomes for the children and families with whom we work the court environment needs to be a safe and inclusive environment in which families and professionals can feel that their voices have been heard.' Here is a short extract from that blueprint:

> In ethical terms this requires lawyers representing parties in Family Court proceedings should be courteous and respectful to their opponents, to litigants representing themselves, to parties and to witnesses. The imperative of courtesy includes the need to demonstrate understanding, tolerance and patience. Members of the Family Law Bar Association must ensure that their conduct does not expose others to harassment or bullying. If harassment or bullying occurs, the Family Law Bar Association will provide support to its members as described in this policy. Members of the Family Law Bar Association should demonstrate by our actions and responses that we listen to our opponents, to professional and lay parties and to witnesses. Advancing the client's case must be done without aggression or discourtesy. Disagreement, robust challenge and holding people/organisations to account can and should be delivered without being unduly harsh about a party/witness or by the undermining or insulting of opponents. Criticisms required should be made in a respectful, and where possible, constructive way. We must demonstrate recognition, empathy and respect for everyone's social, cultural, racial, religious, and sexual background or disability and make appropriate adjustments to our approach to respond to the needs and vulnerabilities of the parties and/or witnesses. The

language we use should be clear and direct. We should avoid words and phrases that are obscure or meaningless and use plain language and avoid jargon. Inflammatory or loaded language should be avoided and we should strive to diminish rather than escalate conflict. We must treat others as we wish to be treated ourselves. We should be supportive of those we observe being treated in a manner that is not compliant with this respectful working policy.

As individuals, when we see or hear inappropriate conduct directed at a colleague we need to support them *in that moment*. We can rise and deflect the judge's attention even if we do not tackle the words said directly. By standing up (metaphorically and in reality) we can distract the judge's focus from their target, giving that person time to think, compose and breath. We can make a note of the judge's demeanour as well as comments in case our colleagues want to check their own experience against that of a neutral observer: 'Was I overthinking it? Was I imagining it?' We can check in on them. We can make them see they are not the problem, so their confidence is not crushed. And we can report the judge to Spot.[33]

Some chambers have taken steps to provide direct support. Queen Elizabeth Buildings Hollis Whiteman being the first chambers to do so to my knowledge. They asked themselves 'What can chambers do? Represent their members.'[34] They set up a panel of barristers within chambers to address complaints of bullying by judges, solicitors, court staff and other barristers:

- Any barrister, pupil, clerk or member of staff within chambers can make a complaint to any individual member of the panel.
- That member must respond within seven days and can escalate the matter to the full panel.

---

[33] https://www.barcouncil.org.uk/support-for-barristers/equality-diversity-and-inclusion/talk-to-spot.html

[34] https://www.counselmagazine.co.uk/articles/bullied-in-court-what-chambers-can-do-about-it#:~:text=An%20article%20by%20a%20former,says%20Bar%20Council%20Chair%2C%20Legal

- Escalation must be considered by the panel within seven days of receipt.
- The panel then has a range of options available, including making complaints to the regulators signed by the panel and our heads of chambers.
- All decisions reached in the first and second instance must be recorded in writing and filed confidentially.

All escalated complaints are reported by chambers to Talk to Spot. Their panel will involve senior judges or other heads of chambers if appropriate. If paperwork is required for a formal complaint they will draft it. As they said, '*the quiet phone call has only taken us so far: it is time concerns were recorded formally. Our policy includes that the person making a complaint does not necessarily have the final say over what actions are taken. Our chambers policy is designed to make sure bullying does not go unnoticed by the right people*'.[35]

The problem isn't going away

Year on year the Bar Standards Board and Bar Council are told of the problem.

In December 2023 the Bar Council published its report on 'Bullying, Harassment and Discrimination at the Bar' taken from the Working Lives Survey of that year.

> Barristers have been increasingly reporting that they have experienced or witnessed bullying, harassment, and discrimination. In our most recent survey of Barristers Working Lives 2023, 44% of respondents said they had experienced or observed this behaviour while working either in person or online. This is an increase from 38% in 2021 and 31% in 2017.[36]

---

[35] The Harman review will contain updated data which will inform the awaited Bar Council update.

[36] Bar Council, 'Bullying and Harassment', 2025, https://www.bar council.org.uk/support-for-barristers/bullying-and-harassment. html#:~:text=Barristers%20have%20been%20increasingly%20report ing,either%20in%20person%20or%20online

Notably, there have been several recent findings against judges for bullying or unacceptable behaviour. These include:

- Lord Justice Clive Lewis was found to have behaved in a rude and hostile manner towards counsel in the hearing. The JCIO issued Lewis LJ with a formal warning for misconduct and found that he 'had intervened excessively in counsel's submissions, throughout the hearing, in a manner which became increasingly harsh and rude and to the extent that it constituted judicial bullying'.[37]
- District Judge Stephen Harmes was issued with a sanction of formal advice for misconduct after asking a female advocate if she was pregnant in open court. The JCIO found while the comment was not intended to offend 'it was objectively likely to cause embarrassment when asked of a female advocate, and to cause offence to others hearing it'.[38]
- His Honour Judge Nigel Gerald was issued with formal advice for misconduct after the JCIO 'considered that HHJ Gerald had been discourteous towards counsel by raising his voice and making remarks which showed irritation and a degree of contempt for counsel's submissions'.[39]

Illuminating as these examples are, Bar Council research and anecdotal experience suggests they represent the tip of the iceberg. Clearly not all 44 per cent of those describing bullying, harassment or discrimination in their questionnaire responses related it to judicial behaviour. As the report says, it arises from the behaviour of those who are in positions of power or influence; judges, more senior barristers, senior clerks and practice managers, but the plain fact is that it's a stain on the reputation of the judiciary to have judges

---

[37] The Statement from the Judicial Conduct Investigations Office, September 2023, https://www.complaints.judicialconduct.gov.uk/disciplinarystatements/Statement3023/

[38] The Statement from the Judicial Conduct Investigations Office, March 2024, https://www.complaints.judicialconduct.gov.uk/disciplinarystatements/Statement1424/

[39] The Statement from the Judicial Conduct Investigations Office, March 2024, https://www.complaints.judicialconduct.gov.uk/disciplinarystatements/Statement1324/

featuring in those responses and statistics at all – for judges, unlike the others, hold public office.

I make the point now, as I did at the launch of Behind the Gown back in 2017, that bullying and harassment are different facets of the same evil – an abuse of power by one with more to those with less. The Bar Council wants to effect change and has reason to be frustrated at reporting on the issue year on year with ineffective self-regulation by the Bar or judiciary to resolve a well-evidenced problem. Hence why they brought Baroness Harman in. As the Bar Council said when announcing the project:

> [T]he level of reporting of bullying, harassment and discrimination suggest an entirely unacceptable state of affairs. […] The review will seek to identify the reasons for the unacceptable levels of bullying and harassment, including sexual harassment, at the Bar. It will consider the impact of these behaviours, the efficacy of current measures to counter this problem, reporting mechanisms, support services, and, most importantly, it will identify solutions.

Well-intentioned as the review is, the reaction to this initiative has been instructive. One message to me read: 'Why must we yet again recount experiences we would rather forget when we've said them so many times before to so many forums and nothing changes.' For my part, I engaged and urged others to do the same. Having had a lengthy one-to-one session with Harman this year I can say that, for the first time in many years, I feel positive that something new and biting will come out of her report. She has the bit between her teeth and has been indefatigable in travelling around the country to gather evidence. Harman will guide us but it's up to the judiciary to accept and acknowledge they have an internal problem and to embrace the report recommendations. They can't work if judges don't engage or are required to engage. Judicial self-regulation is, frankly, not working. The President tells us to tell him about judges who cross the line. Ironic, when there is at least one current member of the High Court who is known to not just the Bar but to judicial colleagues for their consistently disrespectful and rude behaviour in court. Many will not have the experience or resilience to deal with this and they should not have to.

There are many inhibitors to a barrister speaking back and calling the judges' behaviour out. Respect for the court and judge is ingrained. You might fear that any challenge to the judge's behaviour will impact the judge's perception of your client or their case. Furthermore, a bridge burnt today may not be mended before you appear in front of that same judge tomorrow, or next week, for another client; you don't want to risk prejudicing that future client's case by being out of favour with the judge. Underlying any one or a combination of these possible reasons for not speaking up is the most powerful deterrent of them all: feeling confused, powerless and intimidated.

So, are we nearly there yet?

No. We have made the subject of judicial bullying an open area for debate, and that is a massive advance. But we have not got satisfaction against those who are the most egregious perpetrators of it. We have to light the touch paper marked 'complacency' if we are to stamp out judicial bullying. Quite frankly we have to set the Bar higher and mark achievements harshly. We have waited too long for not enough to change.

6

Women at Work: Glass Ceilings and Sticky Floors

Back in the winter of 2017, I was acutely aware that we were approaching a significant number of milestones on the road towards female emancipation and equality. 10 January 2018 marked 100 years since (some[1]) women were given the right to vote under the Representation of People Act 1918. If you have an image in mind for that era, it might be of elegantly clothed Edwardian women, carrying placards and proclaiming 'Votes For Women', politicising the streets and subverting the societal norms of what it meant to be a 'lady' and a member of the 'weaker sex'. If you delve deeper into the recesses of feminist history, into its darker seams of political oppression, then remember Emmeline Pankhurst, the radical suffragette imprisoned for organising and participating in protests involving civil unrest, window-smashing and arson, going

---

[1] The RPA 1918 Act gave the vote to women aged over 30 but only if they were registered property occupiers of premises with a rateable value above £5 (or whose husbands did). That property requirement for men was abolished by the same Act as it was imposed on women: men were granted the right to vote aged 21 whether or not they owned property and men who had turned 19 during their service could also vote even if under 21.

Figure 6.1: This is my penny, struck in 1906 and defaced with the words 'Votes For Women' stamped over the portrait of King Edward VII. At the start of his reign women, along with the poor and criminals, were denied the right to vote. Mutilating coins in circulation was propoganda and direct action – suffragettes spread their message via a coin in common currency, too plentiful and small a denomination to warrant recall, to get the message out far and wide.

on hunger strike in prison and being brutally force-fed as a result. You might also know of Emily Davidson who, while proclaiming the cause for political equality, was killed by the hooves of the king's horse at the Derby in 1913. I confess that until I belatedly started to research the history of women's emancipation, I was largely ignorant of what still had to be fought for beyond the right to vote in 1918.

As Prof Jo Delahunty KC, alumni of St Anne's College Oxford University, I have gained a reputation for my work in the courtroom and beyond that means I get invited to speak professionally nationally and internationally. I have been granted my Jurisprudence[2] degree; I have been called to the Bar; I have sworn my Judicial Oath; I have taken out a mortgage; I have a bank account, credit card and passport in my own name. I can travel without my husband and without his permission. I am married but chose not to 'obey' my husband in our wedding vows. I have maintained my maiden name for all purposes (professional or personal) and my children take it along with my husband's. I have equal rights to care for my children were I to leave him or he me. One hundred years ago I would have been denied all those rights to professional and personal self-determination as a lawyer and as a woman in society for no reason other than I was born a woman. In the eyes of the law pre-1919, I simply did not exist as a legal 'person'. That was a revelation to me. How, as a woman proud to call herself a feminist, could I have been so ignorant of the battles fought on my behalf by those who had gone before me? What follows is the knowledge that I worked to acquire to remedy that deficit. The exercise gave me hope. It gave me courage. It gave me a newfound respect for the heroes of the past – no longer quaint black-and-white press images confined to the annals of history, but vibrant, brave women made obstinate and strong by their belief in a woman's right to justice and equality. Knowledge cannot be taken for granted and is a powerful stimulant to action. As Dana Denis-Smith, creator of the '100 Years Project' says, 'We need an understanding of the past to enable us to learn lessons for the future.'[3]

---

[2] Posh word for 'law'.

[3] https://first100years.org.uk/about-us/. Please check out the First 100 Years project (and now also the 'Next 100 Years Project'). It was created by Dana Denis-Smith, CEO of Obelisk Support. It is a truly ground-breaking history project, supported by the Law Society, the Bar Council and CILEx, charting the journey of women in law since 1919. The project is powered by Spark21, a charity founded to celebrate, inform and inspire future generations of women in the profession. Dana is a powerhouse of a woman, and I am indebted to her for her imagination and drive in making this a centenary year to remember. The First 100 Years Project is a digital museum and historical video collection that celebrates the heroes (and heroines), commends the pioneers and charts the journey of women in law from 1919 up until 2019. Dana has now added to it with the 'Next

Women's campaign to enter the legal profession

Law, and particularly the Bar, was the last profession in England, apart from the Church, to hold out against women's entry. The Sex Discrimination (Removal) Act 1919 had a long gestation. The right to higher education and to advance into the legal profession was the product of decades of campaign work by remarkable women, the men who supported them and the press who got behind and supported their cause. Women had been campaigning to practice as lawyers since the 1870s – women from all walks of life and heritages united by the drive to learn, earn, practice and teach for not just their own betterment but for society's.

As Dr Judith Bourne reminds us:

The first evidence we have of an organised campaign challenging the male exclusivity of the profession is in 1873, when Maria Grey, an educationalist and suffragist, organised a petition demanding the right to attend lectures arranged by the Council of Legal Education. This was rejected. A more indirect challenge was made in 1860 by Maria Rye, a friend of Grey, who opened a law stationer's office to train female legal clerks.[4] In essence, if you were a feminist in the late 1870s, seeking to study law was not just a personal intellectual quest, but a route towards equality for one and all. Qualifying as a lawyer meant that you could use the law to challenge women's restricted legal rights in society. Education was a means to an end for the greater good of equality and society at large. Only a small number of women were able to take this path, as studying law required not just high intelligence but an independent income or the backing of one's family. Lack of funds excluded working-class women from the luxury of an education, and social stigma inhibited access to higher education by the upper class. It was middle-class women who had the best chance of fighting for their right to study and earning it.

While universities welcomed women as students, they denied them degrees upon successful completion of their studies: women had no right to the rewards of their academic labour, having no legal status

---

100 Years Project' passing the baton from the women of the first 100 years to women of the next 100.

[4] https://www.lawgazette.co.uk/commentary-and-opinion/women-who-blazed-a-trail-for-the-pioneers/5069719.article

as people. With that barrier to advancement in place, women could not enter the professions they sought to join. Women who wished to become lawyers faced another, apparently insurmountable, hurdle to emancipation. Inns did not permit women to join their ranks as barristers. The Bar had self-interested reasons to fortify themselves against women's admission to their ranks, for their world was an exclusive professional domain, a gentleman's club imbued with status. It gave rank, privilege, and access to wealth and power. Politicians and prime ministers were drawn from their ranks. It was hot-wired into business and politics. The Bar was the preserve of the male.

A number of strong, bloody brilliant and bloody-minded women took this fight for entry to the Bar to the doors of the Inns. The stories that follow take you through this war of attrition. Women worked collaboratively (not competitively) in a pincer movement to pierce the legal veil. They were dogged and imaginative.

A historical overview

In 1903, Bertha Cave applied to join Gray's Inn (you have to be admitted to one of the four Inns of courts to train and practice as a barrister) and was rejected, despite being supported by two members. Her later appeal was heard in the House of Lords, when she appeared as a litigant in person before the Lord Chancellor – rather proving the point that she had the skills to be a barrister and argue a case you might think. Her case was rejected not because of any lack of advocacy skills but because her point of law rested on gender and her gender disqualified her from entry to the Inn. Bertha was the first to challenge her exclusion from this men's club, but she was not alone. She was one of a band of women who worked over decades to break down barriers to entry to the legal profession.

1903 was the year the suffrage activist Emmeline Pankhurst founded the Women's Social and Political Union advocating the use of militant tactics to win the vote for women, a passion immortalised by the slogan 'Deeds not Words'. Her equally remarkable daughters, Christabel and Sylvia, were activists in the cause. Christabel was a co-founder of the Women's Social and Political Union and became one of the suffragettes' most militant activists.

The year after Cave's denial of admittance, Christabel Pankhurst, a year into her Manchester University law degree and unwilling to accept being barred from the Bar, applied to join Lincoln's Inn. The daughter of a barrister, Richard Pankhurst, Christabel wanted to follow in his footsteps as a son would have the right to do. Richard had been a member of Lincoln's Inn. Christabel was rejected. Her intelligence was not raised as a bar to entry: her gender was the issue.

> Christabel Pankhurst's petition is one of the first recorded attempts by a woman to be admitted to Lincoln's Inn. At a Council meeting, held on 11 January 1904, her petition was put before Council. In her letter she recalled how she had previously applied to the Steward of the Inn on 2 January to enroll as a member. On 7 January she had received a reply from the Steward, 'informing me that as female students have not hitherto been admitted to the said Society, it would be necessary for me to approach the Masters of the Bench by petition … I humbly pray that I may be heard by the Masters of the Bench.' The minutes of the Council meeting note simply that she 'was refused'.[5]

Pankhurst went on to graduate from Manchester University with a first-class law degree in 1906. During her time there she was the first, and only, woman. Having been refused admission to the Inns, Cave and Pankhurst along with other women, took the battle to a second front line: the solicitors' profession. Christabel's brilliant words have not lost their fierceness over decades – I willingly proclaim them afresh: 'Remember the dignity of your womanhood. Do not appeal, do not beg, do not grovel. Take courage, join hands, stand beside us, fight with us!'[6]

In 1913 Gwyneth Bebb, who had read law at St Hugh's, Oxford, gave her name to the case that challenged the exclusion of women from the solicitors' legal profession. She had been the sixth woman

---

[5] The Honourable Society of Lincoln's Inn, 'Christabel Pankhurst', 27 February 2018, https://www.lincolnsinn.org.uk/library-archives/tales-from-the-archive/february-2018-christabel-pankhurst/

[6] https://www.manchester.ac.uk/about/magazine/picture-features/queen-of-the-mob/

to study law at Oxford, and the first woman to achieve a first-class degree in law. Her exceptional (and undeniable) intelligence and long-term association with women's emancipation marked her out to be a very special woman. Bebb had sought to be admitted to the Law Society in 1912, arguing that she was 'a person' within the meaning of the Solicitors Act 1843; that 'he' should include 'she' as a natural meaning given her exclusion as a woman was not specifically provided for; nor was 'there something in the subject or context repugnant to such construction' as required by section 43. The court's response? The statute could not have meant that 'he "embraced" she', 'an interpretation evidenced by the lack of any women solicitors since 1943'. A circular and disingenuous response. Bebb's application was refused simply on account of her sex. She appealed. In *Bebb v The Law Society [1914] 1Ch286* the (male) Law Lords unanimously decided that women were, by the common law, *under a general disability by reason of their sex*.[7] The court ruled that women were *incapable* of carrying out a public function in common law: *to be a woman was a disability* that must remain 'unless and until' parliament changed the law. I have italicised the words that strike the flame of red-hot anger in me. As the *Daily Express* wrote, 'if a woman can take a first class in law at Oxford, what right has the Law Society to prevent her from earning her living as a solicitor?'. Nothing but misogyny.

The public outcry against the Law Lords' rejection of Bebb's case was loud and insistent. 'Are Men Lawyers Afraid of Women's Brains?'[8] asked the (mostly) sympathetic press. The publicity helped to mobilise a campaign for equality. But then came the carnage of the First World War (1914–18), and life and death took priority.

The Great War savagely removed many men from the marriage 'market' and family firms. There were fewer men alive to marry – not all women had to or could be expected to marry to become dutiful wives and mothers – and 'Father and Son' could no longer be inscribed above the threshold to a thriving business with a legacy to pass on to the next professional generation. That void made space

---

[7] https://first100years.org.uk/a-woman-is-not-a-person-a-review-of-bebb-v-the-law-society-1914/

[8] *The Daily Sketch*, 11 December 1913, covering the appeal of *Bebb v. The Law Society*.

for an educational and professional metamorphosis in women's access to education and the workplace. Social and political change was in the air.

A private members' bill, the Women's Emancipation Bill, was introduced in the House of Commons on 21 March 1919 by the Labour MP Benjamin Spoor. It contained three clauses: to remove the disqualification of women from holding civil and judicial appointments; to include women on equal franchise; and to allow women to sit and vote in the House of Lords. It was a radical success. The bill successfully passed all stages in the House of Commons. During its second reading in the Commons, only seven MPs spoke in opposition to the bill. Many spoke in favour of civil and judicial appointments for women, following the logical argument that if a woman had passed all the examinations for her desired profession, she was just as capable to work in that profession as a man with the same qualifications. The government, which opposed the change, did not have its eye on the ball, and the Emancipation Bill progressed at a pace that outstripped its opponent's ability to stifle it. Eventually, the government proposed a weaker, alternative bill – being particularly keen to remove the clause granting equal franchise to women. It created and fast-tracked its rival bill, the Sex Discrimination (Removal) Bill, so as to present it to the Lords, crucially, *two days* before the second reading of the Women's Emancipation Bill. The Peers preferred to back the government's own bill, because it protected their boys' club in the Lords – retaining the Peers' exclusive rights, restricted to men, to sit in their House.[9]

The disgruntled Sir Frederick Banbury informed his Peers in the debate that:

---

[9] By this stage the government Bill had passed its first and second stages in the Commons and passed through the Lords with amendments, the Commons concluding its debates on 26 November 1919. If one reads the Hansard reports for the stages of the Bill's passage between Commons and Lords one can see that while the Commons were clear that the spirit of the Act had required them to pass an Act enabling women to take a seat as a Member of the House of Commons, the Lords resisted this measure for their own ranks: see Hansard, 27 October 1919, vol 120, columns 349+ and the exchanges between the Houses as recorded in Hansard right up to 26 November 1919.

> The Lords are masters of their House, and the House of Commons are masters in theirs. If the House of Commons likes to sit with the fair sex in their midst, and to continue their deliberations assisted by beauty, that is for the House of Commons to decide. ... For goodness sake's let us leave one of the Houses with the old tradition and let there be one House where the deliberations are conducted by men and not by women.[10]

With the Peers on board, the milky government bill was passed and the groundbreaking Women's Emancipation Bill was defeated.[11] Just reflect on the impact that this shift had – as a result of the government and the Lords' actions, women did not win the right to vote on equal terms with men until 1928, nor to sit in the Lords as Life Peers until 1958. What a loss to the country and to womankind.

In January 1919, Bebb applied to join Lincoln's Inn – the same Inn that had rejected Christabel Pankhurst in 1903. They *still* rejected Bebb on account of her gender. In April 1919, after the Barristers and Solicitors (Qualification of Women) Bill was introduced in the Lords, the Benchers of Middle Temple *again* voted not to admit women to the Inn. Self-interest was still holding the majority line against equality, but it could not hold it much longer with the passing of the December 1919 Act. The Sex Disqualification (Removal) Act 1919 received Royal Assent on 23 December 1919, and the impediment to women being admitted to the legal profession was removed. It also enabled women to receive the degrees from university they had earned.[12] But the 1919 Act was an 'enabling' Act. It did not make changes to all rules automatically – it was up to the organisations themselves to change their rules and regulations to comply with the law. Some organisations were proactive and

---

[10] Hansard, 27 October 1919, https://hansard.parliament.uk/commons/1919-10-27/debates/059c3eb6-d7c5-45f1-ab73-7f092ac6dc26/CommonsChamber

[11] With thanks to Gray's Inn archive history for its resume of this history and its article https://www.graysinn.org.uk/history/women/women-the-beginnings

[12] And to serve as jurors and magistrates.

acted in anticipation of applications by women. Others held back to await applications and then decide what to do. Perhaps they thought (hoped) it would never happen. And what of the law? How welcoming were their institutions to the woman they knew had been waiting to join their ranks since the beginning of the century? The Act may have broken down the garden walls to the Law Society and the Inns, but women still had to walk up the garden path and knock loudly, and persistently, on the front door to demand entry to the legal professions.

As Bourne points out, the litigation and campaign work were interlinked:

> Bebb was not a lone agent but part of an organised campaign which included Cave, Normanton and many other women and men. Specifically, she was one of a group of four, including Nettlefold, Costelloe and Ingram. This campaign was eventually successful, and the legal profession was opened up to women. The Sex Disqualification (Removal) Act 1919 was not an altruistic act by the legal establishment because of women's war work; rather, it was a response to this fierce campaign. Bebb, in particular, demonstrates the hostility women had to endure in order to achieve formal equality and the reluctance of the legal profession to admit women.[13]

The women were ready. They collected the degrees they had earned. They went back and demanded entry to the Inns. This time they could not be denied.

On 22 November 1922, the *Daily Mail* published 'Women's Call to the Bar', in which ten women law students were 'screened' for call – Theodora Llewelyn Davis, Helena Normanton, Monica Cobb, Auvergne Doherty, Ethel Bright Ashford, Elsie Wheeler, Naomi Wallace, Lillian Dawes, Beatrice Daly, Dr Ivy Williams. Bebb was not among them.

---

[13] With thanks to Dr Judith Bourne for this helpful summary. The full article is at https://www.lawgazette.co.uk/gwyneth-bebb-the-past-explaining-the-present/5070047.article

Remember Gwyneth Bebb's name, for 'she persisted' until death claimed her aged 31. She would have been on the list of names of the first women to be screened for call to the Bar on 22 November 1922 but her name was absent. Bebb died from complications of childbirth in 1921. She was studying for her Bar Finals at the time.[14] It is incredibly sad and poignant that while fighting for the right to practice as a barrister as a woman, Bebb was killed by the most common killer of women at the time – the act of giving birth. Of the ten women called, some continued at the Bar, some left to pursue a different life or career, and others became 20th-century legal pioneers – all were remarkable women

Just pause and reflect there for a minute before reading on because it is really important to hold in your heart and mind the knowledge of how far women have come, and how hard our forebears had to fight to get us to where we are now. We can be inspired by those who have done bigger and better things before us. We all need heroes. We can learn from the past how to improve our future and those of the girls who need us to fight for them. Bebb typified the women who marched resolutely forwards to achieve educational and professional acceptance.

Did those women create momentum for emancipation and equality at all levels of the Bar, so that as of the 21st century, we can walk into a courtroom or sit as a judge with all of the advantages to career progression denied our professional forebears? No.

Sticky floors and glass ceilings

If history is our teacher, how have we learned so few lessons, when we have had such pioneering women to lead and inspire us? Maybe it's because we just try to get on with the day job, keeping up relationships, juggling all the clashes between work, ambition and home responsibilities. It is a hard ask. Maybe we are so focused on surviving and thriving ourselves that we do not look around to see what is going on in plain sight. That was true of me until a few years ago. After all, I was a professor, a recorder, a KC and a Bencher. Certainly the majority of my clients were women, who often suffered

---

[14] https://first100years.org.uk/gwyneth-bebb-2/

Figure 6.2: 'We Stand on the Shoulders of Giants.' 2022 marked the centenary of the first woman, Helena Normanton, being 'called' to the Bar by Middle Temple in 1922. As part of its programme celebrating 100 years since women were first admitted to its roll call of the Bar, Middle Temple reviewed its archives and chose 100 'Women of Distinction' from its membership to be named as having played a part in the history of the Bar. I was one of those 100 women. It was an honour to be selected.

by virtue of their gender and failed to reach their potential, but they were not me, not *us, not the briefs*. I worked in a world where women were the majority as colleagues. *We* were professional women, using our brains to their fullest extent for personal benefit and public gain. I worked with women as solicitors, juniors and silks. I heard cases and gave judgments on the fate of families as a woman. I appeared before women judges. Hadn't we all done well?

I was wrong. As Bar research makes plain, year after year, women have been and are still being failed by the profession. In examining the reasons why, I became radicalised by anger at the number of hurdles placed in the way of women that not just impeded their progress and progression at the Bar, but seriously undermined their retention by it. In thinking of the place of women at the Bar, I also had to confront the additional barriers faced of social class, ethnicity, religion, parenthood, caring responsibilities and judgement about their life choices and appearance (that would not be levelled against men).

When I added to those biases issues such as sexual harassment, abuse, bullying and discrimination, all of which have a disproportionate impact on women of colour, I had to accept that I could and should not encourage them to join my world unless I publicly 'called out' the obstacles I, with the advantage of seniority, could now see. As told in previous chapters, I first started speaking out, publicly, on this issue in 2017. Press and public interest had been fuelled by the #MeToo movement and the time was ripe for change. So why, come 2025, am I still waiting to see enough of it? Women are still not equals at the Bar and Bench with men, and it is not because we are not good enough. As successive Bar Council research studies show, the stark reality is that the Bar is leaking talent from an entry base of equality. While increasing numbers of women have entered the profession over the past two decades, high numbers of women are leaving the Bar post qualification and practice, and those that remain do not attain silk in equal numbers as men or sit as judges at the same levels and in the same numbers.

When looking at the ratio of women to men at the early stages, whether enrolment on the bar course, call to the bar, pupillage or tenancy, the gender mix is broadly equal. This even ratio continues into the early years of practice. 2023 data (published in 2024[15]) indicates that of the self-employed Bar under five years call, women make up just over 48 per cent. Yet by 15 years+ call this figure dives to just over 35 per cent. This loss of senior junior women barristers reduces the pool from which silk (King's Counsel) applicants are drawn. Out of the 326 applicants for silk in 2024, only 84 were women (around 26 per cent of all applicants). Of those 84 women, 33 were appointment KCs. Women made up less than half of the

---

[15] The 2024 data to be reviewed and published in 2025 is not yet available.

number of male KCs appointed in the same year (72). Moreover, when one adds the issue of ethnicity to the mix, the pressures are disproportionately magnified.[16]

The Bar Standards Board's Diversity at the Bar report 2024, published in January 2025,[17] based on figures from 2023, found that around 3.6 per cent of the Bar, 6.2 per cent of pupils, 3.7 per cent of non-KCs and 1.4 per cent of KCs are from a Black/Black British background. This compares to around 4.1 per cent of the UK working-age population. The proportion of Black/Black British barristers at the Bar has increased by around 0.6pp since 2015 and by 0.2pp compared to December 2022.[18] As of 2024, the Bar Council's 'Race at the Bar' report identified that there are only eight Black female KCs (the same as in 2022)[19] of 25 Black KCs.[20] In the 2024 KC recruitment round, no Black barristers were appointed to KC, despite ten applying.[21]

In all areas of practice and stages of their careers, even at silk, Black barristers earn less than their male colleagues. Notably, in 2023, the 24 Black KCs earned a median income equivalent to 44 per cent of their white counterparts' earnings.[22] The majority are also based in London. When they do apply, women have

---

[16] The 2024 analysis is available at https://kcappointments.org/wp-content/uploads/2025/01/Monitoring-statistics-2024-onward.pdf

[17] This is the latest data at the timing of writing, available at https://www.barstandardsboard.org.uk/resources/bsb-publishes-its-annual-report-on-diversity-at-the-bar.html

[18] Bar Standards Board, 'Diversity at the Bar 2023', January 2024, https://www.barstandardsboard.org.uk/resources/bsb-publishes-its-annual-report-on-diversity-at-the-bar.html

[19] Bar Council, 'Race at the Bar: Time to Double Down on Race Equality Work', 4 December 2024, https://www.barcouncil.org.uk/resource/race-at-the-bar-time-to-double-down-on-race-equality-work.html

[20] Bar Standards Board, 'Race at the Bar: Three Years On', December 2024, https://www.barcouncil.org.uk/static/f1da4b31-7adb-475b-900b6a0f20cf1530/378c2794-0694-4deb-99e32e8130cb092d/Race-at-the-Bar-three-years-on.pdf

[21] The 2024 analysis is available at https://kcappointments.org/wp-content/uploads/2025/01/Monitoring-statistics-2024-onward.pdf

[22] Barbara Mills, 'Inaugural Speech 2025', January 2025, https://www.barcouncil.org.uk/static/3b4dde75-7092-4c37-b2ef9866458be4b6/Barbara-Mills-KC-inaugural-address-8-January-2025.pdf

equal or greater success in being appointed. In the 2024 survey, published in 2025, around 39 per cent of the female applicants for silk were recommended for appointment, compared with 30 per cent of male applicants. This trend of greater success for female applicants has persisted for 23 of the last 29 years, but still, we have too few women applying so the gender gap widens. The Bar Standards Board is well aware of the gender disparity in silk and has sought to understand why. One answer provided is that 'women may face systemic disadvantage in silk applications because of their secondary school, university or area of practice'. Looking at these compounding features might explain why three-quarters of senior practitioners (78 per cent) who take silk went to paying fee-paying secondary schools, went to Oxbridge and achieved a first-class degree. Later analyses look at this granular detail but *Counsel* magazine each year provides an analysis of the online chambers profiles of those who take silk. The analysis for 2024 tells us that applicants who attended Oxbridge continue to be appointed as KCs in large numbers across all practice areas, many of whom achieve first-class degrees, and BAME candidates continue to be under-represented at silk level.[23]

The board responsible for KC applications is aware of this disparity and understands it must be addressed – as it said as far back as 2017:

> We are pleased that the number of women applying and being successful continues to rise, and that the proportion of women amongst those appointed is at its highest level ever. However, we would still like to see more women apply. We have commissioned research to see whether there are barriers which may deter well-qualified women from applying.[24]

---

[23] The 2024 analysis is available at https://www.counselmagazine.co.uk/articles/who-gets-silk-2024

[24] Queen's Counsel Appointments Press Release 2017, https://kcappointments.org/category/2017-competition/

As one contributor said, the 'twelve cases of substance in two years' requirement of the KC application process creates difficulties/puts off women who carry out silk-level work but who may have taken a career break for children.[25]

> [I]f you are a woman who has had a baby or worked part-time to look after children, [to] get 12 silk-type cases is very challenging. Women are still bearing the brunt of childcare on their career. A lot of women say, 'I can't apply because I only have 4 or 5 cases'. … If you are a mother and work part-time, it is difficult to accumulate cases for a good application.[26]

Indeed, while the accompanying notes for the 2024 'applying for silk' event clarifies:

> Having fewer than twelve cases is not a bar to application, although it is possible that fewer cases may not cover the breadth of evidence required. You should make it clear in your application why you are unable to provide twelve cases. It may be worth considering whether there are any cases from slightly outside of the three-year window that could be included.[27]

The end result? Despite good intentions we have not moved on in eight years. The suffragettes had it right; deeds, not words, matter.

---

[25] https://www.lancaster.ac.uk/media/lancaster-university/content-assets/documents/lums/work-foundation/BalancingthescalesupdatedMOAccess.pdf

[26] https://www.lancaster.ac.uk/media/lancaster-university/content-assets/documents/lums/work-foundation/BalancingthescalesupdatedMOAccess.pdf

[27] Applying for Silk Event, 23 October 2024, Accompanying Notes, October 2024, https://kcappointments.org/wp-content/uploads/2024/10/Applying-for-Silk-event-23-October-Accompanying-Notes.pdf

This wastage of talent starts to become clearer the higher up the pyramid one goes. Since the ranks of senior judiciary are largely drawn from the KC coterie, that silk pool, drained of female talent, has a knock-on effect in terms of representation of women and women of colour in the judiciary.

Do not be misled by a headline statistic of women who sit as judges. It is a pyramid structure with women making up a large part of the baseline and becoming more and more invisible the higher up to the apex we look. As of July 2025,[28] we are told by the official statistical website that '[t]he proportions of female and ethnic minority individuals were higher amongst the magistracy than in the judiciary'. Over half (57 per cent) of all magistrates were female. 'Ethnic minorities' made up 14 per cent. In tribunals, female judges accounted for over half (57 per cent) of the most senior roles (presidents). The highest level of female representation in the County Court was among the Deputy District Judges at 48 per cent (the lower tier of the judiciary), with this figure notably declining in percentage terms in higher ranks of the judiciary, including just 25 per cent of women appointed as Deputy High Court Judges. Of the current Supreme Court Justices, we have ten men and two women (Lady Rose appointed in 2021 and Lady Simler appointed in 2023). All the men and women are white. The President and Deputy President positions are held by men. We are going backwards not forwards. As at 2017–2020 we had Lady Hale as the President (she was Deputy President from 2013 until 2019) and she presided over nine men and two women (Lady Black and Lady Arden). All three Lady Justices have now retired. For the first time since 2013, we do not have a woman as either Deputy President or President. We do have a Lady Chief Justice Carr of course occupying the most senior judicial position as President of the courts in England and Wales, but one woman, however superb, cannot be, and represent all the missing women from the roll-call of judges from High to

---

[28] Gov UK, 'Diversity of the Judiciary: Legal Professions, New Appointments and Current Post-holders – 2025 Statistics', https://www.gov.uk/government/statistics/diversity-of-the-judiciary-2025-statistics/diversity-of-the-judiciary-legal-professions-new-appointments-and-current-post-holders-2025-statistics--2?

Supreme Court. Looking at the gender divide in the judiciary overall, far from making progress, we have returned to a position last seen a decade ago.

We, the public, lose out by that lack of representation. Increased diversity in the judiciary will positively shape the development of the law, and it is important that justice is not only administered by, but is seen to be done by, a judiciary which is reflective of the society today.

Where are the women at the Bar? The illusion of inclusion

It is dispiriting to note that what Helena Kennedy KC (Baroness of the Shaws) identified as a problem in terms of progression and retention some 20 years is as true now as it was then. Kennedy concluded that the issues which stifle diversity at the Bar are pretty obvious, pretty basic and invidious:

Practice bias:

> Women are sought to act for men in rape and other sexual assaults, because of the involuntary endorsement they give to the male defendant. A recurring moan of pain is uttered in the women's robing room at the Old Bailey by female barristers who are force-fed a diet of sexual offence cases to the exclusions of all else. The men either make themselves scarce or say they cannot hack it if children are involved. In a skewed effort to flaunt their professionalism women not only find themselves conducting these cases but sometimes do them with as much machismo as any man.

Status:

> [F]or those determined to go into legal practice, the majority are steered towards public service law, by which I mean fields largely funded out of legal aid. ... Women invariable do the ill-rewarded work in all walks of life and what follows is a lowering of the esteem of that professional activity.

Income:

> [W]hen governments justify taking the scythe to legal aid, they summon up for the public the notion of the fat cat lawyer, bloated male barristers dining out on public funds, when in fact those who will suffer will largely be committed young women who work tireless for little rewards, and their clients.

Parenthood:

> No one can job-share a murder trial or ask for a three-day week if they are a trial lawyer but if chambers were amenable, it should be possible for women and men to adjust or reduce their caseload to allow space between cases for a well-adjusted family life. The problem remains that chambers often maintain a culture in which saying no to a case is sacrilege. There is a particular machismo at the Criminal Bar which means success is measured by being constantly in court without a day to catch breath. Losing women in significant numbers at this stage also dilutes the pool from which judges will be drawn five or ten years down the road.[29]

This has not changed at the coal face. I gave evidence to the Westminster Panel Inquiry into the Sustainability of Legal Aid in 2021 and heard from other witnesses that this was just as true now as it was in 2005. Dana Denis-Smith of the 100 Years Project and the Next 100 Years Project and I are in accord when we say that *'culturally we seem to need our female leaders to be perfect and at the top of their game while mediocre men climb the ranks all the time by simply being capable of doing their job'*. Indeed, the adverse effect of working practices and pay on women's wellbeing at the Bar is a key contributor to such disparity in retention rates. Women's caring responsibilities are disproportionately high compared to male colleagues. At the

---

[29] Helena Kennedy, *Eve was Framed*, Penguin Books, revised edition 2005, pp 34, 2, 2, 47.

independent Bar, there is little flexibility, with late service of evidence and skeleton arguments requiring urgent responses, often after-hours and following long days in court. This leaves little time for family life. This is exacerbated by ongoing government cuts to legal aid in real terms year on year.

Whether we practise in Family Law or Criminal Law, Immigration or Housing – all sectors of the publicly funded bar – cuts to legal aid have resulted in a loss of income to all. Days of court are not remunerated, meaning that time off for caring responsibilities for elderly parents, sick partners, children, and so on, results in further loss of income. In comparison to employed practice, with its more regular and flexible working hours, holiday and sick pay plus pension, it is easy to see why women leave the Bar. Lynne Townley, former[30] chair of the Association of Women Barristers, has said that the attitude at the Bar '*has got to change. … Until ways can be found to retain women, you will find this relentless imbalance at higher levels in the profession*'. As we know, this brain drain reduces the pool of experienced women who ought to be applying for silk.

But the attrition factors that lead to a loss of senior women do not explain why those who do stay the course and take silk have less visibility, professionally and publicly, than their male colleagues. That has, I suggest, to be down to institutionalised industry bias.

Mikolaj Barczentewicz, a public law lecturer at the University of Surrey, designed an algorithm that analysed all the cases heard in the Supreme Court and generated a database of all barristers who had appeared before it. He has very generously shared his report with the public, the only request being that it is made plain that it is a work in progress. What he has produced offers a valuable insight into the visibility of women in the highest court of our land. As Barczentewicz indicated in an article for *Counsel* magazine in March 2022, statistics revealed a 'clear rising trend for male leaders' in the Supreme Court, commenting 'there is a much higher proportion

---

[30] 2018–21.

of male-led teams including women than at any time in the past'.[31] Whilst I acknowledge the positive point made in that comment – that more women were appearing in the Supreme Court in absolute terms – that must not detract from the harsh reality that the proportion of teams led by women silks was and remains low. But while women might be being seen in the Supreme Court, they are not being heard, because the speaking parts (taken by the silks appearing on the front row) are overwhelmingly male. Women are the juniors: not the leaders.

Karon Monaghan KC, a highly respected colleague, is a discrimination specialist at Matrix Chambers. Karon says it like it is, in an article published in *The Times* on 24 October 2019: 'The near absence of women silks will be no surprise to anyone who appears in the Supreme Court.'[32] Karon represented Claire Gilham, a district judge, in her successful challenge to the Ministry of Justice over her right to be classed as a whistle-blower. Karon said that solicitors and clients too often chose men to represent them because they thought they would have more gravitas. As Karon says, 'Men therefore appear in greater numbers. ... Those men then get a reputation for being good in the Supreme Court, as having the ear of the court and as silks who can be relied upon to perform well, so continuing the cycle.' Let me make plain that this is no sour grapes from Karon. She is one of the women who is most regularly instructed to appear at the highest court in our land. When women like Karon say that 'the persistent under representation of women is likely to do with straightforward prejudice and stereotyping, and it is self-perpetuating', she is telling it as it is. I endorse without hesitation what she says.

On 8 November 2023 the Lady Chief Justice, Master of the Rolls and Heads of Divisions issued a joint statement encouraging the participation of junior counsel in general, and female counsel in particular, in advancing oral argument in courts and tribunals

---

[31] https://www.counselmagazine.co.uk/articles/gender-at-the-supreme-court-bar-; https://barczentewicz.com/post/2021-03-15-empirical-study-supreme-court/

[32] https://www.thetimes.co.uk/article/qc-attacks-gender-bias-in-top-court-jn3j6bsxh

hearings.[33] Judges will be expected to ask whether this has been considered. On 7 March 2024, Lord Reed, President of the Supreme Court, issued a practice note stating that the court similarly expects a speaking part for junior counsel in all suitable cases, or at least confirmation that this has been considered. It was explicitly recognised that 'experience in advancing oral argument is essential if junior counsel are to progress, and experience of advocacy in the highest court can have particular value'.

I am watching to see evidence of implementation – then impact.

We need women to be *visible and vocal* at the highest levels of achievement in law: as silks, as judges in the High Court, as heads of divisions, in the Court of Appeal, appearing in the televised cases coming from the Supreme Court and in the Supreme Court itself. Just consider how much of an impact it made around the world when Brenda Hale, as President of the United Kingdom Supreme Court, gave the judgment on the government's decision to prorogue Parliament? Images of her composed and assured delivery of the court's unanimous judgment, upon one of the most controversial issues to be determined by that court in recent years, were beamed around the world. Even her broach attracted its own fan base: the spider emoji became a symbol for female empowerment and support across countless social media platforms. That illustrates the power of visibility: show us a strong, confident, brilliant woman, doing her job superbly, and you can inspire others to aim high. That sends a powerful message to the young who watch.

As Dana has said, 'one hundred years ago the battle was for participation in the legal system. With more women than men now entering the profession, what we need now is equal numbers of men and women in leadership positions, receiving the same remuneration'.

Why are we haemorrhaging female talent? Think back to the previous chapters. Women are the most likely targets of discrimination or harassment, and if they are Global Ethnic Majority (GEM) women the risk is higher. Successive Bar Council Working Lives reports have found the main reasons for women leaving the Bar

---

[33] https://www.judiciary.uk/encouraging-greater-participation-of-junior-counsel-in-courts-and-tribunals-hearings/

were current and future income, the impact of legal aid cuts, child caring responsibilities (mainly those aged 35–44) and an increase in expected pro bono work. Frankly, what reason does the Bar give for women to stick with the profession? The present is grim enough and the future holds out fewer hopes for progression to silk or to the Bench.

As Kennedy says: 'As in other professions, there is a glass ceiling for women, which means that getting to the top floor involves a detour out through the window and up the drainpipe, rather than a direct route along the charted corridors of power.'[34]

The gender pay gap reports by the Bar Council: where are we now?

The Bar Council found that the disparities between male and female pay were not readily explained. It made several key findings, which include that the disparities between male and female pay were not readily explained:[35]

- In the 0–3 years post qualification experience (PQE) band, the earnings gap between men and women has been between 9 and 13% each year for the last three years.
- In each practice area and at each PQE band (0–1, 1–2, 2–3) an earnings gap is always present, with no exception.
- The gap is present right away at 0–3 years, widens and then peaks around 11–15 years PQE, before narrowing again among juniors. It is extremely pronounced among silks. The earnings gap remains present among both barristers who have caring responsibilities and those who do not.
- Women are more reliant on legally aided work than men but, even among all those who rely on this work for more than three

---

[34] Helena Kennedy, *Eve was Framed*, Penguin Books, revised edition 2005.
[35] Bar Council, 'New Practitioner Earnings Differentials at the Self-employed Bar', April 2024, https://www.barcouncil.org.uk/resource/new-practitioner-earnings-differentials-at-the-self-employed-bar-april-2024-pdf.html

quarters of their earnings, women at 0–3 years PQE earn 13% less than men.

In response to the report, Sam Townend KC, the then Chair of the Bar Council, said: 'The earnings gap between men and women at the self-employed Bar is a structural problem that presents a collective challenge for the Bar. We need to reconsider the ways in which we speak about and address money, billing, work opportunities, work and personal choices.'[36]

Voices at the Chancery Bar report: what does this say and what points of greater application

Published in 2021, the Voices of Women at Chancery Bar report is based on data and roundtable discussions from 2019 summarising the recurring concerns about women's pay.[37] The report called for a multifaceted approach to address unequal pay and other institutional challenges.

Female barristers at the roundtable discussions highlighted the issues in the allocation of work, with one barrister noting that '[Work] can come in in your name and it can end up with somebody else down the corridor.' Another barrister's feedback was 'We get the kind of clever but less well paid [stuff] … company law, insolvency.'

In a raw article in *Counsel* magazine by Marcia Shekerdemian QC we read about what was to follow: 'The IBC is fully engaged in the task ahead. Lucy Barbet is coordinating roundtables with Chancery sets' senior clerks to address the issues raised – especially fairer and more transparent work allocation practices and, critically, the gender pay gap. As for that, I cannot not refer to the BMIF's

---

[36] Sam Townend KC's comments are available at https://www.barcoun cil.org.uk/resource/mind-the-early-gender-earnings-gap-at-the-bar-new-research-from-the-bar-council.html

[37] Voices of Women at Chancery Bar Report, Chancery Bar Association, December 2020, https://www.chba.org.uk/for-memb ers/library/consultations/consultation-responses/voices-of-women-at-chancery-bar.pdf/view

data; this indicates that on average, men in Chancery practice earn almost 100% more than women. Why? How can this be allowed? What is being done to stop this? Inexplicable and inexcusable. It. Must. Stop.' And yet – the problems highlighted in those round table meetings appear to linger.[38]

At the Bridging the Bar event in June 2025 I spent some time with a young tenant at a commercial set who rapidly broke down in tears at describing how she felt she was under a level of scrutiny unlike her male peers. How they appeared to get the speaking roles that she did not. How despite her leader trying to apply good practice by giving her a speaking role in court, client choice took that option away. She was consistency obliged to take a lesser role in a case compared to equally experienced men. That was impacting on her confidence, fulfilling an assessment of her that had filtered down as not being as confident as her male peers. She was in a chambers dominated by older affluent white men with certain expectations. She had no female role models to follow. I signposted her to the support flagged in this chapter.

The report's key concluding recommendations urged chambers:

- Clerks should be active in curating the practices of individual members of Chambers.
- Raise awareness of the duty to monitor fair allocation of work.
- Put in place active monitoring of work allocation and ask the clerks to take the initiative on raising discrepancies.
- Arrange regular anti-unconscious bias training for clerks and members.
- Implement Parental leave policies, which are in line with Bar Council recommendations.
- Rather than assuming that something can or cannot be done (including as regards our fees), what clerks should be doing is actually asking women.
- Actively consider your marketing methods and how they are disadvantaging women in Chambers.

---

[38] https://www.counselmagazine.co.uk/articles/voices-of-women-at-the-chancery-bar

- Recognise that the culture of the Bar has a negative impact on women's confidence which is not their 'fault'.
- Consider not only formal mentoring processes but also formal reverse mentoring. For example, a senior woman mentoring a younger man. Or just women (of whatever seniority) mentoring men (of whatever seniority).
- Consider bespoke mentoring and advice to encourage women to apply for silk.

The Women at the Criminal Bar (WICL) report on 'Women at the Criminal Bar' also highlighted the pay gap divide between men and women at the junior end of the criminal Bar.[39] In 2019, female criminal barristers earned 39 per cent less than their male counterparts. WICL identify three solutions to address the pay disparity:

- Accountability for those with briefing power – solicitors, clerks and other public organisations need to encourage gender equality and commit to collecting data on fees.
- More female criminal clerks – clerking remains a male profession, criminal sets should actively seek to recruit female clerks and analyse how all clerks promote different barristers.
- Challenging gender stereotypes – incorrect perceptions about the type of work women are suitable for example, women are seen as better for 'emotional' clients and men are more suitable for complex fraud work must be addressed. The industry must work to challenge these preconceptions to enact change.

The point surely is this. The Bar Council cannot lead the way with its powerful 'We are the Bar' campaign that seeks out to attract aspiring barristers from under-represented sectors if the Bar, as an industry, and chambers as its engine hub, is not willing to make changes to embrace them. How are heads of chambers, senior clerks, practice managers going to monitor and intervene? Are they prepared to

---

[39] Women in Criminal Law, 'Women at the Criminal Bar: Fair Access to Work and Fees', February 2021, https://www.womenincriminallaw.com/post/women-at-the-criminal-bar-fair-access-to-work-and-fees

do that and how will they do that when we are a collective of self-employed individuals who have no employer? How, and who by, is change going to be tracked? Are members going to sign up to it if it means they may receive fewer briefs and lower-paid ones? Gender stereotypes may be latent not patent – how are they to be uncovered? Is training to be mandatory? I'm not saying that the WICL proposals do not have the capacity to deliver change, I just want to know, practically, how they can be made to be effective. For if they aren't, we are selling a falsehood to the pupils the Bar Council is actively seeking to welcome into our midst.

Intersectionality matters

Our experiences as women cannot be pigeonholed. We think of leaving the Bar, and do leave, not just because of our struggles as women, but because of the difficulties we may face from not being white, or straight, or having family support to get us through lean times. We might be skint working in legal aid, especially in crime. We may be wrung dry by working on the sex cases which, again, female barristers carry the burden of disproportionately. We might not be able to afford the essential childcare needed to get to court. We may be one or any combination of those things. Being a woman is the lowest common denominator – but it is not the whole sequence.

We cannot talk about women in this chapter and not talk about colour.

When interviewed for *Counsel* magazine in September 2023, having been elected as vice chair of the Bar, Barbara Mills KC, the first GEM woman to be so elected, spoke plainly about how 'talent was not enough' to succeed as a woman or person of colour, 'It requires access to all available opportunities'.[40]

Spot on

The Bar Council's 'Bullying, Harassment and Discrimination at the Bar 2023' report revealed some stark differences in experiences of

---

[40] https://www.counselmagazine.co.uk/articles/-talent-on-its-own-is-not-enough-barbara-mills-kc

working life as a barrister, particularly in intersectionality by sex and race, and regarding experiences of bullying, harassment and discrimination at work. More than half (52 per cent) of female barristers from ethnic minority backgrounds reported bullying or harassment, compared with 17 per cent of white male barristers. That is almost over three times the likelihood. We (the Bar) cannot tolerate that.

We (the Bar) have to own that and confront it. As women we have more than earned our place in chambers and in court, but we have to do more for more to make it a place of equality of opportunity and advancement. Significantly, whatever our gender, we (the Bar) have to make active changes to get colleagues of colour onto the front row and with top billing as judges.

Barbara had some advice to give on how to carve out your place as a woman of colour at the Bar: '*First, put your blinkers on and ear plugs in to drown out those who will tell you that it is, "too hard" or "not for you". If you want it, there is no reason why it is not a profession for you. You must take your CV seriously. Be as highly qualified as you can be. Quality in terms of qualifications and expertise is irrefutable. Be strategic from the very beginning, and aim to secure internships, mini pupillages and funding. ... It can be a lonely and very opaque journey. So, find your tribe which includes a "mentor plus", someone willing to be with you and sponsor you throughout the long walk of your career. Be prepared to work hard and know what hard work looks like. It does not mean working until three o'clock in the morning every day but working efficiently and well. Finally, tough as it may be, you must work to eliminate any feelings that you are an imposter. Get involved – active participation in all aspects of life at the Bar has helped many to combat feelings of being "on the outside".*'

It is not the first time Barbara has spoken out honestly and openly about the barriers to retention and progression at the Bar for Black colleagues. As far back as 2019 in her article for *Counsel*[41] she said this:

> The Bar's culture, tradition and shape were informed by the circumstances and experiences of its founding

---

[41] https://www.counselmagazine.co.uk/articles/changing-the-picture-diversity-at-silk-level

fathers – white men from privileged backgrounds. That inevitably created a system which has, at its very core, the notion that whiteness is the norm and as a result it perpetuates structural and systemic unfairness obstacles to those who enter the profession from a variety of other backgrounds and heritage.

And the unfairness continues to stain our profession. We cannot otherwise explain why, as Barbara points out, 'Black female barristers are the lowest earning group across the whole Bar … it is not a coincidence that there is a prevalence of Black barristers in publicly funded, and therefore underpaid, work'. Barbara referred to the data which unequivocally evidenced that female barristers are likely to earn less than male barristers and Black female barristers are the lowest earning group across the whole Bar. It was no surprise to Barbara that more than half of Black barristers surveyed by the Black Barristers' Network thought that race had negatively affected the allocation of work or were uncertain whether it had been:

> Clerks must consistently implement systems to ensure Black barristers (particularly women), get a fair share of the junior briefs … the Bar cannot afford to keep looking away. While it may increasingly say it strives to represent equality and inclusivity, it currently does not look like the population it serves, and at the current rate, is unlikely ever to look like that society.[42]

Nor is this injustice just about gender. Able men and women are impacted on by prejudice.

The focus on racial inequality, particularly in the judiciary and at the Bar, has been increasing. The Bar Standards Board has reported. The Bar Council has reported. The Black Barristers Network has reported. Middle Temple's Race Working Group and several other Bar organisations including the Commercial Bar Association have

---

[42] https://www.counselmagazine.co.uk/articles/changing-the-picture-diversity-at-silk-level

also reported. All reports highlight significant racial inequality. Inequality in terms of representation and progression were to some extent already visible. Racial inequality in remuneration and adverse experiences in practice are clear. As with other sectors, the problematic use of data for a group described 'BAME' has been recognised. Comparing BAME barristers with their white counterparts or Asian or 'Minority' groups, masks very different outcomes for different racial groups.

Evidence now confirms what we knew anecdotally: under-representation is most acute in relation to Black African, Black Caribbean and mixed heritage practitioners.

The Bar Council's 'Race at the Bar: Three Years On' report of 2024, as touched on earlier, laid bare the impact of gender and race on incomes.[43] Regardless of practice areas and seniority, GEM barristers still earn significantly less than their white counterparts. The income gap of £16,000–18,000 is present at the start of a GEM barrister's career. The gap only grows, within barristers' 11–15 years of PQE before lessening among senior juniors. Among silks, Black KCs typically earn £200,000 less than their white and mixed/multiple ethnicity background silks.[44]

In all areas of practice and at all stages of their career, Black and Asian barristers earn less than white barristers. At the self-employed Bar, white barristers' median earnings are around 32 per cent higher than Asian barristers' and 54 per cent higher than Black barristers. Black barristers are also less likely to get immediate tenancy and are the most likely ethnic group to go onto a third six.[45]

---

[43] Bar Council, 'Race at the Bar: Three Years On', December 2024, https://www.barcouncil.org.uk/static/f1da4b31-7adb-475b-900b6a0f20cf1530/378c2794-0694-4deb-99e32e8130cb092d/Race-at-the-Bar-three-years-on.pdf

[44] There has been no update to this. To flag, the Bar Council did publish gross earnings by sex and practice area in 2025 but this refers to figures from 2023 and does not differentiate between ethnicities.

[45] *The Law Gazette*, 'Race Report Reveals "Limited" Progress for Black Barristers', December 2024, https://www.lawgazette.co.uk/news/race-report-reveals-limited-progress-for-black-barristers/5121741.article#:~:text=In%20all%20areas%20of%20practice,those%20of%20a%20black%20barrister

As a group, both Black African and Asian Bangladeshi barristers had the lowest incomes. This much was pointed out by the work of the Black Inclusion Group (BIG) commissioned by the Commercial Bar Association, the Chancery Bar Association and the Technology and Construction Bar Association, who shared a wish to tackle racial inequality, and Black inclusion in particular, across their spheres of influence. They summarised their work for *Counsel* magazine.[46] BIG reported that the specialist commercial Bar was failing to attract, recruit and retain Black barristers, as demonstrated by the relatively low success rate of Black applicants for pupillage, the paucity of Black silks and the complete absence of a single full-time Black High Court judge. The outcomes for Black barristers are notably worse than for other ethnic minorities. As they said: 'The Specialist Commercial Bar is missing out on available Black talent'. They noted that

> The experience of some Black barristers in practice is one of substantial hurdles and barriers along with profound levels of isolation, dislocation and an absorbed sense of not belonging. Some contributors talked of 'being highly visible while being overlooked', 'always being on trial', finding and understanding 'the requirement for Black excellence'. They also described experiences of overt racism.[47]

As they say:

> Those accounts were supported by the fact that 47% of those who responded to the survey (the majority of whom are White) reported witnessing race or ethnicity-based unacceptable behaviours during their professional lives. Behaviours that would be contrary to the Code of

---

[46] https://www.counselmagazine.co.uk/articles/black-inclusionand-the-commercial-bar-

[47] https://www.counselmagazine.co.uk/articles/black-inclusionand-the-commercial-bar-

Conduct. That confirms, shockingly, such behaviour is going on in plain sight.[48]

Bleak

If we look to the judiciary we see no better a picture. The government's statistical report on diversity of judicial appointment[49] reported that 'ethnic minority candidates made up a much higher percentage of applications than their representation in the eligible pool, and their representation decreased between each exercise stage, from application to shortlisting to recommendation for appointment'. That was the case whether the applicants were Asian, Asian British, Black or Black British. Looking at data from 2021 to 2024, '[f]or three of the legal exercises over the past three years, there is evidence to suggest disparity in the recommendation rate from eligible pool in favour of white candidates compared to Asian candidates'. In the courts, the proportion of judges from ethnic minority backgrounds was highest for district judges in magistrates' courts (15 per cent) decreasing to lower proportions for the more senior appointments – 13 per cent deputy High Court judges, 9 per cent High Court judges, 3 per cent Court of Appeal judges and none in the Supreme Court.

What message does that whiteness of the judiciary send? It's definitely not welcoming. It's clearly not inclusive.

That message of stagnation was reinforced by the Ministry of Justice's own report, 'Diversity of the Judiciary: 2025 Statistics'.[50] The report found that since 2015, the number of judges from different ethnic minority backgrounds had increased from 7 per cent to 12 per cent, but the number of Black judges remained at 1 per cent of all judges.

---

[48] https://www.counselmagazine.co.uk/articles/black-inclusionand-the-commercial-bar-

[49] https://www.gov.uk/government/statistics/diversity-of-the-judiciary-2025-statistics/diversity-of-the-judiciary-legal-professions-new-appointments-and-current-post-holders-2025-statistics--2#ethnicity-1

[50] https://www.gov.uk/government/statistics/diversity-of-the-judiciary-2025-statistics/diversity-of-the-judiciary-legal-professions-new-appointments-and-current-post-holders-2025-statistics--2

> Responding to the publication, Barbara Mills KC, Chair of the Bar Council, said: 'Every year we are told that there is gradual progress being made towards a more diverse judiciary, but it's far too slow for Black lawyers and this is no longer good enough.
>
> The representation of Black judges has remained at 1% across the judiciary for a decade with only gradual increases of people from other minority ethnic backgrounds. We want to see real progress and a commitment across the board to ensuring that there is support and investment so that our judiciary reflects the diverse communities we live in.
>
> We are concerned that candidates from a minority ethnic background, and in particular Black lawyers, are disproportionately ruled out at each step of the recruitment process. We are told that this data is not statistically relevant. We disagree. It is relevant and requires scrutiny.'[51]

In July 2025 the UK Association of Black Judges was launched and Barbara Mills KC went to the front line again. She attended to speak about her experience and offer her support to the association as chair of the Bar and as a deputy High Court judge. Of that she said:[52]

> The launch of this association, and the attendance and presence of voices from across the legal profession, including Lady Chief Justice of England and Wales Baroness Carr, is a testament to our collective commitment to shaping a legal system that truly reflects the society it represents.
>
> To me it is important that we as Black judges show up in a system that doesn't always feel like it shows up

---

[51] https://www.barcouncil.org.uk/resource/progress-on-judicial-diversity-is-too-slow.html
[52] https://www.barcouncil.org.uk/resource/progress-on-judicial-diversity-is-too-slow.html

for us, to ask hard questions and be part of a respectful solutions-driven conversation.

This year's report also expanded its data collection on disability, and for the first time, the Judicial Diversity Forum introduced data on social mobility, measured by type of school attended. Of that, Barbara said:

> We know that there are many people across the legal profession working to have a positive impact on our judicial system and the individuals within it. We are pleased that the report has also started to monitor social mobility. Initiatives such as the pre-application judicial education programme, SBA and circuit judicial outreach initiatives and our judicial appointments mentoring programme continue to offer support and insight, but the statistics suggest much more needs to be done.

Champions for change

Barbara Mills became the chair of the Bar in 2025. The impact of that was felt immediately and continues to grow month by month. Her energy and input is quite simply staggering to behold and read. Barbara is a woman of firsts: the first woman of colour to be elected as vice chair; the first Black woman to be the chair of the Bar; the first GEM woman to take up that role. She is the first family practitioner to be so appointed in 35 years. She was also made a deputy High Court judge in 2022. In Barbara we have a role model we can look up to, learn from and be inspired by. As is evident simply from the speeches I quoted earlier, Barbara speaks up when it is needed and counts and does so with courage and a directness that is breathtaking in its vitality. Barbara is a woman of principle and huge ability. I know that not just from what she has achieved and written but by what I have seen in chambers. Barbara is a beacon of hope for many of us going forward, not just for what she has done so far but for the message she is sending out that will be heard long after her term ends. She has set a bar for action that needs to be a marker we check back on to see if the challenges she has set for our profession have been met.

We have Kirsty Brimelow KC appointed as vice chair of the Bar for 2025. Kirsty is also a woman of firsts. Kirsty was the first female chair of the Bar Human Rights Committee (2012–18). She was appointed as a deputy High Court judge in 2021. In 2021–3 Kirsty led the Criminal Bar Association – serving as vice chair and then chair – during the criminal Bar action and negotiations with government that secured the increase in legal aid fees. Kirsty is a fighter for justice and change. She is fearless. On her election Kirsty said: '*I will work to change the Bar's own backyard by taking solid steps to eliminate the gender and race pay gaps at the Bar and I will extend the championing of social mobility and diversity, as well as expand the Bar's environment commitment.*' Kirsty is a woman who can be relied upon to persist.

As of 2025 the Bar Council trod new ground and it was women who walked into the history books. With Barbara as chair and Kirsty as vice chair, along with Lucinda Orr as treasurer, 2025 delivered the first all-female officer team for the Bar Council in its 130-year history.

What can we do to make sure that these incredible women have colleagues to follow in their wake? We do not want to repeat the high of having Brenda Hale as our President of the Supreme Court only to experience the loss when she went and the Supreme Court, and we, were left impoverished by her absence. We have Sue Carr as our first Lady Chief Justice, who is ready to step into her shoes? Agreed we have the next generation of leaders for change in Barbara, Kirsty, Shona Jolly KC, Karon and Brie, but every generation needs men and women who are prepared to make a difference. We need role models to look up to and emulate. Brie has the words for the moment – '*leadership is the art of inspiring a consensus of big upward ideas*'.

What can we take from this?

Be ambitious

Take every opportunity to advance your skill set. Be hungry to improve, for how else will you have the framework to build upon for more senior roles? Ask to take a role in conferences with clients, in professional conferences, in court. If you fail in an application for silk, for recorder, for deputy district judge, apply again. Even Barbara did not get silk first time around as she has publicly shared her experience to encourage others not to give up when feeling defeated. Look at Alexandra Wilson and the story of her progressions in her book. As Alex has said in the past of her experiences trying to make her way at the Bar, *'people stood in my way'*, but she pushed past them. She practised in crime before coming to 4PB to specialise in family law, then moved to the United States to expand her experience and horizons. She is soaring in the legal world. She has a Master's from Columbia Law School, is now associate attorney at a prestige law firm and has published her second book, this time a thriller, *The Witness*. She has not stopped yet. I expect more of Alex. I am proud of her and for her.

We have initiatives by chambers and because they are few in number compared to the number of sets we have in London, they warrant special mention – other sets can learn from and emulate them.

11KBW: scholarships for Black students on the Bar Practice Course

In response to the lack of representation across the Bar of Black barristers and students, 11KBW awards an annual £30,000 scholarship to fund the cost of a Black student on the Bar course. Alongside the cost of fees and maintenance, the recipient also receives mentoring from members of chambers during their qualification and pupillage, an assessed mini pupillage and a guaranteed interview for pupillage (provided they meet a certain score during their assessed mini pupillage).[53]

1COR: assessed mini pupillage

To aid diversity and social representation at the Bar, 1COR launched an assessed mini pupillage scheme in 2015 targeted at socio-economically disadvantaged applicants. Chambers now offers ten

---

[53] https://www.11kbw.com/knowledge-events/news/2024-11kbw-scholarship-for-black-students-on-the-bpc-open-for-applications/

mini pupillages each year which offer applicants a guaranteed first round interview provided they meet a minimum standard.[54]

New Square: social mobility mini pupillages

New Square Chambers offers a social mobility mini-pupillage scheme designed to enhance access to the Bar for individuals from under-represented or socio-economically disadvantaged backgrounds. This initiative provides participants with an opportunity to experience the daily life of a barrister, gain practical insights into legal practice and receive personalised mentorship. Chambers also reimburses candidates for reasonable travel expenses. The scheme aims to equip participants with the knowledge and confidence needed to pursue a career at the Bar successfully.[55]

12KBW: social mobility mini pupillages

12KBW runs a social mobility mini-pupillage programme focused on supporting students from less advantaged backgrounds. Through this programme, participants gain hands-on exposure to the work of barristers, one-on-one mentoring and practical advice on navigating a career in law. Mini pupils are not assessed, instead, the initiative seeks to foster equal opportunities and break down barriers, creating pathways for aspiring barristers to thrive within the legal profession.[56]

Library of opportunity

Bridging the Bar have recognised the importance of sharing information about sets who embrace diversity and inclusion. To that end they have started to publish a 'directory'[57] of those chambers who

---

[54] https://www.1cor.com/london/about-us/equality-and-diversity/
[55] https://newsquarechambers.co.uk/join-us/social-mobility-mini-pupillage/
[56] https://12kbw.co.uk/pupillage/social-mobility-mini-pupillage/overview/
[57] https://bridgingthebar.org/diversity-directory/

have partnered up with Bridging the Bar who support its aims. That type of visibility really makes a difference. A statement on a chambers website that says it positively welcomes candidates form non-traditional backgrounds extends a hand of welcome but detective work to track those chambers is not always as easy for some potential candidates as others. Access to tech/privacy/time to use it are not always there as of right for the most disadvantaged. A library of opportunity gives those candidates a start point, along with encouragement, that there may be a place for them in this extraordinary profession.

We don't have to wait for collective action. We can each play our part.

Become mentors and be mentored

Mentors bridge the gap (or try to) between stages of a career that are otherwise a cavernous void to the junior member. Mentors can pass on advice and contacts, but the real value they have, I believe, is in making senior roles more accessible and relatable to the young: and if they are relatable, they can be emulated. No one is suggesting that the junior mentee try to become a younger carbon copy of the senior mentor: that would be a waste of the individuality upon which the Bar thrives. But: it makes aspiration more real, and career dreams more ambitious.

The Association of Women Barristers started the ball rolling with a student mentoring scheme in 2020, which offered students the opportunity to be appointed a mentor to meet with on a regular basis. The aim was, and is, to increase diversity and inclusion by supporting aspiring female barristers. Mentoring schemes are also run by Women in Criminal Law, Women in Family Law[58] and the Black Barristers Network to name just a few. Each was set up to support and inspire, mentor and socialise, empower and encourage.

Mentoring is not just for the beleaguered public law legal aid sector. We need more women and people of colour in commercial work. I was deeply encouraged by the initiative set up by some commercial sets to reach out to applicants. One Essex Court, Brick Court, Essex Court and Fountain Court chambers (power houses in the commercial sector) collaborated to create a series of

---

[58] Set up by my forward-thinking and principled friend and colleague, Hannah Markham KC.

events at a number of universities directed at gender diversity at the commercial Bar. One Essex Court has, in addition, set up a mentoring programme,[59] and has publicly said its needed because '[f]ewer women than we would like are applying for a career at the commercial Bar'.[60] To shift that perception, they hold career clinics, pupillage workshops and pupillage interview workshops. Where they lead, other commercial sets should follow. Just as impressive is their public statement that

> We welcome applications from candidates from all backgrounds. We are not looking for someone to fit a particular 'mould' and there is no 'One Essex Court barrister'. Our members have diverse backgrounds, pathways to the Bar, interests and personalities. For many of our members who worried that they might not 'fit in' elsewhere at the bar, One Essex Court was a natural choice.
>
> Our focus is simply on finding those individuals who show the best potential to become excellent barristers.
>
> We particularly welcome candidates from backgrounds that are under-represented at the Commercial Bar, including (but non-exhaustively) women, people of minority ethnic origin, people with disabilities and those who are LGBT+.
>
> Pupillage is only offered to those who are thought capable of becoming tenants. Pupils are not in competition with each other, and we are committed to taking on as tenants all pupils who meet the standard. Over the past five years, more than 90% of pupils have been offered tenancies.
>
> All pupillages come with substantial funding.

The message from our specialist associations is support and inspire, mentor and socialise, empower and encourage.

---

[59] https://www.oeclaw.co.uk/pupillage/women-at-the-bar/
[60] https://www.oeclaw.co.uk/pupillage/women-at-the-bar/

Be role models

The Law Society's 'Women in Leadership Law Report'[61] has some signposts to point the way forward: I do not see why they are not as relevant to the Bar as a law firm. They suggest:

- *Leading from the top and by example*: it is crucial for leaders to be aware of their biases, to prevent them from influencing business decisions and colleagues alike.
- *Humility and acknowledgment of bias*: ensure individuals and leaders/managers are completely conscious of their biases and the unconscious biases that persist within the organisation. This can help to underpin a culture of awareness that is the foundation for change.
- *Raising awareness as a starting point*: organisations should implement unconscious bias training for everybody within the organisation, supported by the right policies that address inappropriate workplace attitudes/behaviour and the right senior leadership commitment that creates inclusive workplace cultures.
- *Recruitment and selection processes*: law firms and in-house legal teams should be committed to making decisions purely on competencies, quality and attributes on the individuals involved.
- *Support during work*: supporting women in the workplace is important to prevent bias.

The 'Transforming Women's Leadership in the Law' report surveyed 56 female lawyers and aspiring lawyers to collect their testimonies on how the legal profession needed to break down its structural barriers to become a more diverse workforce. The report concluded that law firms, businesses and organisations must provide more flexible working arrangements to retain junior

---

[61] Women in Leadership in Law Report: Findings from the women's roundtables 'Influencing for Impact: The Need for Gender Equality in the Legal Profession', Law Society, March 2019, https://www.lawsociety.org.uk/topics/research/women-in-leadership-in-law-report-need-for-gender-equality

lawyers and better recruitment so aspiring lawyers from underrepresented backgrounds can access opportunities like internships or summer programmes.

Perhaps to be a role model, more legal firms, chambers and other organisations should take inspiration from the Mansfield Rule, which was initially piloted in the United States and provides standards for law firms to measure diversity. By adopting the rule, organisations agree to:

- Track and document the population of candidates for all governance and senior lawyer roles, and equity partners and leadership promotions openings.
- Consider a candidate pool that is 30 per cent women, LGBTQIA+ and lawyers of colour.
- Provide transparency of the appointment, nomination and election processes.

As of October 2024, around 360 US law firms achieved a Mansfield certification in the United States.[62]

Make women visible in the profession – to your peers, to the judges, to the clients

Take the 2024 Practice Direction of Lord Reed, President of the Supreme Court, into the heart of your practice, whether in conference with a client, when taking a platform in a professional conference to legal colleagues, or in court itself.

Leaders can give the microphone to junior colleagues, women colleagues, colleagues of colour when they lead. It confers confidence and gives experience. It can happen in client conferences and in court. Leaders need to be proactive. They can agree 'equality of arms' with the other side and perhaps agree in advance with their opponents which points might be dealt with by juniors. Alternatively, the juniors

---

[62] Miles Gillhespy, 'DE&I: Is the Mansfield Rule Still Relevant for Today's Legal Industry?', SSQ, January 2025, https://ssq.com/articles/dei-is-the-mansfield-rule-still-relevant-for-todays-legal-industry/?utm

themselves should raise the possibility with their leaders and/or each other. But it is no good giving the juniors just the points that the leader expects to lose. That is unfair on the junior. It is much better to find discrete points of law or cross-examination topics which can be conveniently dealt with by a second person. The prospect of the juniors on both sides dealing with those points can then be raised internally and with the other side well in advance of the hearing.

Look out for the men that can support women

As Lady Hale has said, 'Not all women are feminists, but many men are, and women would never have got anywhere unless some men had realised that if the law treated them in the way it treated women they wouldn't tolerate it'.

We have male champions for change in the likes of Eduardo Reyes, features editor of the *Law Society Gazette*. We had them in Kieran Priender when Senior Legal Advisor to the International Bar Association. We have them in the likes of Darren Howe KC, who has sat alongside me in many a meeting about harassment and bullying. There is room for so many more and there are ways to help men do this.

Know and circulate the Law Society's 'Male Champions for Change: Toolkit'. This document acknowledges that the importance of 'proactive participation, promotion of gender balance and efforts to understand how gender inequality limits the ability of individuals and businesses to reach their full potential' should not be underestimated. The Toolkit suggests: 'As champions of change, men can work towards the positive transformation of social norms and can take action to hold other men accountable and encourage them to join in.' The Toolkit offers insight and guidance on what individuals can do to accelerate the rate of progress within the legal profession as a whole. It warrants adoption by our profession. It would make a fine companion to Lord Reed's Practice Direction.

We must proclaim our achievements like men do. When I was made Gresham's Professor of Law in 2016,[63] a position I held until

---

[63] Only the second to hold that post in Gresham's long history, which dates back to 1497 – the honour of the first such appointment goes to my supporter and mentor Baroness Ruth Deech.

2020, I did not use the title 'professor' outside of Gresham at any point. Why? I did not feel like I earned it. It was not until my successor, Leslie Thomas KC's appointment was publicly announced and within minutes I saw he had changed all his public 'tags' to add the prefix 'Professor', that I realised how stupid I had been. I had done precisely that which I had told so many other women not to do. I had held back from marking my career advancement, because I was not sure I had earned it. A man would not do such a thing, and indeed had not. Within the hour, I made up for lost time to the extent that I could. My Twitter handle, my LinkedIn page and my work signature were all changed to 'Emeritus Professor of Law'. When I was approached by the President's office to ask how I wished to be addressed by the Court of Appeal in the seminal case of *Re H-N and Others (children) (domestic abuse: finding of fact hearings) [2021] EWCA Civ 448*,[64] I replied 'Professor', and henceforth was called that in a live-streamed hearing. That was the first time I had claimed the title in court. Five years late, but it had been done.

We must always 'own' the titles we have earnt through competition, hard graft and brains. If we do not celebrate what we have achieved, why should others look to us as role models?

Be inclusive

Adopt some of the steps advocated for by the BIG[65] and agitate for them with your specialist association and in chambers. The principles can be applied across every sector where recruitment and support matters:

- *On outreach*, they recommend that the SBAs (Specialist Bar Associations) develop an introduction programme for Year 12 and 13 students and build connections with universities that

---

[64] Three interlinked cases grouped together so the Court of Appeal could give guidance on how the family courts should treat allegations of rape, domestic abuse and coercive controlling behaviour – the first review in 20 years. I successfully acted for one such abused appellant woman.

[65] https://www.chba.org.uk/for-members/library/consultations/consultation-responses/black-inclusion-group-final-report.pdf

have higher proportions of law and non-law students from Black backgrounds.
- *On recruitment*, they recommend that the SBAs should proactively collaborate with existing groups already supporting aspirant barristers of Black heritage seeking pupillages and to hold joint sessions offering practical guidance and support on completing written pupillage applications and preparing for pupillage interviews.
- *On retention*, they recommend that the SBAs:
  o invite member chambers to monitor and measure the allocation of junior briefs by silks, to ensure fair allocation of opportunities (particularly junior briefs), which are likely to enhance career development and progression;
  o collaborate with existing Black practitioner networks and organisations to provide regular mentoring and sponsorship opportunities for Black juniors with leading practitioners in their practice areas; and
  o arrange workshops with the editors of each of the principal legal directories concerning the Bar, to address under-representation and other identified disparities affecting ethnic minority barristers being included in the directories, particularly Black practitioners in the SBAs' practice areas.
- *On progression*, they recommend that the SBAs:
  o provide focused mentoring programmes and sponsorship opportunities for junior Black practitioners contemplating applications for silk and judicial appointments; and
  o hold annual events, to which representatives of the judges of the Business and Property Courts are invited to assist in explaining to practitioners the evidence required to support a positive reference for the KC Selection Panel.
- *On culture*, they recommend that the SBAs:
  o facilitate Black practitioners at the specialist networking events; and
  o consider when planning all initiatives and events whether there is an opportunity to encourage senior white barristers to engage proactively with supporting the inclusion, retention and progression of Black practitioners.

Make sure your chambers' website has a positive statement of inclusivity welcoming under-represented candidates, that is, those from non-traditional backgrounds, from all heritages, with disability, with neurodiversity.

Know when it is time to hand the baton over and not to over speak

While I can talk, from experience, about the importance of social mobility and gender equality issues, I am a straight, white woman. I cannot begin to know what it is like to be judged on the name I have on a form, or by the colour of my skin. Nor can I understand what it is like to fear that one's choice of sexual partners might affect one's reputation and career options. Nor can I know what it is like to be a person with a disability, that invites judgement and adverse preconceptions of one's ability and potential. Unconscious bias and discrimination through disability, sexuality and race are all areas that the Bar must challenge.

Just as I expect strong men to support strong women to achieve gender equality, as a strong woman it is my duty to support equality of opportunity for my GEM, disabled and LGBTQIA+ colleagues. It is clear we need more voices to champion the cause of equality for disabled, neurodiverse, LGBTQIA+ and GEM people at the Bar and in the judiciary.

Final words: diversity matters, visibility matters, voices matter

Consider this text from a 1978 careers advice book, which advises readers that 'an advocate's task is essentially comparative, whereas women are not generally prepared to give battle unless they are annoyed. A woman's voice, also, does not carry as well as a man's'. Women like myself and others I have long admired, like Baroness Helena Kennedy KC, do not just 'give battle': we invite it, revel in it and fight to win it. The women I know go not only into battle, but do so with panache and skill. We dance with words and, when compared to a man, we can proudly adopt this line (apropos Fred Astaire's skills): 'Sure he was great, but don't forget that Ginger Rogers did everything he did, backwards and in high heels.' We need champions for change at the Bar to be visible, vocal and honest about obstacles placed in their path to seniority. We need more senior men and women to step up to the mark and become activists for change, and to call it out when positive action does not follow fine words.

Every generation needs men and women who are prepared to make a difference.

The task I believe we face as we look forward is to unflinchingly identify and tackle barriers to gender advancement, even if it paints our profession in a poor light. The Bar offers a service that is unique in the world. It is worth putting up a fight for – for its practitioners – for the public.

We need to confront sexual harassment, male and white bias power politics. We need to be prepared to hold inhibiting factors such as allocation of briefs, chances to be led and to speak at professional seminars (at the Bar) and non-family compatible courtroom working practices up to the light for scrutiny and accountability. Just as important is the duty to take actions oneself: not simply look to others for leadership. Again, as Brie says, 'make small changes happen and big changes will grow in the same ground'.

For my part, I strongly believe that it is the responsibility of those who have climbed the ladder not to knock away the rungs, but to lean down and pull others up it. The people I have celebrated in this chapter did not rise to prominence by being quiet and avoiding controversy, nor by acting in competition with other disadvantaged colleagues. Collaboration matters. When we fight for equality we should stand alongside one another, arms linked, advancing as a force to make change happen in our professional lifetime. This is our collective fight to make the Bar a more inclusive meritocracy. We have to Set the Bar for those that follow.

7

Advocating for Change

'The Garrick scandal'

In March 2024, the Garrick Club made headlines for its male-only membership list of the rich famous and powerful. Photographs and names of senior members of the judiciary were published over successive newspaper editions, the web and social media. They were all white, male, old/er men. Women were photographed carrying placards demanding (and being refused) entry to the Garrick gates. 'No More Boys' Clubs in Justice' read one. 'Deeds Not Words' another.

Why was this important? The Garrick was a relic of the past that represented all the worst connotations associated with the Bar. *The Guardian* had gotten hold of the membership list, which included a serving Supreme Court judge, five appeal court judges, eight High Court judges, dozens of serving and retired judges, current and former ministers in the Ministry of Justice, around 150 silks and numerous senior solicitors. If ever we needed a reminder of how weighted the Bar and senior judiciary are in terms of gender, this was it. While the ostensible rule of the Club is not to talk business within its walls, do we really think that likely to be respected, with drink at hand and companionable gossip always having currency? And while case details might not be shared, the mention of a tasty point of law, or a hearing, a brief coming up might be acceptable? But whether anything case related is discussed or not, names and faces, likes, dislikes, opinions become familiar. Status is absorbed like osmosis. In terms of careers, a face remembered or voice heard is going to be in the conscious or unconscious mind for a brief, a supportive word for silk or judicial appointment. In the legal world membership oils the wheels of confidence, even arrogance. The Garrick is Old Establishment. The judges who are members decide the law that affects us as citizens. And who are 'they' at the Garrick? They are all men. Power begets Power and that Power is the exclusive preserve of men.

I signed the letter created by Dr Charlotte Proudman and Elizabeth Traugott, barristers at Goldsmiths Chambers,[1] that made headlines in the national press, from broadsheet to tabloid, in late March 2024, but while they lit the touchpaper, the fire had been prepared by Emily Bendell many years before.[2] This time the soundwaves reached the *New York Times*, Al Jazeera and Australia to name but a few places that picked up the piece. This was a deeply unattractive look for the judiciary and Bar. I then went into print for *Counsel* magazine,[3] inviting Kate Brunner KC and Dr Ann Olivarius KC (Hon) to join forces on 7 May 2024.[4]

When I talk of 'We Set the Bar' it has to be more than words muttered in private setting the world to rights. We have to tackle inequality head-on, even when it might embarrass or antagonise. In *Counsel* we spelt out why it was incompatible for those in public service to be members of an exclusive, male-only preserve of politics, power and patronage. I asked, 'how can we trust *public* commitments to gender equality and equity of opportunity and income at the Bar, when in *private* judges are happy to be members of this men only elitist club'? In my view, for judges to maintain

---

[1] https://garrickclubjudges.wordpress.com/wp-content/uploads/2024/03/open-letter-to-judges-in-the-garrick-club-1.pdf
[2] https://www.bbc.co.uk/news/uk-england-london-54062903
[3] I have mentioned *Counsel* magazine a few times by now in this book (https://www.counselmagazine.co.uk/). It has two women at its helm who have been consistently supportive and forward-thinking – Sarah Grainger and Elsa Booth. They are unafraid to raise difficult topics and approach each challenge I embark on with them with integrity and consummate skill. They and their team perform a really valuable service for the Bar through their monthly magazine which informs, educates and entertains in equal measure.
[4] https://www.counselmagazine.co.uk/articles/garrick-gate-a-critical-tipping-point

their membership of the Garrick was fundamentally incompatible with the core principles of justice, equality and fairness, particularly for senior members of the judiciary who significantly shape jurisprudence on gender-based discrimination and inequality and gendered crimes of violence and abuse. The Garrick was founded in 1831, at a time when women were not deemed to be 'persons' in law. Its homepage records its purpose: 'The Garrick was founded in 1831 by a group of literary gentlemen under the patronage of the King's brother, the egalitarian Duke of Sussex.' They announced that the Club would be a place where 'actors and men of refinement and education might meet on equal terms', where 'patrons of the drama and its professors were to be brought together', and where 'easy intercourse was to be promoted between artists and patrons'.[5]

Let me make plain, I am not against exclusive spaces – my LGBTQIA+ colleagues, Global Ethnic Majority (GEM) colleagues and my feminist friends and I all welcome spaces where we are free to be ourselves. There is a place for men-only spaces as for women or other interest groups. The issue with *this* club was that when members of the senior judiciary mix with senior barristers and solicitors in an exclusionary environment, there is opportunity for direct and indirect promotion and allocation of work. It created the stench of unfair advantage and influence on decision-making behind the scenes. The law, and the judges who administer it in our name, must do so without fear or favour and perception of bias. Membership of *this* club for *this* closed group of males, white men in power, was anathema to the principles required of those in public service. As Ruth Bader Ginsberg said, 'women belong in all places where decisions are made. It should not be that they are the exception'.[6]

In 2015 the former Labour MP Bob Marshall-Andrews put forward a motion to amend the club's rules to allow women membership. It failed, receiving support from only 50 per cent of members, less than the two-thirds majority needed to be carried. Among those

---

[5] https://www.garrickclub.co.uk/about
[6] https://www.bbc.co.uk/news/world-us-canada-54218139

voting against the motion were 11 QCs according to a *Guardian* report of the time.[7]

Some members fought from within but with consequences for them (a reminder that not all champions of women need be women — a point well made from over 100 years ago when the first step to equality through legislation required the support of exclusive male voting MPs and Peers to pass). Former theatre producer Colin Brough, a member for 40 years, was expelled from the club in February 2024 after sending a series of emails to fellow members expressing his conviction that women should be admitted immediately. The strongly worded emails criticised the club's 'Putin-style' management, accused the club's committee of thwarting the desire of a majority of members to admit women, and claimed organisers of a poll on how members felt about women joining were biased. He was summoned to a meeting with the Garrick's chairman on 1 February, charged with 'conduct unbecoming of a gentleman' and formally expelled from the club.[8]

The Guardian then 'outed' the private members list. It sent shock waves through the Club. Hurried resignations of some (but by no means all) members of the judiciary followed. We do not know how many other ranks felt sufficiently embarrassed to quietly resign. According to *The Guardian*, which kept a spot light tightly focused on the Club:

> A letter from 13 committee members noted that the media's 'unfair and unwanted spotlight on the Garrick' had already prompted numerous resignations, including 'a number of senior judges, Simon Case, the cabinet secretary, Sir Richard Moore, head of MI6, John Gilhooly, chief executive of Wigmore Hall, and many others, including Downton Abbey producer

---

[7] https://www.theguardian.com/uk-news/article/2024/may/04/garrick-club-vote-women-female-members

[8] https://www.theguardian.com/uk-news/2024/feb/13/the-garrick-expels-colin-brough-tensions-over-men-only-stance#:~:text=Former%20theatre%20producer%20Colin%20Brough,women%20should%20be%20admitted%20immediately

Gareth Neame, who also resigned as chairman of the Garrick Charitable Trust.' In his letter to the club chair, Neuberger wrote that he too would resign if women were not admitted, describing the issue as a 'running sore' that was becoming a 'reputational problem'.[9]

The Garrick called an extraordinary meeting to debate inclusion of women into the club, and at least five women were named as likely proposed candidates. Then Chair of the Bar Council, Sam Townend KC, issued the following statement, summarising the crux of the issue: 'Closed doors and exclusionary spaces do not foster support or collaboration between colleagues. Where progression from the legal profession into the judiciary relies on references, they create the potential for unfair advantage.'[10] Lady Chief Justice Carr, President of the Court and Head of Judiciary of England and Wales, also issued a statement, reaffirming the judiciary's commitment to diversity and inclusion.

As of 1 July 2024 the Garrick admitted Dame Judi Dench and Dame Sian Phillips under a fast-track rule that enabled the Garrick to admit, in its discretion, four members 'in consideration of their public eminence or distinction'. One wonders why, given the 'exceptional circumstances' (as I would phrase it) presented by the intense press and public scrutiny of Garrick's outdated admissions policy, the full complement of four spaces was not given to fellow nominees such as the classicist Dame Mary Beard, Channel 4 News presenter Cathy Newman, the former Home Secretary, Secretary of State for Work and Pensions and Minister for Women and Equalities Amber Rudd, or Scottish broadcaster, journalist and political commentator Baroness Ayesha Hazarika. There are no shortage of news presenters, politicians or peers in the 1,500-strong male membership list. Has Baroness Hale been invited to join this club to sit alongside Lord Sumption amidst the junior male judges she has presided over? It

---

[9] https://www.theguardian.com/uk-news/article/2024/may/04/garrick-club-vote-women-female-members
[10] https://www.barcouncil.org.uk/resource/at-the-heart-of-the-bar-council-is-a-commitment-to-fairness-equality-and-diversity-says-chair-sam-townend-kc.html

would appear not. The last women admitted was Celia Imrie who joins her two 2024 female colleagues and, as at 4 June 2025 we learnt that Julie Etchingham had withdrawn her candidacy to join the Garrick Club, said to be uncomfortable with the protracted process of being vetted by the London club's membership of 1,500 men. *The Guardian* reported that '[t]he broadcast journalist said she would not comment on her decision, but she is understood to have been uneasy at the level of hostility displayed by men opposed to the admission of women during a candidacy lunch at the club, when members have the opportunity to question prospective members'. The article continued:

> Several women from the first batch of female nominees for membership have expressed frustration at the club's 'half-hearted' steps towards admitting women. One woman whose candidacy is being considered by the club described the vote to admit women as a cynical public relations gambit, designed to allow the club to continue functioning quietly as essentially a men-only club. She said she found the vetting process absurd. 'We're all being made to feel we need to beg to join; most of us don't give a toss whether we join or not and think they should be making every effort to persuade us,' she said, asking not to be named to avoid alienating her sponsors at the club. She said it was clear that men who opposed women's membership were continuing to fight against the swift admission of women. 'It's frankly ridiculous and embarrassing. What are they scared of?'.[11]

What indeed. How much have we learnt since the *Daily Sketch* asked on 11 December 1913, 'Are Men Afraid of Women's Brains',[12] after

---

[11] https://www.theguardian.com/uk-news/2025/jun/04/julie-etchingham-ends-garrick-club-application-after-drawn-out-process

[12] https://www.cambridge.org/core/journals/legal-information-management/article/cambridge-women-and-the-law/EF2B682D0B44C8BA3CB0E649486E8BB7

the Court of Appeal refused to admit Bebbs right to be admitted to the Bar.

When I first drafted this chapter back in 2024 I thought we had made a difference. I wrote that the Garrick scandal proved that we could make a difference by speaking up for what we believed in. I naively wrote that thanks to the publicity around this issue, raised by a group of outspoken and confident women, the Garrick was forced into debate and decision on admitting women after resisting that issue for decades, immune to public censure. That much was true. Emily Bendell, Dr Proudman, Elizabeth Traugott and their galvanised supporters had indeed made the Garrick and its members the objects of critical scrutiny. I thought we had made their well upholstered sets of privilege a little less comfortable. Now, a year later, it is obvious how wrong I was to believe the vote had signalled a change in culture. Misogyny lives on within its membership. Those men who resisted change with their outdated attitudes just hunkered down and bided their time so as to be able to sabotage the progress sought by more enlightened members. No high level resignations now.

Figure 7.1: The *Daily Sketch*, 11 December 1913

The over-representation of white men in seats of legal power (at all levels of judiciary and in silk) is and remains symbolised by the Garrick – an institution that defends itself against change and represents a bastion of discrimination. It is an oasis of privilege that divides the insiders from the outsiders, and the Garrick is its watering hole.

There will always be some who do not see the need to change. They embarrass themselves and the profession by their complacency.

Visibility, access and reach

I'd like to think we would be further on to achieving a more equitable, representative, inclusive, healthier profession because what the Bar looks like, how chambers represent themselves and how it behaves towards its young really matters. But slow as it may have been, none the less, change is happening, and we can thank those not so ground down by defeat for many of the successes I highlight here because they have created ways to deliver change that has not relied on the organs of power to enact. They have acted for themselves by themselves.

Mass has spelt out how exclusionary it feels to look at websites not to see a reflection of oneself. Looking at any chamber's website can be a dispiriting window into our world. The Bar retains areas of practice where the diversity of the community fades entirely to white. The depressing side is best represented by chambers who predominantly practised in the private sector – shipping, chancery, commercial, and so on. Even as I write this, I am shocked at how many chambers' websites present image after image of senior white men in silk and senior junior stages of practice. Just a couple of years back, I judged a Chambers of the Year category in our industry awards where one entry had seven white male silks, followed by a gallery of white male senior juniors. Women and people of colour made an appearance only at the staff section as receptionist or clerks. Where was the insight or self-reflection on how this would look to outsiders? I saw no statement of welcome or inclusion for applicant barristers from diverse backgrounds on their application section. This can and should change. Contrast this with the One Essex Court 'welcome':

> We welcome applications from candidates from all backgrounds. We are not looking for someone to fit a particular 'mould' and there is no 'One Essex Court barrister'. Our members have diverse backgrounds, pathways to the Bar, interests and personalities. For many of our members who worried that they might not 'fit in' elsewhere at the bar, One Essex Court was a natural choice ...
>
> We particularly welcome candidates from backgrounds that are under-represented at the Commercial Bar, including (but non-exhaustively) women, people of minority ethnic origin, people with disabilities and those who are LGBT+.

We need symbols of welcome. The impact of seeing Sultana Tafadar KC's image in the press in 2022 as the first hijab-wearing criminal barrister to secure silk was incredible. The fact that Shaheed Fatima KC is also a hijab-wearing silk barely made any news on her appointment back in 2016. While 18 per cent of newly appointed silks were from a minority ethnic background in 2025, none of the Black applicants were successful. Reflecting on the statistics in January 2025, Chair of the Bar, Barbara Mills KC, said: 'It is concerning that this year none of the Black applications were successful. There is a need to better understand the factors that impact the success of Black applicants.'[13]

We are learning to celebrate diversity. We can do better.

Tooks Court, the civil liberty set I joined in 1988 and was proud to have as my legal home for almost 15 years, reflected the society I saw around me. Why have so many other chambers not caught up with the commitment to diversity We Set the Bar at Tooks decades ago? Consider the diversity of barrister photos found on the websites of common law chambers now by random selection and see how many are mixed in terms of gender and culture. If chambers cannot demonstrate inclusivity based on their current tenant make-up, they

---

[13] Bar Council, 'Bar Chair Congratulates New King's Counsel', January 2025, https://www.barcouncil.org.uk/resource/bar-chair-congratulates-new-king-s-counsel-press-release.html

can and should fly a flag of welcome and change, positively inviting applicants from under-represented backgrounds to apply. We should expect that to be the norm and be seen with greater prominence in chambers who so clearly have an unbalanced profile.

We need to see backstories. For those of us who now look to be part of the establishment, because we are white, silks and sit as judges, our chambers' profiles have little on them to indicate what routes we have taken to get to fight for and find our place at the Bar. Our profiles proclaim our achievements; they do not reveal the barriers we have overcome to claim them. As Mass puts it, '*the "achievements" and "education" sections of a barrister's profile can be intimidating for many aspiring barristers to see. It can blind an aspiring barrister to his or her own strengths, on the basis that those strengths might be different to what is currently celebrated on Chambers' websites. That might include having gone to a particular university, having won a particular academic prize or simply, "fitting in".*'

Whether we come from single-parent working-class families, are first-generation UK citizens, went to academies as opposed to private school, had to work to fund our place at Bar School and pupillage as opposed to the bank of Mum and Dad paying for it, our professional portals give the impression that we were always destined to find our place in this profession. We exclude all personal details.

The Bar lags behind the society it serves, because it takes time for up-and-coming entrants, who are changing the face of the profession, to climb the stairs of success. But will applicants even knock on the door of the Bar if they cannot see a path to it? The stereotypical privileged elite image of the Bar trickles down to school level.

Derek Sweeting KC (as he then was – now Sweeting J), on raising the prospect of the law with a teacher, was told '*Well, it's not really something that people from your background do.*' Among our current generation of rising stars, Mass nearly didn't come to us, because he was unsuccessful in applying to Oxford: '*I remember in that moment, I almost had to start again, because I saw Oxford as being the only route to the Bar. And so as soon as Oxford was not possible, I had completely given up.*'[14]

---

[14] https://www.gresham.ac.uk/watch-now/legal-profession-diversity

When non-traditional applicants do get to the Bar, there is often an unequal distribution of success across specialisms, and that cannot be explained by lack of intelligence or motivation. As Stephen Lue astutely puts it, '*You will see Black barristers excelling in crime, immigration, family law. They are often laudably motivated by a burning desire to address social inequality for vulnerable people, and this is wonderful. BUT we are often absent in the chancery division and in other pure civil areas. This has always bothered me, I am worried that the message from the Bar to aspiring students might be, we are happy for Black lawyers to handle the criminals, the immigrants and broken families, but the big money stuff you should leave to the CLEVER people.*'

We need to break down the divide between publicly funded legal aid work and the better remunerated private sector – the commercial Bar. I have talked about the important work of Brie and her colleagues in the previous chapter. Black inclusion in the commercial Bar is now a headline action point. The commercial Bar, the Chancery Bar Association and the Technology and Construction Bar Association, together with members of the Specialist Bar Associations (SBAs), collaborated in an enquiry to tackle racial inequality. The scope of their enquiry and the calibre of evidence was genuinely groundbreaking. In 2022, 'The Specialist Commercial Bar & Black Inclusion: First Steps' report, discussed earlier in this book, made 17 recommendations.[15] Examples include:

- *Outreach*: SBAs develop an introduction to the Specialist Commercial Bar programme for Year 12 and 13 students (this echoes my assertion that we need to get to potential candidates earlier than at university).
- *Recruitment*: SBAs should proactively collaborate with existing groups already supporting aspirant barristers of Black heritage seeking pupillages at the Specialist Commercial Bar.

---

[15] The Commercial Bar Association, 'The Specialist Commercial Bar & Black Inclusion: First Steps', April 2022, https://www.chba.org.uk/for-members/library/consultations/consultation-responses/black-inclusion-group-final-report.pdf/view

- *Retention*: SBAs should ensure the fair allocation of opportunities (particularly junior briefs), which are likely to enhance career development and progression, provide regular mentoring and sponsorship opportunities for Black juniors with leading practitioners in their practice areas, and arrange workshops with the editors of each of the principal legal directories concerning the Bar, to address under-representation.
- *Progression*: SBAs should provide focused mentoring programmes and sponsorship opportunities for junior Black practitioners contemplating applications for silk and judicial appointments; and hold annual events explaining to practitioners the evidence required to support a positive reference for the KC Selection Panel.
- *Culture*: SBAs need to facilitate Black practitioners networking together and consider when planning all initiatives and events whether there is an opportunity to encourage senior white barristers to engage proactively with supporting the inclusion, retention and progression of Black practitioners.

We should demand more transparency from the commercial sets about their recruitment policies and diversity and initiative drives. They have the funds that legal aid sets do not to offer funded scholarships or mini pupillages to overcome access blocks. Trying to find commercial sets that do offer scholarships, mini pupillages, mentoring schemes or marshalling opportunities is exhausting and demoralising. If I cannot find them, and if those I have asked to do the legal research can't either, then how is a council estate kid going to find them from a base point of zero knowledge? They will not. In my view we have not done enough to hold non-diverse chambers to account. They have let sets with a social conscience and the Bar Council take the strain for them. They are allowed to get away with inaction, not exposed nor shamed into explanation for inaction. The Inns have awards and are to be congratulated on how many they offer and the purpose behind them. But how many chambers offer their own? If not awards, then what of community initiatives – professional investment of time if not chambers' finance? It is the collective responsibility of the Bar to act, not a duty to be shouldered by legal aid sets, or those non-legal aid colleagues who have a social conscious.

And what of intersectionality? We should not define a person by their gender, colour or sexuality alone, or indeed any of the single qualities that make up the whole person. What if you are a person of colour and gay and neurodivergent? How many barriers do you have to break down to feel accepted and seen as you are?

Being out and proud at the Bar

As Simon Rowbotham, a barrister at 4PB, said when proclaiming the launch of the Middle Temple LGBTQIA+ Forum back in 2019 as its Vice Chair:

> Unlike the first woman or the first (GEM) barrister admitted to the Bar, there will never be a record of the first gay man or woman, the first bisexual or the first trans person to be called by the Inn. Of course, that's not to say their names are not contained in our archives: LGBTQIA+ people have always existed and, arguably, just as London has always been a queer city (to quote Peter Ackroyd's *Queer City: Gay London from the Romans to the present day* (Chatto & Windus, 2017)) so indeed have the hallowed grounds of the Temple.[16]

Simon rang in the changes made by the Bar and the Inns since the devastating report of Marc Mason and Dr Stephen Vaughan at University College London back in 2017. 'Sexuality at the Bar: An Empirical Exploration into the Experiences of LGBT+ Barristers in England & Wales'[17] found that of the 126 survey respondents (98 male and 28 female), just over half of the survey respondents had experienced some form of discrimination at work or in their professional studies on account of their sexuality. One-third had experienced some form of bullying. Some 26.5 per cent said they had experienced sexuality-linked discrimination 'sometimes', 'often' or 'frequently' and 25.6 per cent experienced such discrimination

---

[16] https://www.legal500.com/fivehundred-magazine/the-bar/theres-never-been-a-better-time-to-be-LGBTQIA+-at-the-bar/

[17] https://papers.ssrn.com/sol3/papers.cfm?abstract_id=3043790

'rarely' (47.9 per cent said 'never'). More recent figures gathered by the Bar Council in 2023 emphasise that LGBTQIA+ barristers continue to experience greater levels of bullying and harassment, with 38 per cent reporting this compared with 28 per cent of heterosexual barristers. The same trend is found in experiences of discrimination, with 22 per cent of LGBTQIA+ barristers reporting discrimination compared with 16 per cent of heterosexual barristers.[18]

Simon talked of the 'catalytic impact' the work of Vaughan and Mason had on the Bar, most notably for the Inns. Each now have LGBTQIA+Forums (or equivalent) for a start. As Simon explained, the Forum exists *because there is absolutely no excuse why now, today, any student should exist under the misimpression that to be LGBTQIA+ in any way disqualifies them from succeeding in this profession, whether they are the youngest member of the Bar or aim to become the most senior justice of the Supreme Court. We would be lying if we were to tell them that they will not face any discrimination or hate, or that there are no colleagues who remain ignorant and on the wrong side of history. But the dinosaurs are facing extinction, and their fossils will soon be confined to the dustbin of bigoted history. We cannot magic away the prejudices that many of our members may still face in everyday life, especially those students who will return to countries less liberal than our own. But we can make sure that their interaction with this Inn is one that is not simply neutral, but positively affirmative: success at the Bar comes from being who you are, not what anyone else thinks you ought to be.*

Back then Simon said '*[s]uccess at the Bar comes from being who you are, not what anyone else thinks you ought to be*', but reinterviewed in 2021 for *Counsel* on the progress made since the Vaughan report, Simon was perhaps a little less euphoric: 'The conclusions are mixed, with the general trend in a happy direction notwithstanding a lack of cohesive initiatives from the central bodies.'[19] He makes the powerful point that 'the visibility of LGBTQIA+ membership in the

---

[18] Bar Council, 'Bullying, Harassment and Discrimination at the Bar', December 2023, https://www.barcouncil.org.uk/static/5a630b6a-8e91-473f-bfa0cca11b707e42/Bullying-harassment-and-discrimination-at-the-Bar-December-2023.pdf

[19] https://www.counselmagazine.co.uk/articles/are-we-nearly-there-yet-

profession has never been higher but there is work yet to be done, not least where reports continue of homophobia and transphobia. There is also room for leadership, particularly where queer voices do not speak as one; the 2019 schism within Stonewall and the establishment of the LGB Alliance involved members of the Bar in a very public way. ... LGBTQIA+ groups should not be left to do the heavy lifting; we are all stakeholders in this profession and the issues that face the LGBTQIA+ Bar require solutions from everyone, queer and Allies alike.'

When checking back with Simon for his take on where we are now, he was full of praise for the '*amazing piece of work*' that is the LGBTQIA+ Charter[20] with so many chambers now signed up. The charter 'aims to guide organisations in implementing best practice with regards to LGBTQIA+ inclusion, allowing them to demonstrate to potential applicants and clients that they are (or are working towards becoming) an LGBTQIA+ inclusive organisation'.[21] As it explains, 'the Charter is a checklist of basic steps which we believe are practical and meaningful. By publicising that they have taken those steps, organisations will send out an important message that they are welcoming to LGBTQIA+ people'.[22] Its principles are clearly set out. Those organisations who sign up to the charter make the following 11 commitments:

1. We are an LGBTQIA+ inclusive and welcoming organisation. We welcome all people, regardless of sexual orientation or gender identity.
2. We always challenge LGBTQIA+ phobic language or behaviour, whether from anyone in our organisation, or directed at anyone in our organisation from anyone dealing with our organisation.
3. [We will ensure that by *DATE* our]/[Our] *(delete as appropriate)* recruitment materials, website and other marketing materials are LGBTQIA+ inclusive including allowing everyone individually identified in those materials to choose their own pronouns, while using only gender-neutral language to refer to people generally.

---

[20] https://freebar.co.uk/resources/the-freebar-charter/
[21] https://freebar.co.uk/resources/the-freebar-charter/
[22] https://freebar.co.uk/resources/the-freebar-charter/

4. [We will ensure that by DATE our]/[Our] *(delete as appropriate)* internal policies and governing rules and procedures use only gender-neutral language, do not discriminate on LGBT+ grounds and are explicitly inclusive of those who identify as LGBTQIA+.
5. We have a policy on transitioning at work applicable and available to everyone in the organisation.
6. [We will ensure that by DATE there]/[There] *(delete as appropriate)* is a gender-neutral option for all toilet and other facilities we offer (including for people with impaired mobility), for which all the signage is gender-neutral.
7. [We will ensure that by DATE our]/[Our] *(delete as appropriate)* IT and other systems allow for non-binary pronouns and we respect everyone's choice of their own pronouns.
8. Our recruitment and selection processes are designed to encourage LGBTQIA+ applicants and to reduce the risk of bias and discrimination against LGBTQIA+ candidates. When placing and drafting recruitment adverts, we take particular care that they will come to the attention of talented LGBTQIA+ applicants and we encourage LGBTQIA+ applicants. We will not use recruitment agencies who do not share our values.
9. [We will ensure that by DATE everyone]/[Everyone] *(delete as appropriate)* involved in managing or overseeing our selection processes has had recruitment equality training which included LGBTQIA+ issues.
10. We have in our organisation people who publicly identify as LGBTQIA+ and/or LGBTQIA+ allies. We encourage LGBTQIA+ people in our organisation to apply for judicial and similar career-advancing appointments. We have designated members of staff and/or barristers for LGBTQIA+ people to go to with any concerns. We bring to the attention of everyone in our organisation and joining our organisation the LGBTQIA+ networks that exist more widely for barristers and all who work with them. We have/we would welcome the establishment of an LGBTQIA+ network in our organisation.
11. We welcome scrutiny of our compliance with this FreeBar Charter. We check, report publicly on, and monitor that at least annually. We are proud of and promote our compliance

including on our website, including by displaying this charter and the FreeBar Charter Mark.[23]

One of the things I find so remarkable about this charter is that it acknowledges an evolving process of adjustment may be required – it 'allows organisations to demonstrate to potential applicants and clients that they are (or are working towards becoming) an LGBTQIA+ inclusive organisation'. Those words in parenthesis are really welcoming. This is a charter that invites collaboration – such an important message – it is deliberately inclusionary. It anticipates a staged process of engagement and guides chambers through it. For straight people like me, who want to know best how to support my LGBTQIA+ colleagues, being able to ask questions and learn how not to undermine (or, god forbid, offend) them is important. We all have hidden biases, and some blatant ones. We need to spot those ingrained ways of thinking in ourselves and others and learn how to challenge them constructively.

Stephen Lue is a perfect gentleman (in every sense of the word) who represents the best of the Bar. Stephen, who is Jamaican/Chinese, gay and neurodivergent, says '*I have often been left with the feeling by some of my white colleagues that no matter how many hallowed institutions I thrive in, I will always be seen as an outsider. Some of my white colleagues have communicated to me that no matter what I achieve, my racial background precludes me from being, truly middle class. Because inherent in a genuine middle-class experience is whiteness. For some of my Black colleagues I am the gay one, and for some of my gay colleagues I am the Black one.*'

Being open about who you are as a person matters, because it adds to all the skills and life experiences one can draw upon for a client. Stephen recounts his experience of representing a trans woman during his pupillage: '*Being LGBTQIA+ didn't mean that I was able to magic up a defence over and above what another barrister could. But it did mean that I could put her at ease. ... It was not about getting her to escape punishment, it was about her feeling like she was treated with dignity.*'

Stephen made a difference by being who he is. That has taken courage. He has walked his own path: '*All the Inns were dismayed when*

---

[23] https://freebar.co.uk/resources/the-freebar-charter/

a survey was put out in Counsel magazine a year or so ago revealing the fact that many LGBT members of the Bar felt very unsupported and unhappy. I have also heard stories of pupils not wishing to be "out" during pupillage but that they would only do so once they obtained tenancy.'

I will let Stephen's words speak for themselves about the importance of being oneself at the Bar: '*I matured into celebrating my entire identity and personhood, and my journey has shown me how everything that I am gives me strengths rather than weakness to make up for. Now they are added strings to my bow that I can deploy in connecting with my clients, the issues in my cases and in networking with my professional and lay clients.*'

We need more role models that that can advertise what we are proud of at the Bar. We have the FreeBar to promote LGBTQIA+ equality and inclusion, connecting LGBTQIA+ people and allies to provide a forum for mutual support. Scrolling though the visibility list is inspiring and a delight.[24]

For my part, to see my friends and colleagues in the roll call, Stephen alongside Brie, Nick Allen KC, Dr Chelvan and Liz Isaacs KC, alongside pupils, practice managers and clerks is inspiring, while for others it may be life-changing and liberating. We have so many more names to celebrate. There is the gloriously flamboyant Oscar Davies who, at just 2018 call, has burst onto the Bar's multicoloured rainbow life with sass and courage. In 2020 they were confident enough to professionally use the title 'Mx' in court. By 2024 Oscar had been named a 'LGBTQIA++ Champion of the Year' alongside being ranked as a rising star in the Legal 500 rankings.[25] They have collected many accolades for their work in court for vulnerable parties as well as their activism. Oscar (they/them) is the first publicly recognised non-binary barrister in the UK. Oscar is someone who, in all aspects of their working and personal life, acts to promote inclusivity, equity and representation, not just in the legal field but across all sectors of society. Just today I watched a couple of wonderful posts on LinkedIn of Oscar delivering a 'Know Your Rights' series covering trans rights and another with Owen putting on their make up, bewigged and begowned, as a 'get ready

---

[24] https://freebar.co.uk/visibility/
[25] Oscar is at Garden Court Chambers and practices in public law, human rights, employment, employment, housing and education law.

with me' post. That was simply glorious. More Oscars please. Being visible and vocal matters.

4PB created the Alan Inglis Memorial Essay Prize in 2024 as an opportunity to honour Alan's contributions to the LGBTQIA+ community. Alan was a much adored and respected door tenant at 4PB and widely known as an LGBTQIA+ advocate, Alan passed away in August 2023. His memory lives on for many. This prize is one way of honouring those who paved the way for others to shine as their true selves.

There was a wonderful celebration on 26 June 2025 called 'Pride in Practice';[26] a landmark cross-profession LGBTQIA+ Pride event, jointly hosted by the four Inns of Court, the Bar Council and Law Society of England and Wales at Inner Temple. This collaboration marks a continued commitment to inclusivity, visibility and unity across the legal world and will provide an opportunity to connect with colleagues, allies and trailblazers from every corner of the legal profession. It included addresses from Barbara Mills KC, Chair of the Bar and Ian Jeffery, CEO of the Law Society, and with a special performance by the Pink Singers, Europe's longest-running LGBTQIA+ choir. The event 'honoured the contributions and resilience of LGBTQIA+ people in law and reaffirm[ed] our shared commitment to equality and justice' and expressly said: 'Whether you're an LGBTQIA+ identifying barrister, judge, solicitor, student, pupil, trainee solicitor or an ally – you belong here.' How joyous.

My roll call of FreeBar heroes must obviously include Master Victoria McCloud, as currently therein described,[27] she being the first transgender judge to be appointed. In that entry McCloud describes a breakthrough moment for inclusivity:

> I was called to the Bar in 1995 and somewhat later it was openly made clear that gay and lesbian people hoping to be judges should not feel obliged to declare their sexuality under the heading of a matter which might embarrass the Lord Chancellor. It was for me a very welcome signal of 'permission to be'. Sometimes the saying of

---

[26] https://www.lincolnsinn.org.uk/whats-on/pride-in-practice/
[27] https://freebar.co.uk/visibility/master-mccloud/

something is necessary to make it feel real. ... Invisibility and disempowerment, so often self imposed, are evil twins. I think that we must always remind ourselves of the need to stay visible and to believe and encourage others to believe that where the will to be our genuine selves is strong, the future often follows confidently in its footsteps.

It was all the more depressing then that in April 2024[28] McCloud, decided to quit after 'toilet politics and death threats' left her feeling she could not continue to sit. She was the first transgender woman on the judiciary, and at the age of 40 was the youngest person appointed a master of the Queen's (now King's) Bench Division of the High Court. But after 18 years' service, pre-retirement age, she has left, feeling unwelcome and isolated, and her position made 'untenable' because 'politicians and others incorrectly cast being trans as a "lifestyle choice or an ideology"'. What a loss to the Bench. In interview with Catherine Baksi of the *Times* she says that in the past she has encouraged other transgender individuals to become lawyers and judges, but now it would be 'much harder' for a transgender person to become a barrister and 'impossible' for anyone to become a judge, advising anyone considering it to 'proceed with caution'.[29]

Behind the judicial corridor change is afoot if reading the regular *D & I Newsletter* is a reliable barometer of mood. Two years ago the LGBTQ+ Judges Association was created and July 2025 saw a celebration of Pride month with a blog introducing the LGBTQ+ working group of the Judicial Diversity Committee with the four members of the group introducing themselves and their plans for the year ahead. However, how widely shared this presence and work is outside the judicial circuit is harder to establish.

I would suggest that whether we are talking Bar or Bench we need to travel further on the road to full LGBTQIA+ visibility.

---

[28] https://www.thetimes.co.uk/article/toilet-politics-and-death-threats-why-transgender-judge-victoria-mccloud-quit-pk27h83bf
[29] https://www.thetimes.com/uk/law/article/toilet-politics-and-death-threats-why-transgender-judge-victoria-mccloud-quit-pk27h83bf

The annual July Pride in London march is always a calendar date to mark. The Bar has its own banner headlined 'Fighting for equality under the rule of law'. Members march with the Law Society and FreeBar LGBTQIA+. They are a visible contingent, wearing a mixture of purple legal Pride t-shirts and full barristers' regalia. They look glorious. Those images are joyful. But such support, symbolic though it is, cannot be a once-a-year pledge. Being Proud during Pride month is not the beginning and end of our duty to be inclusive at the Bar. We should not rainbow-wash the Bar by hoisting a rainbow flag.

Where are our diversity role models?

HHJ Khatun Sapnara (Bengali: খাতুন সাপনারা) has led the way for women of colour, and fought battles on their behalf, for the entirety of her professional career. Khatun, a former colleague at the family Bar at Coram Chambers, my friend for decades, is now an acclaimed Bangladeshi-born British judge. As a child, Khatun left her village in Sylhet District, East Pakistan (now Bangladesh) and arrived in the UK in the wake of the turmoil of the Bangladeshi liberation struggle. She attended state schools in Essex, where she learned to speak English. She graduated with an LLB (Hons) from the London School of Economics. Khatun helped establish a new set of barristers' chambers in Bethnal Green in 1991 at the top of Brick Lane. This was a radical sister set politically to Tooks Court, where I was based along with Wellington Street and Garden Court where colleagues also set out their principled passionate stalls as barristers. Brick Lane chambers was the first set of chambers in London outside the rarefied legal preserve of the Inns of Court, and its members offered its premises and services to community organisations in East London. Khatun later joined Coram Chambers, specialising in family law. Khatun has continued to blaze a trail for women of colour. In 2006, she was appointed a Recorder of the Crown Court, becoming the first person of Bangladeshi origin in a senior judicial position. In 2014, she was appointed as a Circuit Judge to hear cases in the Crown and Family Court. She was appointed by the Lord Chief Justice as a Diversity Community Relations Judge and a Judicial Role Model. She was appointed as Senior Circuit Judge, Designated Family Judge, based at the Central Family Court, with effect from 11 October

2024. She also sits as a Deputy High Court Judge. Her community work continues unabated. Khatun's dedication to charitable causes is evident in her long history of serving on the boards of various charitable organisations. Khatun is a powerhouse of a woman – once met, never forgotten.

The work that HHJ Anuja Dhir KC does to promote inclusivity and diversity is as extraordinary as Anuja is. Anuja was the first non-white barrister to be appointed to sit full-time at the Old Bailey in 2017 after 23 years at the Bar (taking silk in 2010).[30] She is rightly proud of her Indian/Scottish heritage and speaks openly of her challenging journey to the Bar coming from a background which didn't expect that to be a path her life would take. Social, educational and professional mobility is something Anuja had to negotiate. Anuja is generous of her time outside of work and explores every avenue to make the law an accessible career for those who come from disadvantaged, non-traditional Bar backgrounds. What makes Anuja stand out isn't simply her professional accomplishments but her warmth and humbleness. Not all champions for change need to come across as formidable warriors – kindness and approachability are just as effective. I am very proud to have met Anuja through a diversity at work event and then through Brie, a woman who makes it her mission to bring passionate, principled women together.

As of January 2025, we welcomed Barbara Mills KC, who I highlighted in earlier sections (in particular in the discussion of intersectionality) as our first Black chair of the Bar. She represents a beacon of hope and achievement nationally and internationally. Barbara is a woman of principle and huge ability. We have a role model who we can look up to, learn from and be inspired by.

What can we do to make sure that Barbara has brothers and sisters in spirit and colleagues of colour to stand alongside and follow her as she advances further up the career ladder (as she will surely do)?

We have role models within Sikhs in Law, founded in 2020 by the far-sighted Baldip Singh. As Baldip said in an interview for *Counsel* in June 2024:[31]

---

[30] https://en.wikipedia.org/wiki/Anuja_Dhir
[31] https://www.counselmagazine.co.uk/articles/sikhs-in-law

> [W]hile the Bar has come some way in addressing diversity and inclusion challenges, in many ways it has become even harder to pinpoint discrimination and unspoken biases ... with hundreds of years of unsociable working hours, a drinking culture and old boys' network, a number of groups carved out a space within the Bar in order to preserve their religious and cultural identities. Sikhs in Law emphasises four core values of honesty, integrity, fairness and humility as set out by the Sikh gurus. Sikh values and customs are preserved in a safe space, with an emphasis on events which are free from alcohol and meat. We also put on family-friendly events. By not asking our members to choose between career development events and spending time with the family, the Association actively encourages and promotes family life. Sharan Kaur Bhachu, Master of Advocacy at the Association and a family barrister at 42BR, is a strong advocate of this particular aspect. As a mother to three girls, she often has to balance the needs of life as a Mum against that of a successful barrister. Being able to attend events with her husband and children, bringing them into the world of the Bar, is a significant factor in balancing these difficult and competing worlds.

Sikhs in Law has, among its appointed number, many a person who are role models in their own right; Baldip, Sharan and Mani Singh Basi[32] are three who take the lead for others to follow.

We have young women already making their children and families proud of everything they bring to the Bar as young mothers and carers. Emma Hughes is a role model, not just as a young mother but also as a young carer. As Emma explains: '*I was a carer for my late uncle who suffered with dementia. I truly understood the need for a reasoned,*

---

[32] https://www.4pb.com/barristers/mani-basi/; Mani is a man of many accolades, including Legal Personality of the Year 2024, Legal Aid Barrister of the Year 2024 and Junior Barrister of the Year 2024, among many others.

thoughtful advocate when someone loses their litigation capacity.' Emma brings all those skills to her workplace for her clients.

We have role models who 'own their past' without shame and bring the richness of their experience into the courtroom. I am thinking of Shelly Glaister-Young again, for, as she writes to me:

> I know now, from the work I do, the impact on children of having parents who are emotionally unavailable through mental ill health. I know first-hand what it means to be the rope in the tug of war and have the police at your door to calm your parents and ask you to somehow proffer the impossible solution that all adults will agree to. I not only understand why I react to people and stressors in the way I sometimes do, but I also understand, intimately, the value of supportive adults and sibling relationships, all of which underlines the importance of what I do and my need to do it.

Shelly is an icon for many at the bar with her facial piercings and body armour tattoos. She plays with and takes risks with her image – she rocks it.

The way to welcome candidates to make the Bar inclusive and diverse is not rocket science – we can share our histories on professional platforms, we can speak at events, we can mentor. Through the involvement I have in charities like Bridging the Bar, Speakers for Schools or organisations such as Young Legal Aid Lawyers I can see shoals of talent swimming in my direction. But they cannot travel without hope, and one has to be ready to lean in and scoop them out of the incurrent before it ebbs.

It is incredibly important that, if we see there is a gap between our chambers' composition and the society we live in and serve, to at least demonstrate an awareness of that imbalance on our chambers' portals and make our welcome clear. Not just with words but with evidence-based examples of what we are doing to try to redress the imbalance. We might have a section on journeys to the Bar, for example – something to break down misimpressions that might emerge from a photo and educational biog alone, and whatever chambers may or may not do *we* can make a difference. We can go public on social media, LinkedIn articles for the profession and the public about what we want for the Bar and how we embrace others in that journey. We can take a platform, or support those who already do it, in debates.

We cannot change the past of the Bar, but we can, and should, do all we can to challenge, change and curate its future.

Disability at the Bar

Do I have a disability? Apparently so. Aged 59, I found out. It was a revelation.

Neurodiversity and my experience

In 2022, 'Resolution', the community for family justice professionals, held its national conference, at which I gave the keynote speech, sharing the mic with District Judge Howard Kemp. We were given free rein to address what lessons had arisen for us out of the COVID-19 pandemic. I chose to talk about the benefits and pitfalls of remote working, and the emerging awareness of how this can impact neurodiversity. I am known for publicly raising issues around recruitment, retention and progression at the Bar, but this was new territory, and difficult to find a path through when I had few examples around me to illustrate and amplify what I wanted to say. Nonetheless, I spoke openly about the need to destigmatise neurodivergence, and my emerging awareness of how undiagnosed ADHD, dyscalculia and dyslexia may have affected me. My awareness of my condition was awakened by one of my children, who as an adult had been diagnosed during the pandemic as being autistic and as having ADHD. I wanted to send out the message that inclusivity of those with neurodiversity (which may not always be diagnosed) matters for the future health of the legal profession, and that we need to be alert to (sometimes false) preconceptions of 'normality' versus neurodiversity.

I need not have worried about the reception I would get. During the speech, Twitter (as then) was awash with messages of support. After the conference, I decided that, if I was to be true to my word, if I meant what I said to my child (and the Resolution audience) about not viewing a neurodivergent diagnosis as a 'burden', then I ought to put myself forward for professional assessment to know the psychiatric 'truth' about my own functioning. It almost didn't matter if I was or was not identified as neurodivergent as a result – it was about demonstrating, by being prepared to put myself in the psychiatric arena for analysis, that there was nothing to be ashamed of in saying 'Am I?' and, if so, then 'Hello' to learning more about the way my brain functions. As someone used to reading psychiatric and psychological reports and questioning the authors on them, it was curious to be on the receiving end of questions. It made one appreciate the vulnerability, the exposure of oneself and one's past, that we routinely ask of parents in proceedings. As matters turned out, the outcome was clear. I was diagnosed with ICD-11, 6AO5.2 Attention Deficit Hyperactivity Disorder, Combined Presentation (symptoms of inattentiveness and hyperactivity/impulsivity). It is a classification that falls within a defined disability.

With the support of *Counsel*'s editors, Elsa Booth and Sarah Grainger (who have been in the vanguard of constructive, educative debate through their work in this publication for many a year), I went into print with my psychiatric diagnosis. They put me on the cover, getting the message, literally headlined, front and centre, out to our profession, barristers and the judiciary alike.

The editors headlined this 'Taking the Neurological Lead'.[33] *Counsel* enabled me to make my diagnosis public because, as I said within its covers, 'one has to lead by example if I say there should be no stigma attached to being neurodivergent at the Bar'. Stigma and silence around neurodiversity in wider society is present in the Bar's history and culture, but ignorance about its prevalence is exacerbated by our isolated working practices. As self-employed practitioners, while we join forces when working collectively via chambers, we are rarely together physically; moreover, remote working or hot desking is the new norm, and we move from case to case in different parts of the country with different colleagues. Isolated working practices mean that barristers create their own work adjustments or coping strategies, honed over years, which become their 'normal'. As a result, we are not very good at recognising, let alone applauding, the things that make us different.

---

[33] https://www.counselmagazine.co.uk/articles/taking-the-neurologi cal-lead-professor-jo-delahunty-kc

Figure 7.2: *Counsel* magazine cover, 'Taking the Neurological Lead', March 2023

Source: © *Counsel* magazine

When the COVID-19 pandemic forced me to go paperless, I realised just how rigid my case preparation process was. It was a struggle to make the transition, particularly in the context of what I now know to be my ADHD experience. The need to change to be able to work effectively digitally forced me to deconstruct my prep technique. Marking up papers by flagging them up in a tab or colour format only I could understand was a winning process ingrained into my silk DNA: paper, working on it physically, was my intellectual 'comfort blanket'. Looking back, I can now see it as instinctual adjustment to a neurodivergent me. When I looked for people to talk to about neurodiversity at the Bar, I found very few discussing it openly at my practice level and I could not believe this to be representative of reality. I felt it needed to be brought into the open for discussion. I was asked by my Resolution interviewer, '*Did your work on bullying at the Bar inspire you to highlight neurodiversity, with the aim of forging a more inclusive and accepting culture?*' Good question. Having already broached other uncomfortable topics for the Bar, it seemed right to discuss this one – to start a conversation around it.

We pride ourselves on our individuality at the self-employed Bar. The Bar welcomes individuality: it is what marks us out for instruction. My skill set is different to that of my peers, and that is in part due to my ADHD. Neurodiversity manifests itself in many ways – I now know that my ADHD screams out in my way of working. My brain is an intrusive, noisy, busy, hectic organ, and the only way to switch it off is to do something that absolutely engrosses (simultaneously) eye, hand and brain (silver smithing, throwing pots, drawing) and crowds out intrusive work thoughts. It also explains my very particular case prep methods. My ADHD means that I hyperfocus – I concentrate intensely for long periods of time, working for hours without pause, not breaking to go to the loo or get a cup of tea. I zone out from the outside world and its distractions. My brain is at its best at these times. I can make intellectual and conceptual leaps between facts: they literally move, like some mental mind game, from their place in the papers written by others, to the place they will find in the case as I reframe it. My ADHD means I am massively motivated by short deadlines and short-term goals like trial performance. That works with my court-based life as a barrister, and performance life as a public speaker. I now know that 'hyperfocus' often happens if the individual is doing a job that they enjoy and find interesting. While hyperfocusing, the person can improve their performance, meaning they work even more efficiently. This process allows them to complete a task without any distractions, and the outcome is often of great quality. I would like to think that's the case with me.

If one in seven people might be neurodivergent, my point is that the perception of the Bar (and of the skills needed to be a part of it) needs to change to fit reality. We can and should recognise that many of our ways of working are already suited to varying neurodivergences; that we are already here, just quiet or (as I was for many years) oblivious to our neurodivergence and neurodivergent needs. We can publicise this variety, diversity and flexibility. I have taken the platform for Bridging the Bar on many a stage to make the point that having a disability or fearing one is neurodivergent is nothing to be ashamed about. In 2025 I created the Prof Delahunty KC BTB Essay prize and asked entrants to 'consider the legal framework and practice guidance that the UK has in place to accommodate the needs of neurodiverse individuals in legal proceedings. Does it achieve its aims? Discuss'. It came with a £500 prize. Handing the award over this year at the graduation ceremony was a delight for me as much as I hope it was for the winner, Monique Fremder.

We need, each year, to get the message out to the new hopefuls who do not know what they can and cannot express of their needs. By doing that we promote reasonable adjustments, acceptance and understanding of neurodiversity. I hope that my openness about my diagnosis is a demonstration of how being neurodivergent is nothing to hide. I hope it shows that a person with ADHD or other neurodivergent condition can be successful in the legal world. I hope it will encourage others to learn about it, to be open-minded about it, and for colleagues with ADHD and other neurodivergent conditions to be proud of themselves and more confident to 'go public' with it, should they wish. I wish for those with neurodiversity to unashamedly see the skills they have to offer because of it, and to know they can add value to the Bar by claiming it and not hiding. I want to challenge the preconceptions and myths of what it takes to work at the Bar. We should all feel able to bring our authentic selves to work (and wider society) without fear of criticism or adverse judgement. When completing my Bar Council data for the mandatory certification and accreditation process – for the first time since being called to the Bar in 1986 – I entered 'yes' against the question 'Do you have a disability?'. That was a powerful moment. I OWNED my disability. It is important that it is seen and counted.

My neurodiversity does not make me a 'better' barrister. It makes me JDKC, and I am successful as JDKC. Being diagnosed as neurodivergent late in life is becoming far more common, particularly for women who do not 'present' in a stereotypical way and are extremely skilled and self-taught 'maskers' or 'mimics' due to their powerful observational abilities. I am acutely aware that I now have the privilege of being firmly established in my field. I have status, authority and accolades. It is far less of a challenge for me to be open about my own ADHD and see what response that brings, than it is for an aspiring pupil or junior barrister just starting out to speak about their status.

The reality of this was illustrated (in April 2024 and March 2025) by anonymous articles in *Counsel*,[34] the first written by a junior autistic barrister, the second a junior ADHD barrister. Both pose salutary questions about how inclusive the Bar is.

In the first article, X, describes how they were open to their chambers about their diagnosis of autism, in an attempt to explain its impact on their capacity to cope with a colleague's conduct towards them. Rather than their disability being accepted and supported, they found that it was ignored in practice, at best, misunderstood and maligned, at worst. Their distress was so profound that they contemplated suicide. As they eloquently write:

> My rumination went into overdrive, and I had to take time off sick. I was having panic attacks at court, barely concentrating on paperwork, and avoiding chambers in case I ran into the barristers who had so utterly invalidated my experiences and damaged my self-worth. In May 2022, I went on holiday to escape. After spending most of the week considering whether to jump off the hotel balcony, I realised I needed to leave chambers or the damage to my health might be permanent. So, I moved chambers, and it has been a revelation. When I disclosed my autism, they actually asked me what reasonable adjustments might

---

[34] https://www.counselmagazine.co.uk/articles/valuing-autism-in-chambers

assist. Then they put them into action. For example, unpredictability stresses me out, so I have an allocated desk instead of hot-desking, and an arrangement always to be emailed rather than telephoned. I was invited (but not pressurised) to address chambers on my personal experiences as an autistic barrister, so that members could learn more. And when I mentioned an accessibility issue that impacted my participation in tribunal hearings, multiple members rallied round and, collectively, took action on my behalf.

Firstly, and unfortunately, it shows the Bar has a long way to go before it is truly inclusive of neurodivergence. ... Secondly, and more positively, my story proves it does not always have to be like that. ... My autism does not stop me being an effective barrister; other people's attitude to it nearly did. If your current practice environment is holding you back, seek a new one. I am proof things can be better.

Well said.

In the second article, published April 2025,[35] the author was writing during Neurodiversity week, and their story made painful reading.

She writes after her diagnosis aged 38 and 15 years call, and after describing it as self-revelatory and self-validating, continues poignantly that it

> made me unutterably sad. It was difficult not to look back on my life and wonder what I might have been able to achieve if I'd been diagnosed earlier. Part of me wanted to contact all those who had been witness to my previous screw-ups, waving my diagnosis like an alibi: 'Look! There's an explanation! It wasn't my fault!' – but that would not solve things. While I am close with the solicitor who first nudged me towards diagnosis, she is the only client of mine who I have told. The reasons for this will be obvious to others at the Bar: it

---

[35] https://www.counselmagazine.co.uk/articles/adhd-barrister-

is a competitive arena, and much as we like to think we live in a world that is understanding of disabilities, I'd be a fool to let myself believe that clients are lining up to instruct a disorganised barrister who struggles with deadlines and misses emails.

She then talks about the (literal) cost of her condition with a frankness that is courageous and sad:

> In some ways, the Bar is a good fit for me. New cases and the flexibility of combined practice areas mean I haven't given in to the impulse to suddenly change career, which is common in those with ADHD. My dopamine deficiency means I'm great under pressure; and a lifetime of light-speed thinking means I am very good on my feet. But written work does take me longer, so almost all my bills get knocked back or knocked down. I can't explain to my solicitors, or the costs judge, or the LAA, that that advice really did take me 11 hours 46 minutes (I timed it), because I have ADHD. So I take the hit, every time. And the stress of the compensating measures I take to mask my ADHD adds up. The extra load I carry is not limited to the physical weight of my over-stuffed handbag.

Her final words are profound:

> The data show that neurodiversity is severely underdiagnosed, particularly in women. Since finding out more about it, I've often noticed traits of it in others at work. I wonder whether they have been diagnosed and, like me, choose to keep it to themselves – or whether, like the me of years gone by, they feel a sense that there is some unspecified and shameful thing wrong with them. It is partly for that reason that I'm writing this: to encourage others to find out more, and seek a diagnosis. While we don't yet live in a world where neurodiversity is unremarkable and accommodated, I hope we can at least stop beating

ourselves up in the interim. For me, at least, it has been far better to know.

Going into print by each junior took courage but their experiences show we have far to go and evidence how much easier it is for seniors to speak up for them, and that is what we must continue to do and what others should do. We must Set the Bar for others.

Physical disability

We can and should celebrate the likes of the young people who set up Bringing [Dis]Ability to the Bar (BDABar),[36] a group run by and for disabled aspiring barristers 'working to dismantle barriers affecting disabled aspiring barristers & improve accessibility at the Bar through research, education, mentorships & more!'. BDABar has initiated a two-way mentorship scheme offering 'the mutual benefit of a barrister mentor who can support as aspiring disabled barrister in their passage at the bar whilst giving them the benefit of lived insight into how to manage disability'. The posts of Konstantina Nouka aka @wigonwheels, founder and chair of BDABar, posts with clarity, intelligence, wit and style about her journey to the Bar and also the sheer physicality of it. When Konstantina talks of her 'journey' she takes us through the access issues that bedevil her working day, from public transport to the court and into the courtroom. Her posts have done more to bring the reality of the thoughtless physical hurdles the fully able-bodied place in the way of those without free movement than any individual I can name.

Consider also how remarkable it is that while a pupil, Charlotte McDonald, with creativity and courage, launched her 'Disability's not a bar' podcast. Charlotte, with her co-creator Haleemah Sadia Farooq, talk passionately about pursuing a career at the bar with a disability and have a guest speaker on each episode sharing insight and advice and raising awareness of issues faced by people with a disability at the Bar and while pursuing a career at the Bar.

Konstantina and Charlotte are resilient, determined ambassadors for disability at the Bar. These young people[37] have already done

---

[36] https://www.bdabar.org/
[37] https://www.bdabar.org/meet-the-team

brilliant work. Notably these are *juniors*, pupils, signposting the way ahead for those in a position of power to change traditional practices.

We also have Neurodiversity in Law,[38] who have a brilliant ethos illustrated by their motto 'No mind left behind'. This organisation was, again, founded by a very young team and launched with a tweet on 8 May 2020. The very medium chosen to launch the organisation was an example of the effortless way the young use social media as a platform – for challenge, inspiration and change. A group of aspiring and qualified legal professionals connected to form a mix of lived experience and allyship, with a common goal: to promote, support and destigmatise neurodivergence in the legal professions. How bloody brilliant is that?

And now, we have a new bright spot to look to for education and inspiration – 'Neorodiversikey', set up by three young people, Charlotte Clewes-Boyne, Danielle Gleicher-Bates and Emma Llanwarne. Already they are winners of the 'Legal Sector Neurodiversity NPO (Not For Profit) 2024', having been finalists in Women and Law Diversity Awards 24 and others. They want to 'unlock understanding' around neurodivergence and neuro-inclusion.

The fact that we have these young organisations already making waves is proof that change, and challenge, can come from the young – as elders, we simply need to see and hear and support them. As we know, words matter, names matter, images matter – but deeds matter even more.

The winds of change

We have some incredible examples of positive affirmative action that demonstrate what can be done by barristers who care enough to make change happen.

Following the Black Lives Matter protests of 2020, bloggers started to investigate historical legal figures, including 18th-century Lord Chancellor Lord Hardwicke for whom Hardwicke Chambers was named. He was found to have been one of two authors of the Yorke-Talbot opinion in 1729, which was relied on by slave owners as providing legal justification for slavery for many years.

---

[38] https://www.neurodiversityinlaw.co.uk/

In response to this, the chambers changed its name to Gatehouse Chambers. Brie, joint head of chambers, explained the motivation behind the name change: '*The discovery of the provenance of our business' name did not sit comfortably with our values as an organisation, or the inclusive and diverse nature of our people and our clients. We have spent many years building up a reputation for excellence, innovation and diversity. We are proud to move forwards with our new name which accords with who we are as an organisation.*' Perhaps we can change the past of the Bar after all.

I have already touched upon the work of Baldip Singh, specialist barrister at No 5 Chambers, a champion of our era who set up and created the Sikhs in Law association.[39] Baldip conceived the Sikhs in Law association in 2020 with the aim of promoting, empowering and recognising Sikhs in the legal profession. It grew to become the largest network of Sikhs in the UK legal profession. Committed to promoting the rule of law and civil liberties while remaining independent and non-political. The inauguration ceremony was held in the Supreme Court in 2023, with Lord Leggatt praising the contribution of prominent Sikhs to the Rule of Law, such as Sir Mota Singh and Lord Justice Rabinder Singh. By 2024, Sikhs in Law had set up its own Sikh Court. I was present at the inauguration of the Council of the Sikh Court in April 2024 as an invited guest. The colour, noise, passion, belief and faith colouring each word of the Ardas as the prayer rang out of Lincolns Inn was truly uplifting. I was truly proud of my friends and colleagues of the family Bar, Baldip, Mani Singh and Sharan Kaur were sworn in as judges. To then be called to be awarded the Panth Seva Award for my services to the community (one of only two non-Sikhs to be honoured) for my championship of neurodiversity, was an honour I had not expected and was overwhelmed to receive especially at such a groundbreaking and august event.

We can clearly look to the likes of Brie Stevens-Hoare KC, Mary Prior KC, Mary Aspinall-Miles, Stephen Lue, Marina Sergides, Colin Wells, Srishti Suresh and Shelly Glaister-Young, Ian McCardle, Mass Ndow Njie, Eve Robinson and the many others who have contributed to the shared goal of this book. They, WE, Set the Bar. But not all my

---

[39] https://sikhsinlaw.co.uk/about-us/

champions are senior barristers, secure in their place at the bar. Emma Hughes is the impressive young woman who, as I write this, is now a tenant in a great family set after a number of patient attempts to gain entry to the Bar. For too long, she felt as though she had to 'make up' for having a child as a very young mum, though Cai is in reality her inspiration and drive in life. I was saddened to learn this, but not surprised. Women who are young mothers will not know if there is anyone in chambers they can see as a role model, as we do not say if we are working mothers or carers. We too rarely see chambers statements of principle and inclusion about respecting applicants who are parents, carers, neurodivergent or disabled. And where are the signs to signal a welcome to immigrant applicants, working-class kids (white or people of colour), those who are neurodiverse, non-binary or disabled? We need to be more open about our individual characteristics and struggles in order to represent a positive example.

So – what should we do and be seen to be doing? Raising awareness is an essential starting point, and please do not accept anyone's assurance that they are not biased in one way or another. We all are. It is crucial for leaders and decision-makers to be aware of their biases to prevent these from influencing business decisions and opinions of colleagues on recruitment. We need to understand what our conscious and unconscious biases are before we can hope to be able to correct them. A culture of awareness is the foundation for change. Practically, we need to demonstrate cultural inclusiveness, such as a place for private prayer, alcohol not always being the norm for work-based socialisation or PR, accessible chambers for those whose mobility requires it. We need paternity policies that work. We need flexible clerks and colleagues when childcare or caring duties impact on our working availability. The task I believe we face is identifying and tackling barriers to equal access and advancement. We need to look at unconscious bias. We need to address power bias and bases (like the Garrick).

We need to Set the Bar higher for action and accountability

What can the Bar Council do?

I cannot praise Sam Mercer highly enough for all the work she has done behind the scenes. She does not work alone. Her work on Spot, on diversity and inclusion, on making the Bar a heathier environment, is too vast to be itemised. Invisible though she may be to the public Sam is a driver for visible change and campaign at and for the Bar working alongside many dedicated committee members, officers, vice chairs and chairs. In summer 2018, the Bar Council launched '#IAmTheBar', a campaign that profiled the experiences of those who have succeeded at the Bar from non-traditional backgrounds, launched to increase social mobility across the Bar and support fair access to the profession. It has run to great acclaim every year since then – a visually attention-grabbing concept, it worked on X and Instagram to perfection, getting to a public not reached by professional publications – great images, short text. Aspirational and inspirational – it is a good start. In 2019 the campaign won the LexisNexis Legal Award in Legal PR and Media Communication for its progress in raising social mobility at the Bar.

Due to the success of the campaign, the Bar Council launched several spin-off series, including I am the Bench in 2018 on X and Instagram, where the judiciary shared their stories to encourage people from diverse backgrounds to apply to the judiciary. HHJ Sandy Canavan detailed her working-class background and pointed to the economic costs as one of the key challenges facing aspiring judges: '[T]he cost of doing a degree and then going on to do Bar Finals undoubtedly puts off a lot of talented but poor kids who don't have the safety net of the bank of Mum and Dad behind them.'[40] Her account sheds light on the significant economic challenges that deter many talented individuals from entering the judiciary.

'Becoming the Bar' in 2021 profiled recent and current pupils from under-represented backgrounds. Adiba Bassam identified that her background as a non-Oxbridge and non-Russell Group student made her feel like she was on the back foot at networking events. While on the Bar Professional Training Course (BPTC) she shared:

---

[40] Spin-off series: I Am the Bench, https://www.barcouncil.org.uk/media-campaigns/campaigns/iamthebar/spin-off-series-i-am-the-bench.html

> It was made clear to me … while I had a first-class degree it was a 'Westminster first' and amounted to less. At careers advice, I was told that I had an interesting American accent, but this could be held against me as it is not typically what barristers sound like. I was also told that I looked quite young. I did not know that my accent or physique would impede my chances of pupillage before this.[41]

Her story underscores the bias and elitism that can create significant obstacles for aspiring barristers.

The latest campaign, I am the Future of the Bar, in partnership with Bridging the Bar, spotlights stories from aspiring barristers. Zahra Dalal, a now commercial barrister, shared: 'As a South-Asian woman looking into a career as a barrister, I was struck by how this lack of diversity was mirrored. My desire to change this intimidating landscape has motivated [me] to become a barrister and stand as a role model for other young women like me.'[42] Her story highlights the need for visible role models and a more inclusive profession to empower future generations.

What can circuits do?

Gather together a pool of recorders and judges who would be willing to have students from non-traditional backgrounds to marshal with them in court so they can see law in action and inspire them to become the next generation of barristers.

What can associations do?

We need to be prepared to identify and challenge the election of speaking parts on the professional stage at conferences and seminars. We want to see mentoring schemes and the success stories from them.

---

[41] Spin-off series: Becoming the Bar, https://www.barcouncil.org.uk/media-campaigns/campaigns/iamthebar/spin-off-series-i-am-the-future-of-the-bar.html

[42] Spin-off series: I Am the Future of the Bar, https://www.barcouncil.org.uk/media-campaigns/campaigns/iamthebar/spin-off-series-i-am-the-future-of-the-bar.html

What can chambers do?

The Western Circuit Women's Forum has suggested some excellent policies in this area.[43] Such as:

- The right to return after a generous period of parental leave – suggested two to three years.
- An extension to the minimum flat rate rent-free period beyond six months – recommends 12 months.
- An option to take all or part of the flat rate rent-free period after returning from parental leave.
- An agreement to limit a returning parent's geographical area of work if requested.
- A requirement for diarised agenda-based meetings to prepare for leave and return.
- Mentoring and wellbeing policies and programmes in addition to parental leave and flexible working policies.
- Arrange and implement reverse mentoring between senior barristers and pupils and juniors from non-traditional background and minority sectors of the Bar.

What can a judge and a silk do?

The initiative by the Supreme Court designed to giving a professional and legal platform to juniors that I discussed in the previous chapter gives real expression to the way in which we can reflect an image of the Bar that is less white and male than the roll call of impressive men we see on our screens and in the law reports. We give way to juniors in cases at appropriate points, we cede the floor to them. The silk is expected to give advance thought to speaking slots and the judge is expected to enquire of them.

What can the court service do?

His Majesty's Courts and Tribunals Service should make the courts accessible to all users (staff, clients and lawyers alike). We need better

---

[43] https://westerncircuit.co.uk/wp-content/uploads/2019/11/wcwfbacktothebarguide-final.pdf

facilities for women and non-binary people at court centres. We need and deserve to have appropriate facilities in place for women who are breast-feeding and for non-binary people.

Concluding remarks

My mantra (you will by now be familiar with it): Diversity matters. Visibility matters. Voices matter.

We need champions for change at the Bar to be visible, vocal and honest about obstacles placed in their path to seniority.

We need more senior men and women to step up to the mark to become activists for change and to call it out when positive action does not follow fine words.

We have talented professionals who are 'out', proud and outspoken. We have men and women of disability and neurodiversity showing us how we can welcome them to the Bar and into our courts. We have GEM men and women raising their voices to speak of what advances have been made and what has yet to be done and how to do it to achieve and deliver equity. We welcome them teaching us about what distinguishes them as individual groups within the outdated BAME acronym. We have to be more specific in our talk and direct in our targets. Men and women can, and should, lead from the top and by example: it is crucial for leaders to be aware of their bias to prevent it from influencing career and workplace decisions and for colleagues to call it out if they are in a state of ignorance. We can acknowledge that we have biases (individual and institutional) which creates a foundation for change. We can raise awareness as a starting point in discussion with colleagues in chambers, in professional associations, in the Inns and with the judiciary. Most importantly, we can offer our time and name by being mentors (or simply by being visible and vocal) to the less senior members of the Bar. It is a non-delegable duty to act.

The guiding principles of our law are justice, fairness and equality. If we believe in them at the Bar and in the judiciary, we should agitate and act to achieve change to ensure that fairness and equality are visibly embodied within our ranks. We must support those who carry the load for us. Being silent is not an option. Letting others take the strain of the campaign for equality and diversity is not good enough. Every senior member of the Bar and judiciary has a responsibility to lead the way. Our juniors are often there before us. We can support them.

The point is, we at the Bar have to set the standards we want for its future health. We Set the Bar, and we have to set it fairly. We have gone beyond the stage of wanting *equality* of opportunity. If we are to Set the Bar, we do not just need, we must demand, *equity* in terms of access, retention and promotion.

8

Is It Worth It?

One sunny Saturday on 15 April 1989, 97 children, women and men went to a football match and did not come home. Liverpool families, whether at the match, watching on TV, listening to it on the radio or hearing the excited chatter in the streets, approached the kick off at 3pm with hope in their hearts and a smile or song on their lips. That all changed at 3.04pm. There was a fatal human crush at Leppings Lane, the Liverpool fans' end, during the match at Hillsborough Stadium. It was televised live. Of those who died, 37 were teenagers, most still at school. Twenty-six of the dead were parents. Some families lost more than one family member. Scores of fans who survived the crush were injured physically, more psychologically than can be accounted for. Attending or not, few, if any, Liverpudlians were left unscarred by the events of that day and its aftermath. Many were traumatised to the point where recovery was impossible. Some found the strength to fight for answers. The families of the bereaved had to fight and wait for 27 years to hear a jury deliver their verdicts on when, why and how their loved ones died.

These are the words of Julie Fallon, sister of Andrew Sefton who died at Hillsborough. Andrew was 23, a Spurs supporter who agreed to drive and go with his Liverpool mates to the FA Cup Final. His friends survived. Julie said:

> Being forever young is something to be desired but there is nothing to be desired for being young forever because you haven't experienced life. I miss what Andrew didn't

become. My mum collapsed as we identified Andrew in the hospital corridor. I saw two police men coming down the corridor and they just stepped over her. The vast majority of the families found it very hard to find any kindness that night. The very first question (the police) asked was 'had Andrew been drinking?'.[1]

This chapter asks, 'Is it worth doing the job we do'? Having talked as a barrister for the preceding chapters I wanted to give first voice to a client in answer to this question. This is what Julie said when I later asked her thoughts on the value of our work as barristers.

Our family's first encounter with the legal system after the Hillsborough disaster in 1989 was pathetically naive and desperate. ... Everyone in that room was as innocently and blindly unaware as each other of the coverup unfolding somewhere else, beyond our collective imagination.

It took time, and lots of it, to realise that who and how you were represented legally was vitally important, no, central, to your success or failure, I know it sounds sad! We sound unintelligent, but we, like the vast, vast majority of the public had grown up spoon-fed on the intrinsic belief that the British judicial system was fair. Everyone in it, whilst they might not all be top barristers, were at the very least, of higher intelligence, moral, ethical and would fight your corner!! ...

At the same slow painful rate that it became obvious to us that it was of make-or-break importance that we ultimately needed to find legal representation that could understand and grasp the magnitude of our grievances, we also became increasingly aware of the role that money played! We had very little of it and we had long since realised that without it we would continue to be ridden roughshod over.

As an experience, meeting our legal teams for the first time, in a huge room in Anfield on a Sunday afternoon, arriving with that awful 'here we go again, more system serving tossers to deal with' was like being in the scene in the Wizard of Oz when the action moves from black and white to breathtaking technicolour. We stumbled away from that meeting. We doubted what we'd heard. We disbelieved what we'd been told. But most of all we couldn't believe that for the first time in 20-odd years, we had been spoken

---

[1] Julie being interviewed for the S4C documentary, *Hillsborough: The Long Nightmare*, which aired in January 2017.

to by members of the legal profession as intelligent, informed, courageous, meaningful equals! It continued for three years in that vein, and the rest as they say is history!

So, as families we are forever in the debt of our outstanding second inquest legal team, armed with their humanity, expertise, talent and recognition and respect for what we as a group had already achieved, not because when it came to it they did what was expected of them but precisely but because, based on all that we had come to know of the way families like ours are ritualistically treated, they did what wasn't!

On 31 March 2014, 96 inquests were formally opened in Warrington, and over the course of a gruelling 296 days, a jury heard evidence about the events leading up to the disaster, how it unfolded and its aftermath. Their task was to decide when, how and why the dead had died. It was the longest case ever heard by a jury in British legal history. Its outcome redressed a long-standing historical wrong. Many of the relatives had attended almost every day of the inquests. On 26 April 2016, the jury returned unanimous verdicts concluding that the 96 victims had been 'unlawfully killed',[2] and exonerated the fans who had carried the slurs of *The Sun* and others as 'Scum', responsible for the death of their own kith and kin, for so long.[3] In 2022, a 97th victim was added to the death toll, when life support was withdrawn from Andrew Devine who had suffered life-changing injuries at the match.

---

[2] In English law, Irish law and Northern Irish law, unlawful killing is a verdict that can be returned by an inquest in England and Wales and Ireland when someone has been killed by one or more unknown persons. The verdict means that the killing was done without lawful excuse and in breach of criminal law.

[3] In its verdicts, the jury concluded:

1. Planning errors 'caused or contributed to' the dangerous situation that developed on the day of the disaster.
2. Senior officers failed to issue specific instructions on how crowds were to be managed at the Leppings Lane end of the stadium.
3. The response to a build-up of fans at the Leppings Lane end was 'slow and uncoordinated'.
4. Commanding officers failed to appreciate that ordering the opening of a gate would increase pressure in the terraces.

I was one of the lawyers chosen to act for the HFSG[4] families in that historic inquest. With 97 deaths and 766 injuries, it was the highest death toll in British sporting history, and at 96 inquests being heard simultaneously 25 years after the event I was one of few able to be there for the reckoning.[5] The 96 then, 97 now, had held fast to the belief that 'they never walked alone'.[6] For a while, in Warrington, we lawyers walked with them step by step. That is what being truly trusted by a client creates – Responsibility and Respect. Fear No One. Do Right.

This chapter deliberately gave Julie, my former client and now constant friend, the first words. Why? Because that is what a good barrister does. They listen to, they amplify the voice of, and they tell

---

5. Police and the ambulance service caused or contributed to the loss of lives by an error or omission after the crush in the west terrace had begun to develop.
6. Fans were not to blame for the dangerous situation.
7. The design of the stadium, home to Sheffield Wednesday football club, contributed to the tragedy.
8. Club officials should have requested the match to be delayed when they became aware of the huge number of fans still outside the Leppings Lane turnstiles.

[4] Hillsborough Family Support Group, now the Hillsborough Support Alliance, dedicated to providing support and therapy to those affected by the disaster (https://www.hsa-us.co.uk/).

[5] The list of lawyers involved acting for the (then) 96 families in the inquests are too many to name. But all were chosen by the families. The solicitors, trainees, barristers for each family grouping worked collaboratively and closely to achieve the joint aim of their respective clients – accountability and justice. My role for the HFSG (a gathering of 76 bereaved families) was investigating the medical response to the disaster and asking whether lives were lost by negligence that could have been saved as the families believed (the jury answered 'Yes' to that question). Its hard to single out names but I will always be in debt to Marcia Willis KC (Hon) and the superb team of solicitors she led, and my colleague counsel led by the indefatigable Mike Mansfield KC and his right-hand man Patrick Roche.

[6] Originally a Broadway song, it was re-recorded by Gerry & The Pacemakers in 1963. On the day after the tragedy at Hillsborough, 13,000 people gathered at Liverpool's Roman Catholic Cathedral;

the story as the client needs it to be told. The barrister who becomes the story is letting Self come before Service.

Being a barrister and being entrusted with trying to make a difference to a case that, for the client, may change the direction of their life, is a privilege and a burden. Never think that duty is not respected.

Last year, I entered a trial acting for a father facing non-accidental injury allegations just before the fact find hearing, all the experts having concluded from a paper review that multiple fractures to a baby had been inflicted non-accidentally. The likely time frame for when the fractures had occurred scooped not just the parents but the maternal grandfather, paternal grandmother and grandfather in its vice-like grip. The case had poisoned the well of happiness this first-born child, the first-born grandchild, had brought into a family recovering from the loss of the adored maternal grandmother from cancer during her daughter's pregnancy. The maternal and paternal families were engulfed by grief when the baby was removed from the parents' care at just a few weeks old. The case seemed hopeless on paper given the unanimity of the experts' opinions on causation. And yet, over the course of just ten days we turned an apparent cast-iron case, fought with relentless prosecutorial zeal by the local authority legal team, into a case woven with straw that could not withstand forensic scrutiny when tested. Medical hypothesis was laid bare with all its contradictions and uncertainties. Speculation was replaced by incontrovertible evidence of the exceptional quality of care given to this adored first-born child and grandchild by his family. The judge made no findings. The case was dismissed.[7] Precious months had been lost

---

5,000 in the church, and a further 8,000 spilling into the streets outside. 'You'll Never Walk Alone' was sung by a lone choir boy, offering both comfort and hope to a city in mourning. The song has become a symbol in the fight for justice for the victims of the disaster in order to change the narrative behind their deaths. It's now Liverpool Footballs Club's anthem. The passion behind the fans' singing hits deep into the soul.

[7] https://caselaw.nationalarchives.gov.uk/ewfc/b/2024/209; see also *Re M, A Child [2024] 209.*

to the parents after their baby was taken from them – they missed his first words, his first steps – but his childhood is now theirs to treasure. He is back home where he belongs – adored and cared for. At the end of the trial, knowing the judge's decision, they gifted me one of the most thoughtful presents I have ever received – a huge crystal gin goblet personally engraved for me. *'Filled with the bitter tears of her opposing Counsel'* it read. They had seen, at first hand, what legal aid defence lawyers do to change outcomes that seem bleak on paper. Even now, a year on from our trial, this extraordinary strong family gift me pictures of their baby, now a toddler, with updates on how he is progressing.

They have gifted me this letter, written from the heart. It speaks eloquently and powerfully of the desperation our clients faced when accused of the unimaginable, with the prospect of losing their child threatening their future as a family, as a couple, as parents. This letter ties together a recognition of so much of that I have tried to explain in previous chapters.

> We were falsely accused of non accidental injury. (Jo's) true dedication to immediately learning the case not only during 'standard' working hours, but also throughout the night and early hours shows that she was giving her absolute everything and leaving no opportunity for errors that could have led to detrimental consequences. Her medical knowledge is astounding and without this, we would not have rightfully had our baby back in our care. Jo was able to tear apart every mistake that the experts made in order to find the answers for our baby. Her cross-examination skills shone in the courtroom, and she led with such confidence in her knowledge that she was doing the right thing for our child and family. Jo is analytical, powerful, and persuasive. Always one step ahead of anyone else and with a mind so wonderfully complex that she left professionals speechless. Her compassion throughout such difficult times is what set Jo apart from anyone else. She was reassuring and kind, yet honest and ready to answer any questions/concerns I had. She adapted to my needs when explaining anything, and ensured

she paused the courtroom when legal terms became too complicated for us to understand so that she could turn to us and explain what was happening. She gave our family and I a voice in the courtroom. Her ability to adjust to her clients is exceptional and yet it comes so naturally. Jo was my anchor in the storm, and I will forever be grateful for having her as my KC. She saved our family.

This letter speaks of my work, but for every mention of my name add to it the extraordinary legal team I led. My junior in that case, Delia Minoprio, and my solicitor Ryan Booth, worked more hours than I could ever count, pro bono, to help me get the result our client deserved.

As a silk we do not act alone in these cases. We are part of a close-knit team of dedicated professionals. Their behind-the-scenes work is the anchor that the case is tethered to. to make a difference. Delia and Ryan placed their own families on hold to fight for our clients' right to regain their own. They are each remarkable people. So many of the people I am privileged to work with are quite extraordinary in their dedication. Max Konarek (solicitor) and Chris Barnes (counsel) to name but two. It is no coincidence that Max and Ryan are work colleagues in the same firm and Delia and Chris are close friends. I find quality and dedication seeks out like-minded professionals. Colleagues become friends. It is that camaraderie that supports us when we lose faith in the value of what we do.

These parents are not the only ones to emerge from the horror of care proceedings to reassemble their fractured family lives when we, the legal aid Bar, alongside dedicated solicitors deliver a first-class service to the client under the watchful eye and alert ear of an attentive, conscientious judge.

In this next case, reported April 2025, we got things right for a mother.

I was again instructed by Ann Thompson (who I had worked with on *Al-Alas* for Chana, our young bereaved mother), now joined by Amina Gillani, both superb solicitors at Goodman Ray. I led Emily James (made a silk in the 2024 list – then an excellent junior). We were a formidable team united in securing the just

Figure 8.1: 'Filled with the bitter tears of my opposing counsel'

outcome for a client I described to the judge in closing submission as a woman '*Raised to be a wife, born to be a mother*'. She was a vulnerable, isolated Afghan refugee and one of the lucky ones to escape on one of the last planes to depart to the UK when the Taliban took control of her homeland and the lives of so many she knew and left behind.

I'm going to let the judge's words speak for themselves as the judgment (reported publicly as *LB Croydon v D (Critical Scrutiny of the Paediatric Overview) [2024] EWFC 438*[8]) is as much a testament to a fair and just process over which HHJ Major presided as to my work.

Dr Cleghorn was the jointly instructed paediatrician in which role, in an alleged non-accidental injuries case, her overarching opinion as to the cause of injuries carried a huge amount of weight in terms of outcome. The local authority had relied on her report to prove non-accidental injury. All experts were against us. By the end of the case, after I had called and cross-examined the community, treating medics and social worker, and then exposed the discrepancies between the primary fact and the expert assumptions of, and flawed opinions on it, the judge said this:

> 97. Dr Cleghorn was subject to a detailed and forensic cross examination by Prof Delahunty KC on behalf of the mother. It was nothing short of a demolition exercise of Dr Cleghorn's evidence. No other party needed to cross examine after she had concluded. Dr Cleghorn conceded in cross examination that, in parts, her evidence was 'appalling'. That there were multiple examples of her lack of 'due diligence' in the preparation of her report, addendum report, and in terms of her preparation for and participation in the experts' meeting for which she apologised.
>
> 98. Counsel for the child for in closing submissions refers to Dr Cleghorn's evidence as 'terrifying' and from a safeguarding perspective for children an utter 'disaster'…
>
> 107. The impact of Dr Cleghorn's evidence goes beyond her own individual evidence. Her errors and closed mind contaminate the professionals meeting. She closed down the conversation around the parents' account of being told how to resuscitate H by shaking as being inherently unlikely. Their account and its credibility or

---

[8] https://www.bailii.org/cgi-bin/format.cgi?doc=/ew/cases/EWFC/HCJ/2024/438.html&query=(major)+AND+(lb)+AND+(croydon)+AND+(v)+AND+(D)

otherwise is a matter for the court not Dr Cleghorn (of course, we know now that there have been serious issues of misunderstanding and failures in the provision of interpreting services for this family, especially the mother). The duty of the experts is to consider all possible mechanisms.

108. Dr Cleghorn's evidence in cross examination is entirely at odds with her written report and opinion. It is entirely supportive of the case advanced by the parents as to the cause of the injuries to both babies.

109. Dr Cleghorn's approach in this case is a cause for serious concern. There are real world consequences for children where the professional medical evidence is flawed, factually inaccurate and lacking in enquiry and analysis. Children could be removed from perfectly safe home environments or alternatively children at risk could remain placed with abusive carers. This case demonstrates the importance of advocates with a detailed knowledge of the case and the facts being able to robustly and critically cross examine experts and fully explore their client's case.

The children went home. We – myself, Emily, Amina and Ann – made a difference to the outcome. We worked ourselves to the bone but it was worth it for this outcome. It was a privilege to work with each of these remarkable women and to do so before a judge that brought to the case an open mind marked by a keen intellect and a fundamental belief that hearing evidence transparently tested by specialist counsel, to be analysed and resolved by the court, is what fairness requires.

The case gained a degree of fame in our working world. Consider these headlines: 'Expert evidence: this is just about as bad as it gets: expert concedes that parts of their evidence was "appalling": one of the parties described it as "terrifying"';[9] 'When experts get it

---

[9] https://www.civillitigationbrief.com/2025/04/04/expert-evidence-this-is-just-about-as-bad-as-it-gets-expert-concedes-that-parts-of-their-evidence-was-appalling-one-of-the-parties-described-it-as-terrifying/

wrong';[10] 'UK High Court judge dresses down doctor over medical evidence errors in care order case'.[11]

Why? Because the judgement came out at a time when we, as legal aid lawyers, felt we were facing an unprecedented challenge to the right to, and value of, our cross-examination experts, especially where, on paper, there was unanimity as to cause of injury. That is a terrifying prospect because it is based on a dangerous premise that united experts present an insurmountable challenge to parents who, obstinately, remain in denial as to their guilt. That is so so wrong. *Re M* and *Re C* evidence the falsity of that construct for in both cases the experts were united in their opinion that the cause of injury was inflicted. In both cases that confidence was undermined by cross-examination. In both cases the judge failed to follow that opinion evidence. In both cases babies returned to their families. Cross-examination secured vindication and reunification.

My extraordinary colleague, Paul Storey KC, led the challenge against Guidance issued in November 2024 by McDonald J, approved by the President, that was widely seen as reducing the capacity to challenge expert evidence to the smallest pool of cases. The Guidance, 'Local Practice Note: Ensuring Adherence to the Public Law Outline in London',[12] contained this exhortation under a heading 'Limiting Expert Evidence': 'a direction for the attendance of the expert at the final hearing will be an exceptional course'.

Paul's case, argued alongside equally committed legal teams, questioned the premise of exceptionality. He and they led the charge for many of us. Paul and his colleagues were produced hard evidence in support of their passionate assertion that experts' views were not

---

[10] https://www.se-solicitors.co.uk/article/102k88b/when-experts-get-it-wrong/https://www.se-solicitors.co.uk/article/102k88b/when-experts-get-it-wrong/

[11] https://www.canadianlawyermag.com/news/international/uk-high-court-judge-dresses-down-doctor-over-medical-evidence-errors-in-care-order-case/392077

[12] https://www.judiciary.uk/wp-content/uploads/2024/11/Local-Practice-Note-Getting-Back-to-the-PLO-in-London-Final-28.11.2024-1.pdf

determinative of outcome and cross-examination was an essential tool to test and challenge their opinions. They created, with the support of many of us uninvolved directly in the case, a library of over 68 cases where children had been returned home after experts' opinions were put to the test, in court, by skilled specialist advocacy. The dialogue in court between Bench and Bar was mutually respectful, engaged and skilled. I exhort anyone wanting to understand that dynamic to read Lucy Reed KC's blog, 'Cross examination of medical experts – exceptional or exceptionally important?',[13] which conveys the proceedings with the elegance and skill she herself saw deployed in court.

Judgment was handed down in *A Local Authority v X (Attendance of Experts) [2025] EWFC 137*.[14] The test as to whether expert instruction was appropriate, as with their call to court for cross-examination, was one of necessity.

We thus live to fight another day.

Our work with a family may be fleeting in terms of our career line but our impact can be lifelong for our clients. That is why we strain every sinew for them.

When we act for clients, we cannot do less than bring our whole selves to the task in hand. As barristers, we are the bridge of communication between client, their case and the courtroom. Brie astutely points out: '*The reality is that by starting litigation the claimant hands control of the parties' dispute to a stranger who does not know the parties and does not have to live with the consequences, and they commit to fight by rules that they do not understand. It is not possible for a litigant to be or feel in control of litigation. When working directly with a client to help them understand the case or identify and explain all the potentially relevant information and evidence for me requires the full range of intellect and emotional intelligence. Helping my client give the best account they can of themselves, and their truth is always a challenge which can be hugely rewarding.*'

If I reflect on what qualities I see amidst my colleagues that unite us, despite our many differences, specialisms and life experiences, I will say we are self-motivated learners. We ask the questions that

---

[13] https://transparencyproject.org.uk/cross-examination-of-medical-experts-exceptional-or-exceptionally-important/

[14] https://caselaw.nationalarchives.gov.uk/ewfc/2025/137

no one else is asking. We are self-driven. I clock off not when the clock says I can, or when my body and brain yells at me that they are tired, but when I think I've done the work needed in order to get to court the next day and do the best job I can for my client. We all doubt ourselves, but we perform, I think, whatever our age, we are perpetually curious and questioning. We are determined, obstinate, stubborn and driven, yet prepared to learn, to be adaptable and to be humble enough to ask for advice.

'*My profession*', once said Sir Edward Marshall Hall KC, '*and that of an actor are somewhat akin, except that I have no scenes to help me, and no words are written for me to say. There is no backcloth to increase the illusion. There is no curtain. But, out of the vivid, living dream of somebody else's life, I have to create an atmosphere – for that is advocacy*'.

I love this quote. It speaks of the work my colleague, friend and king of the non-accidental injury Bar, Paul, can achieve in court. It is what my sister-in-spirit at the Bar, Alison Grief KC, does trial by trial. It is what Mike Mansfield KC does, even now after some 55 years plus at the Bar. John Vater KC and Nick Goodwin KC bring different but wholly valuable and valued skills into every case they are in. John is a fighter for the people. He has raw energy and a passion for justice. Nick is smoothly elegant, devestatingly effective through coolly delivered cross examination. We each bring something of ourselves into court. I learn from the best. It is what I strive to do and do do. We reclaim the narrative from the professionals who thought they knew the family history better than the family. We make vivid the colour of their lived experiences and actions. We bring alive their dreams and aspirations and place their failings in context. We reintroduce humanity and balance where premature judgement had deemed them culpable. We create, in court, through cross-examination, submissions and speeches, an atmosphere that demands attention.

However hopeless the case on paper I never believe it is not mine for the winning, argument by argument, witness by witness. And because I achieve this far more often than predicted I believe I can do it every time. When I do not I feel a failure. Then I turn to friends for support and succour.

I will never get used to the responsibility we have to fight for our client to the best of our ability. What I fear the most, however, is being deprived of the opportunity to do so. I have become increasingly worried at the message driven relentlessly home to the family

Bar – cut down the time cases take to get to trial. Do that by cutting down on the medical experts you want to instruct. Why do you need experts when you have clinicals? If you win the argument to instruct an expert and you get their (invariably negative reports in) why doesn't your client accept that? What can you possibly ask to make the expert reconsider? Why does that need to be done in the course of cross-examination? Ask your questions in writing after the report (draft them for free), put them to the expert in writing for the experts meeting (draft them for free). Why are you still claiming there is more to challenge by calling the expert to trial? What relevance is the research? Why not just put the parents in the witness box if they want their day in court? Why do you need an intermediary? Why do you need more than a five-day or ten-day trial? Why do you need a fact find at all? The outcome is clear on paper –the issues resolution stage is when we can sort this out (a directions hearing with no evidence). Such questions are posed dismissive of what experience shows to make a difference to outcome. I have explored this in many a lecture, article and speech.[15] In summary – experts give their opinion on the material they read in the papers, it is given on the 'facts' as then presented and known. But when that factual landscape changes as community, health visitor, hospital paramedic, family evidence is called, their expert analysis must consider and reflect that. On challenge the expert's opinion can, and often does in my experience, evolve. Research is tested in conjunction with the developing factual narrative. Events not thought relevant to the parents so barely explored on paper now assume a significance that warrants careful reflection in cross-examination. Parents give

---

[15] Perhaps dip into this article discussing the consequences of the SIHIS (Suspected Inflicted Head Injury) pilot published in the January issue of *Family Law* 2025 (https://www.familylaw.co.uk/news_and_comment/what-are-the-intended-unintended-consequences-of-the-sihis-pilot-report) or these lectures I gave for Gresham (there are more on the subject from me there too): 'Medical Experts in the Family Court: Where Two Worlds Collide', https://www.gresham.ac.uk/watch-now/medical-family; 'Expert Witnesses: A Zero Sum Game?', https://www.gresham.ac.uk/watch-now/expert-witness-zero-sum-game; 'Guilty until Porved Innocent', https://www.gresham.ac.uk/watch-now/guilty-until-proven-innocent

evidence in a way the local authority prosecuting the case had not anticipated and the experts have not seen and heard but the judge sees and hears it all. It is they who bear the responsibility of decision-making – not the expert. We know outcomes change in trial after careful, skilled cross-examination of witnesses of fact and experts of medical opinion. That chance to have a birth-family life should not be a matter of historical reminiscence – each child now coming into the family justice system deserves no less. Adoption is not a panacea and for many children it is not viable – the state will take on the child. How many times have we read of instances where children have languished or come to harm in care homes, been moved between countless foster carers, lost the chance of consistent education through care moves, and so on? We do not solve the problems the family justice system inherits by passing on the cost to cash-strapped local authorities, the health service, the police and the community.

We have a long and respected history to call upon when we argue for the bare bones of justice to be respected and upheld in the family court. A classic example comes from Baker J (as he then was) in the case of *Devon County Council v EB [2013] EWHC 968 (Fam)*:

> 155. I conclude with a few closing observations. This case demonstrates yet again the importance of a full and thorough forensic examination of cases of suspected child abuse. A full and thorough investigation involves a number of elements. First, it requires judges of sufficient experience who are able to manage cases through the course of the proceedings. Judicial continuity is a crucial component of the modern family justice system. …
>
> 156. Secondly, this case required the involvement of a range of experts from different disciplines. If the case had been decided purely on the basis of the treating doctors, the outcome may have been very different. …
>
> 157. Thirdly this case demonstrates that whilst it will be possible to conclude the vast majority of cases in 26 weeks under modernisation reforms, there will still be a small minority of cases, exceptional cases, where the investigation takes longer. …
>
> 158. Finally this case demonstrates yet again the crucial role played by the specialist family Bar and solicitors.

The role played by all the representatives has been of the utmost importance. ... Not enough recognition is given to the contribution to the family justice system by family lawyers.

Baker J (now Baker LJ) is someone we look up to. But his words are not simply for historical reference – up and down the land myself, my colleagues at the Bar and solicitors alike, senior and junior, are involved in trial after trial where we change a child's life by the very process and engagement that Baker LJ identified as being crucial to the justice of the case so many years ago.

Non-accidental injury cases engage, in medical terms of causation and presentation, the area where science has evolved and is evolving, and with it we develop our understanding of how natural cause can mimic abuse. As Dame Elizabeth Butler-Sloss, at [23] of *Re B (A Child) [2004] EWCA 567*, said so profoundly, 'the judge in care proceedings must never forget that today's medical certainty may be discarded by the next generation of experts or that scientific research will throw light into corners that are at present dark'.

Two decades later that wisdom holds true. We now have a library of cases in which the significance of EDS4 has cast a different light on injuries previously thought to have been inflicted by excessive unreasonable use of force.[16] We are learning about the effect of omeprazole on bone strength in premature and young babies.[17] We are still learning about the unique complexity of the human body and the interplay of external factors upon its strength.[18]

This is not the time to deaden the role of science in the courtroom. It is a vibrant, ever-evolving, world of surprise and wonder at the uniqueness of the human body.

One only needs to be reminded of the words of Hedley J (as then), in *Re R (Care Proceedings: Causation) [2011] EWHC 1715*

---

[16] See *A Local Authority v M & Ors [2024] EWFC 2388*, for one example.

[17] *Re M case (A Child) (Non-Accidental Injuries: Wider Canvas) [2024] EWFC 2099*

[18] Consider my *Re M case*, in which the increasing evidence around the use of omeprazole was determined relevant to causation of fractures in young children. The local authority in that case failed to prove inflicted injury.

Fam: 'It simply recognises that we still have much to learn and it also recognises that it is dangerous and wrong to infer non-accidental injury merely from the absence of any other understood mechanism. Maybe it simply represents a general acknowledgement that we are fearfully and wonderfully made.'

We currently have a postcode lottery for family justice. The worry is that those courts with the most attractive statistics for cutting through cases in the least time and lowest cost are those being held up as models of good practice – not those courts where experienced judges, often with a superb history as advocates at the Bar, committed to doing right by the child and family before them, devote their time and skill to hearing the evidence fairly – allowing for an outcome other than the anticipated adoption. There is a mood of despondency at the public law family Bar. Things are equally bleak for our colleagues in crime, albeit in different ways; they have retained their right, without challenge, to have their experts of choice for the defence independent of the prosecution (unlike in family trials where we have to agree a single joint expert as between all parties to the case and rarely have the option of a second opinion) and our criminal colleagues have the right to cross-examine the witnesses and experts of their selection and election but their problem is equally profound – they can gather the evidence but lack a court to hear it after decades of cuts and closures.

When we feel we are facing a war of relentless challenge to our principles and professionalism, and when these messages are delivered in court to barristers by a judge who is dismissive, rude, even incredulous at the submissions you make resisting this direction of travel, then despair can suffocate our pride in our job and reduce our self-esteem to ground zero levels. The remarkable thing is, we continue to fight. We believe things will get better if we try hard enough. We treasure the support we have. We remember the stories of the families who have been reunited through our efforts. We push on.

To survive and thrive at the Bar you need to lean into its camaraderie to get you through. As Shelly says, when asked to consider what she would tell her younger self about the place she has now carved out for herself as a family barrister: '*I'd want her to know the rewards will be immeasurable; that she'll meet colleagues, other professionals, lay parties and family members who embody the very best of humanity. I would tell her she'll find a place she belongs, beside people every* bit as awkward and fabulous as her. I would urge her to more readily accept support that is given and, when the time comes, pay it forward knowing it will be appreciated.'

It is encouraging to hear this sentiment echoed by Mass: 'I have found myself surrounded by individuals who have been willing to drop everything to help me, or to answer my questions. I have found myself inspired by people who are committed to ensuring that they leave the profession in a better state than they found it in.'

Those of us who have the position and confidence to speak out about the things that need correcting in our profession should do so. I and others are increasingly doing that. The Secret Barrister did more with their first book to expose the demands placed on the criminal Bar by a disrespected and underfunded criminal justice system than any number of lectures, or talks to the great and good, achieved. Their subsequent books and postings on X continue to drive debate. Alex Wilson's book, *In Black and White*, heralded a whole new conversation about colour at the Bar. 'Crime girl', and the likes of Mary Aspinall-Miles and Dr Chelvan on X, are a force for positive change, because they challenge the status quo and are unafraid to call out injustice. We do so, not because we want to discourage others from entering our profession, but because we want to make it a better place to welcome them.

I was called to the Bar in 1986 and took silk in 2006. The year 2026 will mark 40 years as a barrister, 20 in silk. Aged 17, full of anger and indignation, ambition and energy, I had no idea where my path would lead into adulthood. I'm now a proud parent of three, in my 60s, still with the boyfriend I met and fell in love with aged 17, and I have done more with my professional life than I ever thought possible. I do not take any of that for granted nor must I bury the personal cost of that career trajectory. I often feel burnt out and disillusioned in private and say as much to my family and close friends.

I am tired. Tired of having to fight harder and more often for what I believe to be the unarguable and inalienable rights for the families I represent to have a trial that reflects the seriousness of the consequences for them. I am tired from the relentless volume of the material I have to consume to get to the bones of the case. I am tired of the sleepless nights worrying about emails I have not replied to, the skeleton arguments I have yet to write, the cross-examination lines yet to finesse. I am tired of the travel away from home. I am tired of waiting to be paid for work done many years ago, upon which I pay tax as aged debt, but have no idea when the funds will be mine, losing value all the time I wait. I am tired of being a post-menopausal woman whose body is slacker and slower than my brain is.

I am tired of it all, except the buzz and the prospect of success. For reasons that defy logic I cannot give up the Bar.

When repeatedly asked by my family to slow down I demur. When I am told by colleagues at the Bar who know me and are dear to me to stop taking so much on I fall silent. When I am told by so many people at work and at home I respect to take time off I promise to do so but am poor in following up with action. I am vulnerable to casting myself to being the professional for hire in the last chance saloon. Its egotistic, I know, to believe I can change a case from hopeless to vindication. And yet I do. I believe that every case demands that confidence. Above all, I cling onto the belief that I, Professor Jo Delahunty KC can make a difference and, if I could, I should.

My family believed in working hard and playing hard. They didn't take from the community they grew up and lived in – they gave back. My mum gave me a passion to succeed beyond my expectations that has not dimmed – though she has long ceased to see the light from her spark. Mum died four months after I took silk. She died of cancer which took her life before the Alzheimer's trapped her in a living death. I am in reach of that age now and I want to live my life to its fullest. I have a world outside the Bar that is hidden to most. I draw. I have a studio and craft jewellery from precious metal and gems. I throw pots. I play with image and have not yet done with the tattoos and piercings nor experimenting with an image that defies age-related assumptions of dress codes. I throw myself into these activities secure in the knowledge that my future holds worth in ways that I am still exploring with people I have not yet met. But being a barrister is a core part of who I am. I cannot see how I can sever it from my being without the loss of that which I hold tight as being essential to my sense of self-worth.

Above all, when I ask myself if being a barrister is worth the cost it exacts, I look not for answers within myself, but those I get from the colleagues I am proud to stand alongside in the courtroom. Those I would follow into an empty void if they simply clicked a finger.

The men and women I would want to act for me if I needed them. These people are marked out by their courage – their preparedness to be the lone voice, and to step forward when others step back. I have listened to these icons and been left in awe at their command of the courtroom. They consistently produce magic in court. They make one listen to their every word, producing apparently effortless advocacy that is anything but effortless to produce. It is a beguiling, mesmerising performance, singular to that person, impossible for the onlooker to reproduce. They have panache, cunning and commitment above and beyond the call of professional duty. If I had to name three of those people it would be Mike Mansfield KC, Alison Grief KC and Paul Storey KC, but there are more than that triumvirate, many more.

So, is it worth it?

Yes. An unequivocal, heartfelt yes. We can change the law. We can change practice. We can change lives. When it works, it is a feeling like no other. When it works, we can change someone's life, and those who love them, to profound effect. There is no other buzz like it.

We come to the Bar to make a difference. When we do, the lengths we have gone to achieve our place fade into nothing, and we would not think twice before doing so again.

Postscript

Baroness Harriet Harman's report was published in September.[1] It is an excoriating analysis of the abuse in chambers and the court room I describe in this book and have long campaigned to call out and stamp out. To have my work expressly paid tribute to was bittersweet given the silence and criticism I have endured from colleagues who I expected to have support from and who, only now the message is no longer 'difficult' to hear, clamour to say they will support change. Will they though when it places them in conflict with authority? As Harman says in her October piece for *Counsel* magazine, 'The culture of collusive bystanding needs to be recognised, called out and ended.'[2]

October saw the Bar Council and Law Society unite to host an international conference that called for an end to attacks on lawyers; Barbara Mills said *'Barristers have told us they have faced death threats and rape threats, threats to their family members, threats made by politicians, physical surveillance and lawyers have been traduced in some parts of the media both at home and abroad.' 'There must be no impunity for governments or non-state actors who target the profession. There are patterns of intimidation that show we are facing an increasing hostile environment for lawyers globally. It is vitally important for us to support the profession at this critical time, emphasise the value of independent legal practitioners and promote adherence to the rule of law.'*

And we approach the end of the year we see no end to the maladministration of the MOJ that led to our legal aid data being

---

[1] https://www.barcouncil.org.uk/support-for-barristers/bullying-and-harassment/review.html, chapter 7, page 68, para 199.
[2] https://www.counselmagazine.co.uk/articles/the-bar-s-strengths-are-also-its-weaknesses

compromised by a hack seen to be a risk since 2021 and was wider, deeper and more longstanding than we had been told.[3] The contribution of the Chief Executive to parliament's Public Accounts Committee served up word soup – and not as nourishing. And still no one cares.

I have already gone on record when asked to talk about mental health at the Bar to proclaim 'I was f****** furious, not mad'.[4] This book has picked up on key themes that undermine the work we aspire to do for those most in need. It is prescient. The fight must go on. We, and our clients deserve better than this.

Legal aid is the fourth emergency service. We are crying out for life support by way of injection of funds and respect from the government and our better paid colleagues.

It's time we were heard. It's time for action. It's time our absence was feared.

JDKC
1 November 2025

---

[3] https://www.civilserviceworld.com/professions/article/mps-grill-legal-aid-agency-over-cyberattack-that-prompted-system-shutdown

[4] https://www.barcouncil.org.uk/resource/the-emotional-cost-of-legal-aid-work-if-you-ask-me-what-needs-to-change-it-s-not-us.html; https://www.linkedin.com/posts/professor-jo-delahunty-qc_the-emotional-cost-of-legal-aid-work-activity-7342281344166576129-8F1F?utm_medium=ios_app&rcm=ACoAAAeLVGgBmZI01UgefNm8JegUOcvEmhSImeg& utm_source=social_share_send& utm_campaign=share_via

Index

References to figures appear in *italic* type. References to footnotes show both the page number and the note number (1n1).

1 Crown Office Row
  (1COR) 211–12
3 Plowden Lane 45
4 Brick Court 45
4PB 240
8 New Square 39, 41, 43–4
10KBI initiative 57
11KBW 211
12KBW 212
36 Family 123
1000 Black Interns Project 57

A

accents 42, 48, 52–3
Ackroyd, Peter 234
Advisory, Conciliation and Arbitration Service (ACAS) 146–7
Advocate (pro bono charity) 54
Al-Alas, Chana 78–9
Allen, Nick, KC 239
applying for the Bar *see* becoming a barrister
Arden, Lady 192
Ashford, Ethel Bright 185–6
Aspinall-Miles, Mary 6, 50–1, 65, 87, 147, 280
Association of Women Barristers 213
Association of Women Judges 152
Attention Deficit Hyperactivity Disorder (ADHD) 3, 246–54

B

Badenoch, Kemi 6
Baird, Vera, QC 16n25
Baker LJ 277–8

Baksi, Catherine 241
Banbury, Sir Frederick 183–4
Bar Council
  comments on BSB 133, 135
  diversity and inclusion initiatives 201–2, 257–9
  earnings differentials reporting 198–9, 205n44
  Harman Report xii, 115, 174
  hostile environment conference 283
  legal aid work interview 28, 29–30
  Race at the Bar reports 161–3, 165–6, 205
  statement on private members' clubs 226
  work on bullying and harassment 103n1, 106, 107, 114–15, 141–2, 153, 169–70, 172, 202–3
  working lives surveys and reports 89–91, *90*, 159, 160–1
Bar Standards Board (BSB)
  criticisms of disciplinary processes 125–6, 127, 133, 135, 137–9
  Diversity at the Bar reports 189–90
  Eve Robinson complaint 118–20, 122, 124, 125, 137–8, 140
  reviews of sanctions imposed 135–7
  sexual harassment complaints received 126, 127
  Women at the Bar survey 106n6
  PROCEEDINGS
  Robert Kearney 127–30
  Henry Charles William King 134–5
  Navjot (Jo) Sidhu 131–3
  Alan Wheetman 133–4

285

Bar Tribunal and Adjudication Service
   (BTAS) 119, 125, 130n28,
   135–6, 138
Barbet, Lucy 199
Barczentewicz, Dr Mikolaj 195–6
Barnes, Chris 269
barristers' clerks 44, 179, 199, 200,
   201, 204
Bassam, Adiba 258–9
Bear Garden 43n19
Beard, Dame Mary 226
Bebb, Gwyneth 181–2, 184, 185–6
becoming a barrister
   application process 37–9
   author's story 32–9, *38*
   Gresham lecture 1n1
   non-direct routes 49–51
   personal champions 41, 44–5, 58–60
   pupillage 39, 40, 65
   school outreach 61–3, *62*
   support programmes and
      initiatives 54–7, 63–4, 211–14,
      257–9
Becoming the Bar campaign 258–9
Behind the Gown 116
belonging 51–8, 64, 279–80
Bendell, Emily 223, 228
Bhachu, Sharan Kaur 244, 256
Birmingham Six 25n2, 69–70
Birtles, William 44
Black, Lady 192
Black Inclusion Group (BIG) 206–7,
   218–19, 232–3
body art 52, 62, 245, 281
Booth, Elsa 155, 223n3, 247
Booth, Ryan 269
Bourne, Dr Judith 179, 185
Brannigan, Kate, KC 159
Braverman, Suella 5, 6
Brick Court Chambers 213–14
Bridging the Bar (BTB) 27–8, 54–7,
   63, 212–13, 259
Brimelow, Kirsty, KC 210
Bringing [Dis]Ability to the Bar
   (BDABar) 254–5
Brough, Colin 225
Brunner, Kate, KC 223
bullying and harassment at the Bar
   as abuse of power 107, 111, 174
   author's experience of 109–11, 112
   criticisms of Bar Standards
      Board 125–6, 127, 133,
      135, 137–9

harassment defined 107
internal complaints procedures
   120–3, 124–5
judicial bullying *see* judicial bullying
linked to race 160–7
linked to sexuality 234–5
men's experiences of 108–9
ongoing incidence of 103n1, 106–7,
   108–9, 111, 114–15, 127, 160, 172
specific complaints 109–11, 117–26,
   127–35
tackling the issue xii, 115–17,
   139–43, 169–72, 174–5
talking about experiences 110–11,
   112, 113–14, 116–17, 124–5, 143
types of 107–8
Butler-Sloss, Dame Elizabeth 278

C

Cab Rank Rule 71
Calvert, Barbara, QC 44–5
Canavan, Sandy, HHJ 258
Carr, Sue, LCJ 192, 208, 210, 226
Carroll, Jonathan, HHJ 130
Case, Simon 225
Cave, Bertha 180, 181
Chambers UK Awards 55
Chancery Bar Association 199–201,
   206, 232–3
Chelvan, Dr S 239, 280
Clark, Ross 72–3
Cleghorn, Dr Nicola 271–3
clerks *see* barristers' clerks;
   judges' clerks
Clewes-Boyne, Charlotte 255
Clio Modern Law Awards 86n16
Cloisters 44n22, 45
Cobb, Monica 185–6
commercial Bar
   challenges of Black barristers 206–7
   diversity initiatives 213–14, 229–30
   diversity recommendations 218–20,
      232–3
   gender inequalities 200
   lack of diversity 206, 229, 232
   legal aid sector compared 29–30, 82
Commercial Bar
   Association 206, 232–3
Counsel magazine 149, 152, 153, 155,
   190, 195–6, 199–200, 202, 203–4,
   206, 223, 235, 239, 243–4, 247,
   248, 251–4, 283

INDEX

Counsel's Briefs 97–8
Coupe, Toby 59
court dress 62
Couzens, Wayne 30, 46n25
COVID-19 87, *88*, 92
Cox, Dame Laura 126
Cox, Kharin, HHJ 154
Crime Girl 6, 280
Criminal Bar Association (CBA) 6, 210
Criminal Cases Review Commission 70
cross-examination 79–80, 271–4

D

D & I Newsletter 241
Daily Express 182
Daily Mail 31–2, 185
Daily Sketch 227–8, *228*
Dalal, Zahra 259
Daly, Beatrice 185–6
Davidson, Emily 177
Davis, HHJ 169
Davis, Oscar 239–40
Dawes, Lillian Maud 185–6
death penalty 25
Deech, Baroness (Ruth Deech KC (Hon)) x, 13, 14, 217n62
Delahunty, Lawrence (father) 8, 9, 40
Delahunty, Pauline Alberta (mother) xi–xii, 8–11, 12, 27, 34, 36, 39, 41n15, 281
Delahunty, Professor Jo, KC
  birth and childhood 8–12, 61–2
  family xi–xii, 8–11, 12, 27, 34, 36, 39, 41n15, 280, 281
  education 10–11, 12–14, 26–7
  marriage xi, 31–2, 34, *35*, 39, 40, 42
  political views 26, 27, 40, 43
  journey to the Bar 32–9, *38*
  pupillage 39, 40–5, 109–11
  specialism 15, 83
  Tooks Court tenancy 45–8, *47*, 230
  Garden Court tenancy 44n22, 71–4
  professional portfolio vi–vii, 7–8
  professional ethos viii, 15, 28, 43–4, 48, 67, 79–80, 100–1, 102, 274–5, 280–1

Gresham lectures 14, 53, 68n1, 86, 112, 116–17, 121, 123–4, 152, 153–4, 276n15
Dench, Dame Judi 226
Denis-Smith, Dana 178, 197
Denning, Lord 69n2
Devine, Andrew 265
Dhir, Anuja, HHJ (KC) 243
disability at the Bar
  neurodiversity 3, 14n17, 246–54, 255
  physical disability 254–5
  support initiatives 214, 254–5
Diversity at the Bar reports 189–90
Dodds, Robert Stephen, HHJ 150–2
Doherty, Auvergne 185–6
dress codes 22, 41, *47*, 48, *62*

E

East Finchley Constitutional Club 11–12
Essex Court Chambers 73, 213–14
Etchingham, Julie 227
ethical principles 68–78
Everard, Sarah 30, 46n25
expert evidence 91–2, 92–3, 271–4, 275–9
Eyre, Graham, QC 41

F

Fallon, Julie 263–5
Family Division 91–6, 275–6
Family Law Barristers Association (FLBA) 87, 96, 153, 169–71
Farage, Nigel 5
Farooq, Haleemah Sadia 254
Fatima, Shaheed, KC 230
First 100 Years project 178n3
Fountain Court Chambers 213–14
FreeBar 236–8, 239, 242
Fremder, Monique 250
Fulford, Adrian, QC 46n25

G

Garden Court Chambers 44n22, 45, 71–4
Garrick Club 222–9
Gatehouse Chambers 255–6
gender disparities
  pay gap 198–200, 201, 204
  progression and retention 191, 193–202

representation at Bar 3n3, 43, 188–9
tackling inequalities 215–21, 229–31, 245–6, 257–62
George, Mark, KC 85
Gerald, Nigel, HHJ 173
Gilham, Claire, DJ 196
Gilhooly, John 225
Gillani, Amina 269–73
Ginsberg, Ruth Bader 224
Glaister-Young, Shelly 51–2, 56, 64, 84, 245, 279–80
Gleicher-Bates, Danielle 255
Global Ethnic Majority (GEM) barristers
 challenges faced within profession 2–3, 54, 117–18, 160–7, 202–7, 238
 earnings 189, 204, 205–6
 judicial equal treatment guidance 166–7
 and legal aid work 2–3, 89
 particular challenges faced by women 202–4
 representation in profession 189, 205
 role models 242–4
 support initiatives 57, 211–14
 tackling inequalities 218–20, 229–34, 245–6, 257–62
 taking silk 189
 terminology 2n2
 wellbeing 89–91, 166
Goodwin, Nick, KC 275
Gove, Michael 151–2
Grainger, Sarah 155, 223n3, 247
grammar schools 10–11
Gray's Inn 180
Gresham College x, 7n6, 14
Grey, Maria 179
Grief, Alison, KC 275, 282
The Guardian 222, 225–6, 227

H

Haldane Society of Socialist Lawyers 45–6, 52–3
Hale, Baroness (Brenda Hale) 77, 145, 192, 197, 210, 217, 226–7
Hallett, Baroness (Heather Hallett KC) 111
Hardwicke, Lord 255–6
Harman, Baroness (Harriet Harman, PC, KC) 115, 153, 174, 283
Harman Report xii, 115, 174, 283
Harmes, Stephen, DJ 173
Hazarika, Baroness (Ayesha Hazarika) 226

health and wellbeing 67, 81–7, *88*, 89–91, *90*, 98–9, 166
Hedley J 76, 278–9
Heeley, Michelle, KC 153
Hendy, John, KC 44
Hendy, Pauline 44
Hill, Christine 60
Hillsborough Family Support Group (HFSG) 266
Hillsborough inquests 85, 158, 263–6
HM Courts and Tribunals Service 260–1
Hogg, Dame Mary x, 60
Horstead, Sean 85n15
Howe, Darren, KC 95–6, 153, 159, 169, 170, 217
Hughes, Emma 55, 56, 59, 87, 244–5, 257
Hutton, Professor Ronald x

I

I am the Bar campaign 201–2, 258
I am the Bench campaign 258
I am the Future of the Bar campaign 259
Imrie, Celia 227
In Black and White (Wilson) 167, 280
industrial action 6
Inglis, Alan 240
Inner Temple 36
Inns of Court 36, 235
instructing solicitors 74n7, 97–8
intermediaries 93–6
International Bar Association (IBA) 103n1, 108, 114, 126–7
Isaacs, Liz, KC 239

J

Jackson, Peter, LJ 154
James, Emily, KC 269–73
Jeffery, Ian 240
job satisfaction survey 89–91, *90*
Johnson, Aimbola 165
Johnson, Boris 5n4
Jolly, Shona, KC 210
judges
 diversity and inclusion initiatives 258
 female representation 192–3
 GEM representation 207–9
 judicial authority 144–5
 judicial guidance 146, 166–7, 167–9
 LGBTQIA+ representation 240–1

INDEX

members of Garrick club 222–9
misbehaviour *see* judicial bullying
overall standard of 146
reduced attractiveness of role 146
tackling inequalities 258–62
judges' clerks 60, 144, 162
Judicial Appointments
 Commission 146
judicial bullying
 complaints to JCIO 155
 impact on barristers 148, 150, 158–9
 impact on case 156–7
 judicial guidance 167–9
 parallels with #MeToo 147, 149
 and pressures of courtroom 147–8
 racial assumptions and bias 163–5
 recorded examples of 150–2, 155, 168–9, 173
 speaking out on the issue 147–8, 149–50, 152–5, 156, 175
 tackling the issue 169–72, 174–5
Judicial Conduct Investigation Office (JCIO) 151–2, 155
Judicial Diversity Forum 209
junior counsel, participation at court 196–7, 200, 216–17, 260

K

Kearney, Robert 127–30
Kemp, Howard, DJ 246
Kennedy, Baroness (Helena Kennedy KC) 126, 193–4, 198, 220
kindness of strangers 15
King, Henry Charles William 134–5
King, LJ 151
King's Counsel 3n3, 62, 188–91, 195–6, 205
Konarek, Max 269

L

Lammy, David 167
Larizadeh, Cyrus, KC 86–7, 170
Law Society 182, 215–16, 217, 242, 283
The Lawyer 54
lay clients 74n7
LB Croydon v D 269–73
Legal Aid Agency (LAA) ix, 29
legal aid work
 commercial sector contrasted 29–30
 emotional toll of 67, 81–9, *88*
 impact of 2025 cyber-attack ix, 29, 283–4
 impact on health 67, 81–3
 payment for work 28–9, 30, 84, 92, 96–7, 195
 as vocation 28, 67–8, 82, 100
 workload 97–8
Leggatt, Lord 256
Lewis, Brandon 6
Lewis, Clive, LJ 173
Lexis Nexis Family Law Awards 57n32, 126
LGBTQIA+ barristers
 challenges faced within profession 4, 234–5
 Inns of Court Forums 234, 235
 judicial appointments 240–1
 and legal aid work 89
 LGBTQIA+ Charter 236–8
 personal champions 58–9
 Pride in London march 242
 Pride in Practice event 240
 role models 46n25, 238–41
 support initiatives 214
 wellbeing 89–91
 work yet to be done 235–6, 238–9
Lieven J 95
Light, Jonathan xi, 31–2, 34, *35*, 39, 40, 42
Lincoln's Inn 181, 184
LinkedIn 117–18
Llanwarne, Emma 255
Llewelyn Davis, Theodora 185–6
Lochrane HHJ 58–9
Lue, Stephen 58–9, 89, 232, 238–9

M

Major HHJ 271–2
Male Champions for Change toolkit 217
Malkinson, Andrew 70
Mansfield, Michael, KC x, 45, 46–8, 69, 85, 266n5, 275, 282
Mansfield Rule 216
Markham, Hannah, KC 124, 170, 213
Marshall Hall, Sir Edward, KC 275
Marshall-Andrews, Bob 224
Mason, Marc 234–5
McArdle, Ian 48, 49, 53
McCloud, Master Victoria 240–1
McDonald, Charlotte 254–5
McDonald J 273

McFarlane, Sir Andrew 91–2
  President's Guidance 93–4, 95, 96
McKenzie, Jacqueline 5n4
McMullen, Jeremy (QC) 44
mental health 67, 81–7, *88*, 98–9
mentoring schemes 213–14
Mercer, Sam 141, 169, 257–8
#MeToo movement 116, 147, 149
Middle Temple 36, 184, *187*, 234
Mills, Barbara, KC 107, 202, 203–4, 208–9, 210–11, 230, 240, 283
mini pupillage 128n25, 211–12
Minoprio, Delia 269
mobile phones 43n18
Monaghan, Karon, KC 196, 210
Monteith, Keir, KC 165
Moore, Sir Richard 225
Mullin, Chris 70
Munby, Sir James x, 60, 101, 155
Murray, Paul 84

N

Ndow-Njie, Mass 53–5, 57, 59, 229, 231, 280
Neame, Gareth 225, 226
Neuberger, Lord 226
neurodiversity 3, 14n17, 57n30, 246–54, 255
New Square Chambers 212
Newbery, Freya (HHJ Newbery) 42
Newman, Cathy 226
newspaper coverage *see* press reporting
Next 100 Years Project 178n3
Nice, Sir Geoffrey, KC x
Norman, Al xi, 11
Normanton, Helena 185–6, *187*
Nouka, Konstantina 254–5

O

Olivarius, Dr Ann, KC (Hon) 223
One Essex Court 213–14, 229–30
Orr, Lucinda 210
outreach 61–3, *62*, 218–19
Owen, Becky 85
Oxbridge 12–14, 25, 27, 40, 54, 190, 231

P

Pankhurst, Christabel 180–1
Pankhurst, Emmeline 176, 180
Pankhurst, Richard 181
Panth Seva Award 256

The Paper Chase (TV drama) 26–7
parenthood 3, 43, 53, 87–8, 191, 194, 257, 260
parenting 76–8
Patel, Priti 6
Pender, Kieran 126, 217
personal champions 41, 44–5, 58–60
Phillips, Dame Sian 226
Pink Singers 240
Pink Tape (blog) 6, 47–8
Pitchley, George 60
police 46, 69n2
political rhetoric 4–5, 6, 31, 67–8
Poll Tax riots 46
Powell, Andrew 57
Power, Laurie-Anne, KC 165–6
press reporting 4–5, 6, 17, 67–8, 69, 72–3
Prior, Mary, KC 6, 124
Private Education Policy Forum 19
private members' clubs 222–9
private schools *see* public schools
pro bono work 46
Prochaska, Elizabeth 116
Prof Delahunty KC BTB Essay prize 56–7, 250
professional clients 74n7
Proudman, Dr Charlotte 223, 228
public schools 19, 190
public vs private law 16n20
pupillage
  author's experience of 39, 40–5, 109–11, 112
  competition for 65, 105
  power imbalance during 104–6
  sexual harassment during 109–11, 112–14, 117–26
  stages of 44n21, 104
Purkiss, Kate (HHJ Purkiss) 79

Q

QEB Hollis Whiteman 171–2

R

race *see* Global Ethnic Majority (GEM) barristers
Race at the Bar reports 161–3, 165–6, 205
Reed, Lord 197, 216
Reed, Lucy, KC 6, 147–8, 150, 274
Reyes, Eduardo 217
Robinson, Eve 118–26, 140

INDEX

Roche, Barbara 46n25
Roche, Patrick 46, 46n25, 85n15, 266n5
Rose, Lady 192
Rowbotham, Simon 234–6
Rozenberg, Joshua, KC (Hon) 72–3
Rudd, Amber 226
Ryder, Sir Ernest 152, 155
Rye, Maria 179

S

Saini, Pushpinder, J (KC) 55
Sapnara, Khatun, HHJ 242–3
school outreach 61–3, *62*, 218–19
Scraton, Professor Phil 85n15
Seafarers' Legal Advice Centre 46
Secret Barrister 5, 6, 75–6, 280
Sefton, Andrew 263–4
self-employment 82
Sergides, Marina 87, 99–100
Setright, Henry, KC 154
sexual harassment *see* bullying and harassment
Shekerdemian, Marcia, KC 199–200
Sidhu, Navjot (Jo), KC 131–3, 135
Sikh Court 256
Sikhs in Law 243–4, 256
silks *see* King's Counsel
Simblet, Stephen, KC 85n15
Simler, Lady 192
Singh, Baldip 243–4, 256
Singh, Rabinder, LJ 256
Singh, Sir Mota 256
Singh Basi, Mani 244, 256
slave trade 255–6
Sloane Rangers 41–2
Smith, Marcus, J 168–9
social media 6, 15–16, 97, 117–18, 258, 280
Solanki, Devina xi
Soule, Robin 44
Spark21 178n3
Spearing, Rachel, KC 86
Specialist Bar Associations (SBAs) 206, 218–19, 232–3
The Spectator 72–3
Spencer, Lady Diana 41–2
Spoor, Benjamin 183
St Anne's College, Oxford 12–14, 37, 43
Staple Inn Chambers 52
state school education 10–11, 12, 13–14, 49–51, 89–91

Stevens-Hoare, Brie, KC 33, 50, 60–1, 112–14, 210, 221, 239, 256
Storey, Paul, KC 273–4, 275, 282
'Strong Not Silent' campaign *88*
Sumption, Lord 226
Supreme Court
  composition of 192, 207
  internship programme 55, 56, 260
  Lady Hale as President 197, 210
  Sikhs in Law ceremony 256
  women barristers appearing in 195–7
Suresh, Srishti 49–50, 55, 56, 59–60
Suspected Inflicted Head Injury Service (SIHIS) 93, 276n15
Sweeting, Derek, KC, (Sweeting J) 33, 135, 231

T

Tack, Eleanor 55
Tafadar, Sultana, KC 230
Talk to Spot helpline 141–2, 169–70, 172
Technology and Construction Bar Association 206, 232–3
Thai Bar Association 22
Thatcher, Margaret 26, 45, 46
Theis, J 79
third six (pupillage) 44, 104n2, 205
Thomas, John, LCJ 152
Thomas, Leslie, KC 55, 85, 163–4, 218
Thompson, Ann 79, 269–73
Thornberry, Emily 46n25
The Times 196, 241
Tooks Court 45–8, *47*
Townend, Samuel, KC 133, 199, 226
Townley, Lynne 195
training for the Bar *see* becoming a barrister
Transforming Women's Leadership in the Law report 215–16
Transparency Guidelines 17
Traugott, Elizabeth 223, 228
Trenaman, Nancy 12–13
Trump, Donald J. 31
Trustman, Judith 149–50

U

UK Association of Black Judges 208
unconscious bias 200, 215, 220, 257

University of Manchester racial bias report 164–5
Us Too? (IBA report) 126–7

V

Vater, John, KC 93, 94–5, 96–7, 275
Vaughan, Dr Stephen 234–5
Victoria, Queen 43n19
Voices of Women at Chancery Bar report 199–201

W

Wallace, Naomi 185–6
Wellbeing at the Bar 86, 99n28
Wellington Street Chambers 45
Wellness for Law UK 86
Wells, Colin 48, 52–3, 100
Western Circuit Women's Forum 260
Wheeler, Elsie May 185–6
Wheetman, Alan 133–4
Whitty, Sir Chris x
Wilcock, Peter, KC 46, 85n15
Williams, Dr Ivy 185–6
Willis Smith, Marcia, KC (Hon) 85, 266n5
Wilson, Alexandra 167, 211, 280
women
  as barristers' clerks 179, 201
  emancipation of 176–86, *177*
  and Garrick Club membership 222–9

and minute taking 41n15
state oppression 8–9, 11, 21–2
Women at the Bar survey 106n6
Women at the Criminal Bar (WICL) 201–2
women barristers
  advice on how to succeed 203, 210–11, 217–18
  campaign to enter profession 179–86
  challenges faced within profession 191, 193–202, 257
  dress codes 22, 41, 47, 48
  GEM women *see* GEM barristers
  judicial appointments 192–3
  male champions for change 217
  pay gap 198–200, 201, 204
  ratios of women to men 3n3, 43, 188–9
  role models 209–10, 244–5
  tackling inequalities 215–21, 229–31, 245–6, 257–62
  taking silk 188–91, 195–6
  wellbeing 91
Women in Leadership Law Report 215
Women in Red 7
work ethic 81–2, 280–1
working class barristers 32–9, 42, 48, 52–3, 63
working class judges 258
Working Lives Survey 89–91, *90*
Wray, Rohan 78–9